Historical fiction Book 2025

The Black Princess

Maggie Voysey Paun

CW00762246

MOONLIGHT BOOKS

The Black Princess
FIRST EDITION : 2018
ISBN : 978-81-936313-6-2

Copyright © 2018 Maggie Voysey Paun

Cover design by Rich Voysey at Forge Branding Ltd.

Published by
MOONLIGHT BOOKS
20 Ekjot Apartment, Pitampura, Delhi-110034, India
Email : moonlightbooks2016@gmail.com
Website : www.moonlightbooks.in

All rights reserved. No part of this book may be used or reproduced in any manner whatsoever, including Internet usage, without permission from the Publisher, except in the case of brief quotations embodied in critical articles and reviews.

This book is based upon a true story, however, some of the characters and events have been fictionalized.

The views expressed in this work are solely those of the author and do not necessarily reflect the views of the publisher, and the publisher hereby disclaims any responsibility for them.

Printed by Replika Press Pvt. Ltd., India

*In memory of
Manglakaki
Who also made her home
in many different places*

CONTENTS

Characters

1. LOWER BEEDING
Mrs Helena Bennett
Caroline Golding *later* Budgen, her housekeeper
Mary Piper, her maid
Mary's grandmother (*fictional*)
James Budgen, her tenant
Albert, a neighbour (*fictional*)

2. HORSHAM
Ann and Michael Howes, her friends
Samuel Fuller, their coachman (*fictional*)
Elizabeth Etherton, her friend
Mr and Mrs Aldridge, her friends

3. LUCKNOW
Nur Baksh
The Begum and Captain Baksh, her parents
Faiz Palmer, her sister
Captain, later General William Palmer and British Resident at Poona
   (Pune), her brother-in-law, East India Company (EIC) officer
William junior, Mary, Hastings, Charles and Sarah Palmer, their
   children
Gulzar, her cousin and later close companion (*fictional*)
Zainab, a servant, Sadiq, a cook and later her husband and Razia
   their daughter (*all fictional*)

Captain later General Benoit de Boigne from Savoy, her second husband, a great military commander in the service of Mahadji Sindhia, the leader of the Mahratta Confederacy

Banu, later Ann, daughter of Nur and Benoit

Ali, later Charles, son of Nur and Benoit

Leopold von Wissenburg, a visitor *(fictional)*

Colonel Antoine Polier, Swiss-French engineer and businessman

Doctor and Mrs Blane, Physician to the Nawab and his wife, later friends of Nur in London

Asaf-ud-Daula, the Nawab of Avadh/Oudh

Mirza Abu Taleb Khan, member of the Nawab's household and later traveller who visited Nur in London

General Claude Martin, French businessman and sometime EIC officer

Boulone, his favourite mistress, her sisters Gomany and Amman, James/Zulphikar his adopted son and Sally his adopted daughter

Joseph Queiros, full name Don Joseph Chamois de Quiros Chevalier, his Spanish associate and employee

4. OTHER INDIAN CHARACTERS

Zohra and Ali, Nur's aunt and uncle in Delhi *(fictional)*

The Mughal Emperor, Shah Alam

Mahmud, the overseer in Koil *(fictional)*

Preethi and Sita, two girls employed by Nur in Koil *(fictional)*

Amrita Bose, Nur's servant in Calcutta and London *(fictional)*

5. OTHER EUROPEAN CHARACTERS

Sarah Palmer, William's first wife, now living in London

John their son, a banker in Calcutta

Antony Tremamondo, aka 'Mr Angelo', Calcutta-based cavalry instructor for the British, later Benoit's agent in London
John and Mary Walker, friends of Nur/Helena in London
Warren Hastings, Governor-General of India 1774-85
Charlotte-Eleonore-Louise-Adelaide d'Osmond, known as Adele, Benoit's second wife
Daniel O'Connell, friend of Benoit

OTHER PEOPLE REFERRED TO:
Mahadji Sindhia, leader of the Mahratta Confederacy
Daulat Rao his son and heir
Holkar, one of his Generals
Ismail Beg, a Mughal General and turncoat
Ghulam Qadir, an Afghan leader who invaded Delhi
The Peshwa, ruler of Pune
The Nizam, ruler of Hyderabad
Tipu Sultan, ruler of Mysore
Mihr-un-Nissa and Zinatt, girls 'given' to Benoit
Mohanlal Das, employee of Benoit in Koil (*fictional*)
Wazir Ali Khan, son of Asaf-ud-Daula
Jahanara, daughter of the Emperor
Governors-General of India: Marquis Cornwallis (1786-93 and again in 1805), Sir John Shore (Acting) (1793-98), Lord Wellesley (1798-1805)
Sir Philip Francis, EIC Councillor in Calcutta and bitter opponent of Hastings
James Kirkpatrick, British Resident in Hyderabad and close friend of William Palmer
Philip Wombwell, EIC accountant at Lucknow, sent to sort out endemic irregular financial practices

Johan Zoffany, painter of the British Royal family, for some years resident in Lucknow

Ozias Humphreys, also a visiting painter in Lucknow

Richard Johnson, EIC employee in Lucknow and Calcutta, later Benoit's London agent

Marcel Aumont, Benoit's French batman, later manservant in Savoy who remained in his service for the rest of his life

Michael Walker, son of Mary and John. He and John were later Helena's executors together with Pitfold Medwin in Horsham

'Mr Burke', Edmund Burke one of the MPs who managed the ultimately unsuccessful impeachment of Warren Hastings for alleged crimes and misdemeanours

Din Mohammed, Shampooing Surgeon to the Prince Regent (later George IV), later the successful proprietor of 'vapour baths' in Brighton and London

George Polier, son of Antoine

'Clive', Lord Clive, 1725-74, victor of the Battle of Plassey, who established the supremacy of the East India Company in Bengal

Joseph, Benoit's brother

Mrs Redford, Nur's former, and again later, landlady in Horsham

Cesarine, Charles' wife and Ernest, his oldest son and heir

PROLOGUE

1784 Near Delhi, India

When I was twelve my father took me to meet my husband. The Nawab of Pundri had married me several years before when, having seen me somewhere in Delhi, playing with my older sister, he had asked my father to give me to him. My parents must have told me, perhaps performed some small ceremony, but I had scarcely given it thought since. I rode there on my father's horse, seated in front of him, with the most splendid view of the surrounding country, newly green after the monsoon rains. Of Pundri itself I recall little more than a few hovels, huddled around the high walls of the palace grounds, not a bit like busy Delhi or my mother's lovely city, Lucknow. But the domes and pavilions on the palace roof, the wide terraces screened by stone latticework and the spacious gardens full of trees, flowers and waterways that became visible as we rode through the gates impressed me greatly.

'This will be your home one day,' my father said softly and I turned to him, eyes wide, just in time to see the sadness in his face.

'But you will be there too,' I said, to comfort us both, though I knew it was not true.

Still I skipped quite carelessly ahead of him while a *syce* took care of the horse and came to a stop only at the dark entrance porch, which was guarded by the crossed lances of two fierce Pathans who wore the most splendid red white and gold livery. Of course they lowered their weapons and let us in and, as my eyes grew accustomed to the gloom, I saw him, the Nawab, dressed in purple, seated at the far end of a great hall in a large gilded chair that was raised several steps up from the floor on a platform under a carved marble canopy. A waiting servant led me to the foot of the platform

1

and then disappeared, while another took my father to a room on one side.

Of a sudden I felt as if turned to stone, if stone can feel such fear. Close to, I could see how old he was, the Nawab whose wife I had unknowingly become. Gaunt, hunched, cadaverous, these are words I know now. Then he appeared to me like a giant eagle, hands like talons raised to prise me up when he should choose to pounce, eyes narrowed, glittering, his great hooked nose like a raptor's beak, only the long straggly grey beard and twisted moustaches betraying the man beneath.

'Well, my pretty one,' he beckoned impatiently for me to approach, leaned forward and lifted me eagerly to his lap. 'Hmm,' one talon raised my chin and those beady eyes peered into my face. 'You do not disappoint.' He nodded to himself as if settling a private wager. 'I knew there was true beauty beneath that childish charm. Come, give your husband a kiss.'

My lips puckered, I thought to brush them lightly against his cheek, the one nearest to me, but he had turned to face me and I found instead his pink wet lips pursed and protruding from their hairy nest, opening sufficient to clamp on mine, sucking my mouth into his with such force I fancied he might swallow me whole like some dragon or sea monster. And though I could feel the periodic draught of air from a wide *punkah* attached to the ceiling of the canopy, still could I scarcely breathe with that long nose compressing mine and those bony arms holding me tight, bending me back so far my pigtails brushed the ground. His eyes were shut but mine, casting around for some escape, found instead another pair, bright and warm, set in a young and smiling face which, though upside down, I understood to be that of a servant boy, about my age, whose purpose it was to operate the *punkah*. And in the instant before my husband set me right, the boy winked one eye and I thought perhaps I should laugh not cry.

But the Nawab was not finished with his inspection. His hands were running the length of my bare arms from shoulder to wrist and back again, whence he transferred his attention to my legs and lower body, smoothing my thighs through the silk of my pyjama, weighing my rear quarters in turn as if to estimate their size, kneading and squeezing as if to locate the bones beneath my flesh and breathing

2

heavily the while. Was I to allow such intimate probing? I looked around me in appeal, but my new friend did not meet my eye and continued to operate his fan. It seemed my outrage must be ignored and whatever else occurred I must endure. But just as I decided thus, the Nawab ceased his rude explorations and set me down beside him.

'Aao!'

My father hastened in.

'She is still young,' observed the Nawab, one hand resting on my head in more paternal fashion.

'Indeed.' With what relief my father spoke. 'Her mother says she is not ready.'

The Nawab nodded and raised his hand. 'Then shall I wait on her good opinion and expect to receive your daughter when she is.' And with that judgement he pushed me gently towards my father and stood to indicate our audience was over.

And so I was reprieved for an uncertain period and, though I knew my parents must keep their word to so important a man, yet I felt sure they would extend it to its utmost.

'We are sending you to live with your sister,' my mother informed me a short time later. 'Your brother-in-law has offered you his protection and you may assist her with the children.'

'In Calcutta?' I had visited them there and found it an interesting city with many more Europeans and altogether a different atmosphere to that of other places I have been.

'In Lucknow.' My mother smiled at my delight. 'My son-in-law is to take up a new posting there and your father has promised he will actively pursue a similar new employ.' She hugged me to her. 'How could I live far from both my daughters?'

PART I

Childhood

1

1853 Lower Beeding,
Sussex, England, March

So I am here, still here. I watch the light deceive the velvet drapes, seep through the smallest chink and make the dust motes dance. It makes me smile, though I have seen it many times. But I do not like morning. It is too bright, too unequivocal and demanding of action. Reliable as the sun, comes Caroline to sweep away the darkness and summon me from slumber. She opens wide the curtains, knowing she is not welcome and is defiant.

'Tis a glorious marning, dursn't waste it abed. Surely.'

She bustles out and returns with a breakfast tray, which she had hoped I, meanwhile, would have sat up to receive. But I have turned away from the glare and her, disturbing my two old feline friends as little as I can, and pulled my nightcap over my eyes. Caroline clicks her tongue and sets the tray on the bedside table as heavily as she dare. She wishes she could tell me what she thinks but, apart from my contrary nature, hers is an undemanding situation and I believe she plans to stay with me until the end.

'There's a dosset of fresh churned cream which I daresay will find its way to those cats and not to your cup.'

She is distracted by a burst from below stairs of girlish laughter, followed by a masculine rumble. The daily maid is about her chores and should not have company. Caroline moves swiftly from my chamber to chastise her and shouts down the stairs.

'Stop thy goistering, Mary Piper, the missus is still awaking.'

She is answered by a low murmur of explanation and I hear her descending to investigate. The man's voice is louder and there is an excited buzz of response from both women that does arouse my

6

interest. I push back my cap in readiness for Caroline's return and wonder that Silver did not bark. I fear he is a'roaming and hope he is not chasing sheep - or 'ships' as Caroline would have it - which would not be for the first time. He is a sheepdog, almost pure, but with a wildness that the shepherd who was first his master could not tame and would have been put to death had he not come to me. But that will yet be his fate if lambs are lost.

'Well!' Caroline returns, a little out of breath. She is young but already stout. ''Twere that jug , the fisherman from Brighthelmstone, I have bought some bream off him for dinner. Today he has pictures too for selling. Of the town and of hisself, his boat and the shore and sea beyond, all so clear you could see his face and know t'wuz'e. This is what the girl was so jiggered at. He was telling us that afore long we'll all be getting our likenesses done similar and if we wuz living in Merricur we'd have a passing portraitist knocking on our door soon as ever we knew it!'

She is speaking, I gather, of daguerrotypes, a French invention that has spread like wildfire, especially in America, and which would once have caused in me great fascination. How fast the world is changing while I lie hidden here. How much would I give for likenesses of days long gone, my life before, my dearest ones, to hold, to regard and to display. I have nothing but my memories.

'I had my portrait taken once,' I say now, a little 'jiggered' to find myself this eager to confide. 'Long ago.'

'Did you ever!' Caroline's surprise must be exaggerated, for I know she finds me strange and would surely believe anything I cared to claim. 'Painted I dursay?'

'Many people said it was the most beautiful family painting they had seen, it was not only of me...'

'Your family?' I hear her repeat it, her interest is really piqued, but I wish now to follow my thoughts alone. I know not where in the world that painting hangs and perhaps it is lost altogether, but maybe I can visit the scene of its creation if I let myself be transported...

'Close the curtains,' I tell her. 'And bring my pipe.'

She returns very shortly, holding the green glass base in one hand while supporting the rest of the pipe with the other. The base is already full of water and the head, cover and hose firmly attached. She smiles at my evident surprise.

7

'I keep it ready, ma'am, for just such an urgency.' Her pride has overcome her customary disapproval. 'I only have to set the fire.'

Even watching the preparation of a pipe can be calming and the scent of tobacco alone is pleasant, Caroline acknowledges as much, while refusing to approve that of opium which I find equally sweet. But today I am impatient and take the long hose to my mouth as soon as she transfers the heated coal to the top of the head. It can take some time for the smoke to draw through but, no doubt, Caroline keeps my pipe as clean as the parts of my house where she is allowed free rein and I soon feel the initial signs of bodily relaxation. Sunk on my pillows, I watch her ensure the pipe is safely set, away from furnishings that might catch fire. She seems to take an unfathomable time about this simple task, which is how I know my mind is following my body's example, losing its normal preoccupations, relinquishing perceptions of the everyday world. And then even these slow motions take more shadowy form until they disappear entirely and leave me free to follow my inward dreams.

2

1785 Lucknow, June

'Psst! Nur Begum! Here!'

From the corner of my eye I see her beckoning, just inside the gate in the shadow of the wall surrounding the *bagh,* where the jasmine has climbed so high it spills into the courtyard beyond. She is tall, dark-skinned, strongly built, and she has pulled the end of her white *palav* low over her steel-grey hair, half covering her face, so that I cannot see her expression, though it is mostly stern. She is a serious woman. It is Mary's *ayah,* Zainab, and she is gesturing more urgently. Five-year-old William has seen her too but he turns deliberately away.

'Catch, Nur auntie.' He bats the ball to me and I jump to retrieve it lest it fall into Chandi's eager mouth, which will result in a long chase before we can resume our game. But Chandi is faster than me and, with a yelp of triumph, he seizes the ball and races away from us towards the summerhouse at the far end of the garden. I fear that he will reach this by swimming across the marble bath in front, which he should not do since it is where we also sometimes take a bath, soon hear the tell-tale splash and hope that Zainab has not.

'Auntie!' William is disappointed in me. He has been grumbling constantly at today's various restrictions for he prefers to play in the wider grassy spaces of the Residency grounds beyond our garden.

Three-year-old Mary laughs, claps her hands and begins to run after Chandi and I follow quickly in order to stop her jumping fully-clothed into the water with him, which matters today since she, like William, is wearing fine silk *jamas* ready for the painting. There is another hiss from Zainab and more urgent beckoning, so I take

9

Mary's hand and hurry towards the gate, leaving a disgruntled William to trail after us, chopping crossly with his bat at the poinsettias lining the path.

'The painter is here and he wants us all together.'

Zainab speaks of Herr Zoffany who has these past few weeks been making a portrait of my sister and her family in which I, since I am staying with her much of the time, am included. So also is Zainab, baby Hastings' wet nurse and our cousin sister Gulzar who, being widowed young, has been given a home here by my generous brother-in-law. There have been other sittings but of each of us separately or in small groups.

'Come, William,' I try to take his hand. 'Don't you want to see your portrait? Herr Zoffany will display it for all to see when it is complete.'

Usually I would as soon be outdoors playing with the children as engaged in any other pastime, but I am eager to see how another sees me and know that this painter is very well-regarded in England where he has made his home and has made portraits of the King and Queen and their children. So I seize William by the sleeve, ignoring his protests, and, followed by Zainab, hasten into the house. We go straight to the *sangeet khana*, which is the largest room, where my brother-in-law loves to give music parties, and find the others are already in position.

My sister Faiz is sitting cross-legged on the floor looking down at the baby asleep in her lap. She looks very beautiful in red and saffron silk edged with gold, with several strings of pearls hung round her neck and earrings of diamond that sparkle like small fireworks on either side of her face. She is only five or six years older than I, not yet twenty, but serene and modest like a mature woman. She has already undergone more than three pregnancies with one stillbirth, and Mary and William were so ill with the smallpox two years ago that she feared to lose them also. But I think she is so content because she knows herself so much loved and cherished and, especially now that they have removed here from Calcutta and our mother is near, feels her life to be complete.

My brother –in –law leans over her now from his seat at the centre of the group, his expression adoring, and I think, not for the first time, if only I had a husband like Captain William Palmer instead of the Nawab of Pundri, whose harem I must soon join now that I am grown. Yet again I chase this thought to the back of my mind and, directed by Herr Zoffany, take my place kneeling at my brother-in-law's side. I am quite close to him and leaning even closer to look over the heads of Mary and the wet nurse at Hastings in his swaddling wraps and tiny embroidered *topi*. William is on his mother's far side with Zainab behind him, Gulzar stands some distance behind me. Herr Zoffany squints at us, palette and brush in hand, he is not quite satisfied. We do not fit together quite as he envisaged.

'Straighten your right arm, Captain, and rest your hand with the gloves on your knee. Just so.'

This is the arm that is nearest to me, his hand is now very near mine. Herr Zoffany explains that this is because our figures must be so aligned to draw the eye to Faiz who, though seated to one side of the group, is the true focus of the painting. He makes swift sketches with his brush as I try to hold still, uncomfortable in this new positioning and most impatient to view the result. But the more I long for him to finish, the more he seems to delay and his brush strokes become slower, more hesitant and his person more indistinct. Indeed the whole group is dissolving before my eyes.

I think I hear Chandi barking and am distracted. Did we in our haste leave him shut in the garden? Surely not, for now the barking is approaching, it is near, very near, and I feel his paws on my arm, eager for attention, his tongue licking my face.

3

1853 Lower Beeding, March

'Silver! Where have you been all morning, my lovely boy?'

I scratch his ears and he licks my face and prepares to jump on the bed. The cats have gone, no doubt they smelt, as I do now, the fish that Caroline is cooking. They will have had a fine breakfast of fishheads and other off-cuts, while my own has long gone cold as I lay dreaming.

'No, no, I shall get up,' I push him down, pass him a morsel of bread from the tray and reach for the bell pull. 'And then we shall go adventuring in St Leonards's Forest.'

***

"Through the dell,
Silence and Twilight here, twin sisters, keep
Their noonday watch, and sail among the shades
Like vapourous shapes half seen."

How come you were so melancholy so young, Mr Shelley? Did you have intimations of an early grave? Or perhaps it was November when you walked here and not sweet spring. Though it's true that amongst the trees at any time of year it can be dark and very silent. Despite the sun I shiver and wish there were indeed two sisters walking here and I their friend.

And Silver has gone again, chasing rabbits, squirrels, any furry thing, leaving me alone. No matter, today I have a chorus of birdsong for company, blackbird, thrush, chaffinch, I know you all and there are

12

others too. Spring has sprung once more! Still underfoot the leaves of last autumn yet I am sure, yes there, under the ash, in among the roots are the first primroses and, now I am closer, I spy violets too. Anemones will not be far away. And celandines. Nature triumphant yet again and careless of our woes. 'Mother Nature'. Some mother she.

How well I know these woods, so many years have I been walking here. I do believe it was this very mossy bank on which I sat when Mr Shelley of a sudden appeared and was abashed that I might think him in pursuit and be afraid. For it was night, a summer night, I could not sleep and I was singing one of my favourite *ghazals*. I think he could not have understood it but he must have liked the melody for he later wrote his own and very appropriate words.

"I arise from dreams of thee-
In the first sweet sleep of night,
When the winds are breathing low,
And the stars are shining bright,
I arise from dreams of thee,
And a spirit in my feet
Has borne me – Who knows how?"

Dear Mr Shelley, somehow you spoke my soul although we scarcely spoke!

"The wandering airs they faint
On the dark, the silent stream –
The champak odours fail
Like sweet thoughts in a dream;

It is true we cannot quite recall scents, however much we yearn, as do I to smell champak, just once more.

"O lift me from the grass!
I die, I faint, I fail!
Let thy love in kisses rain
On my lips and eyelids pale.
My cheek is cold and white, alas!
My heart beats loud and fast;
Oh press it close to thine again,
Where it will break at last!"

Ha! You saw me at a particularly bad time in my life and my heart was long broken. Though I was young enough and still good-looking. You would not recognise this old hag that has o'ertaken me. How it gladdened my heart to know that, far away, you had thought of me still, though it was too late to tell you. How willingly would I have given you all these past years and drowned instead, if only such bargains could be made.

Silver! Are you come to see if I am still alive? Good boy, you would protect me if I had need, wouldn't you, like all your namesakes down the years. Chandi warned me, he growled whenever He approached me. He did not trust him.

***

I am chilled to the bone when I return and Caroline allows me to take my food on a lap tray in front of the sitting room fire.

'Tis better take care,' she clucks and bustles, fire irons in each hand, as she stokes the hot coals and adds a large log of the apple branch that broke from one of the Bramleys in last December's gale.

'Why?' I might have asked on another occasion but instead eat heartily, enough to please her, and give only a very little to the cats at my feet. As the log catches and blazes, Silver finds it too hot and takes himself off to the kitchen where the stone-flagged floor better suits his hardy nature.

I have loved fire-gazing since living in Faiz's house. Much as he admired all things Indian, my brother-in-law was not averse to English comforts when they were appropriate. I do not think he would have had need of a fire earlier when they were living in Calcutta, or later when they removed to Pune, but winter months in Lucknow can be cold. He was poking at the heart of an inferno when, upon his summons, I joined him in his study one day. I can see him still, handsome profile aglow, his high clever forehead, his clean-shaven cheeks, the corner of his mouth curved up in what I believed a constant smile.

4

1786 Lucknow, January

He turns his head a little as I approach, indicating that I should take
the other fireside chair, replaces the brass poker in its stand and leans
back in his own leather-bound chair, his elbows on its arm rests, the
tips of the fingers of each hand a little interlaced. My eyes follow his
gaze into the fire's crumbling centre, which just now, I fancy,
resembles a jewelled cave, a cavern filled with rubies, garnets and
yellow topaz, together with elusive flickers of emerald and cobalt, all
of which I know are but the product of gaseous emissions released
from the burning logs. I know this because my brother-in-law takes
an interest in matters scientific and we sometimes read together. I
wonder briefly if he has news of some new discovery or invention to
relate, or perhaps some rare Mughal or Sanskrit document he has
obtained to send to England for General Hastings.

'Your father has sent word,' he looks up and his tone is grave.

My heart beats faster. 'Is all well? My mother?'

'A messenger has come from Pundri.'

I think my heart will stop. I am sent for, surely, my husband
thinks me ready for his bed. It is the day I have dreaded for so long
as I can remember. But what is this I hear?

'The Nawab, God rest his soul, is dead.'

Oh God be praised! I am delivered.

'You must enter mourning for one year. That means - '

No jewels, nor other ornament, plain cloth, a plainer diet and no
amusement outside the home. None of this matters to me.

'But I can stay here?' I hold my breath.

'If you wish.' He laughs aloud at my very apparent joy and
briefly takes my hand. 'Dear Nur *bahyne*, you will always be

15

welcome in my house. And I shall be especially glad that you are here to keep company with your sister, for I am soon to be appointed as representative to Mahadji Sindhia's court in Gwalior and shall not always be here.'

'Why there?'

'It seems he is inclined to friendship with the British and is in any case likely to become the most influential among the Mahratta leaders.' He sighs a little and gazes again into the fire.

'So it will be important to the British to keep close to his heart and mind?' I suggest, wishing to follow his train of thought and guess at his concern, knowing his judgment and powers of diplomacy to be highly valued by his superiors.

'Indeed. Though it is not the position I should have sought as he is often on campaign with his army.'

'Oh we shall miss you.'

He looks away and is silent for some moments before turning back, his worry set aside. 'I shall visit. And there is some happier news.' He pauses, teasing. 'I have engaged a music master for young William and I wish you would share his lessons, for I fear he may resist. You may care to learn an instrument, to sing a little? It may help to pass the time.'

I throw myself on the hearthrug at his feet and kiss his hand. He rests it lightly on my head until a falling log disturbs us.

1853 Lower Beeding March

There is a smell of scorching wool and smoke.

'Mercy, you'll be the death of us all.'

Caroline detected it before me and, implements in hand, has come to quell the flames and shovel up the glowing splinters of the fallen log. Affronted, the cats have fled to the far corners of the room where they are performing a thorough *toilette* to restore their damaged dignity, which makes me laugh. Unwisely.

''Tis no laughing matter, surely. I must put the guard.'

Which is a cage of iron that will enclose the whole fireplace but is mostly banished to the sidelines, for I do not like it, it restricts my view. For the moment, however, I am complaisant. She has had a fright.

'Perhaps the wood is still a little damp and more inclined therefore to spit.'

Caroline shrugs but masks her exasperation. 'Whatever the cause, the cure is plain.' She clanks the contraption into place, stamps on the singed parts of the hearth rug one more time and puffs out of the room.

It is now very warm by the fireside so I stand, a little stiff, and take to the seat by the western window. In my garden the evergreen honeysuckle hedges cast the sleeping rose beds in deep shade and only the water in the birdbath reflects the slight remaining light. A week or two since, I could see the snowdrops' evening phosphorescence but now their time is past and the daffodils are yet too tightly furled. I look beyond to the furrowed field, still bare though softer and more yielding - which I know from the mud that Silver brings in. It meets the darkening sky in a row of skeleton trees and I think, as every year, how many more times shall I see the leaves unbud, the blossom burst, and all my flowers bloom? I will watch until the first stars appear, wishing I were young enough to again go roaming and savour the evening odours of the earth.

5

1787 Lucknow, March

'Let's go *hawa khana*.'

Faiz has sought me out at the end of her afternoon sleep. I have been singing and accompanying myself on the *sarangi* at which after more than a year's instruction and much practice, our master says I am becoming quite accomplished. He is encouraging me to write my own *ghazals* but it is much more difficult than is apparent to the listener. There are strict rules concerning rhyme and repetition, *enjambement* (there must be none) and metre.

'Tell me first, what do you think of this?' I clear my throat and make a small adjustment to one string.

'What is my heart? You take my life
But do as I ask just once
Since you will come here again and again
Carefully observe this place.
What is my heart?
You should come to know.'

Before I have finished the first verse and because there are many repetitions in a *ghazal,* Faiz is singing along with me. She has a good ear and would have made a better performer than I, had she had the time to study.

'Nothing is difficult if you make up your mind.
What is my heart? You take my life.
But do as I ask just once
Please accept.'

'It is very fine,' she concludes.

'From the pen of the new courtesan of whom the town is talking,' I tell her.

'Ah,' she replies. 'I should like to see her perform and would ask my husband to invite her if only I did not fear...'

'I believe this woman to be spoken for. It is said that the son of the Nawab has shown a great interest.' Her expression remains one of sadness. 'You have no cause to fear,' I assure her with all my heart. 'Your husband loves you above all things.'

'Perhaps,' she says. 'Only I feel so heavy and ugly this time.' She is very big with child yet again. 'I can barely mount the stairs. My husband has given orders that a chamber be prepared on the ground floor.'

'You see!' I hug her. 'How he has consideration for you.'

'You are right, and I wrong to doubt him. Come let us go and eat the air now that it is cool, and before all the light has gone.'

Just as we reach the gate to the *bagh,* our mother joins us and it is clear that Faiz has sent a carriage to collect her. As they embrace, I am struck anew by their similarity, especially now that Faiz's shape is more rounded by the expected birth. They could be sisters, my mother still beautiful and fair, her eyes almost unlined and bright, hair thick without a tinge of grey. It is a pleasure to see her, but I wonder at the connivance without my knowledge. The mystery is soon discovered as we stroll down a path edged with orange and lime trees, from which, at this season, most of the fruit has been collected.

'You have been a widow long enough,' she says. 'Your father and I think it is time to find you a husband.'

Did I think I could live forever in such safe seclusion? Surely not, yet, seeing its end suddenly so near, hope fervently for any delay. I cannot oppose my parents.

'We have asked your sister's husband for his assistance in letting it be known amongst his acquaintance that you are free to marry. We should be happy to entrust you to any whom he is pleased to call his friend.'

'We shall host parties again once this baby is born and I am well,' Faiz adds. 'And see whose eye you can catch.'

As she finishes speaking, she gasps, stops abruptly and clutches her belly. My mother and I take her arms to support her but she pushes us away.

'It is nothing, only the baby kicking.'

'Another boy, praise Allah.' Our mother nods with satisfaction as we resume our walk.

'You must take good care,' I tell Faiz. 'For me there is no urgency.'

But, of course, our mother is of a contrary opinion. 'I was already a mother by your age,' she says. 'Which calls to mind another matter.'

Faiz and I exchange amused glances. We both know what she is going to say. For some time now she has been urging Faiz to ask my brother-in-law if they may hold a *bismillah* for Mary to mark the beginning of her formal education. Although William was correctly dressed as a little bridegroom and recited the whole of the *Surah Iqra* perfectly to his tutor, his ceremony was a small private family affair. My mother yearns to display her beautiful light-skinned granddaughter to the world. So far, all the ceremonies marking Mary's growth, for the piercing of her ears and for the first plaiting of her hair, have been very small celebrations indeed, with the distribution of sweets confined to the household.

'I did ask my husband,' Faiz forestalls her. 'The last time he was home. He says that he does not wish to parade too openly his closeness to our faith.'

'Hmph.' My mother stops to nip the dead heads on a bush of heavy pink roses, which I know to be from English cuttings grafted onto our sweeter smelling Indian variety. Some petals fall to the ground and I stoop to collect them, crush them in my palm and breathe in deeply. As the scent reaches the back of my throat it seems indeed that I am eating it.

'Then we must immediately do as we did for William.' My mother has regrouped her forces. 'Mary is rising five and she can already read and write a little in the Arabic script.'

'Indeed, Mother, and I shall be most happy if you would help me with the particulars. So, please, now may we enjoy our walk? I have been looking forward to this evening all the long hot day.' Faiz reaches to take some of my petals and rubs them on her wrists and temples.

'But perhaps you could also ask your husband if we could hold a proper *chhathi* for his new son?' My mother has not finished. 'Which being both a Hindu and Muslim tradition should surely not pose the same problem for him?' She plucks two roses, puts one in Faiz's hair and one in mine and stands back, her head tilted to one side, to survey the effect. 'Such lovely girls I am blessed with. When you were born, I knew how I must celebrate my good fortune.'

Faiz and I laugh at her unsubtle strategem. 'Let us go and sit by the water's edge and you can tell us,' says my sister. 'But hush now and listen!' she holds a finger to her lips. 'I asked the *mali* to turn on the fountains, especially for you.'

6

1853 Lower Beeding March

I can hear water but it is not fountains playing. It cascades from the sky, outside in the dark, and runs in small rivers down my window panes.

I remember my mother's description of the *chhathis* she gave for Faiz and me, when we were carried outdoors to see the stars in the night sky. *'Tare dikhana'.* It is when a child's destiny is written by the watching angel. I have always thought that my own first sighting must have made a deep impression since I have always loved looking at the stars. I have often wondered what my angel thought when he, or she, saw my destiny, whether he suspected mistakes in the reading, so unlikely did it seem. Surely no human would have predicted it nor wished it on any fellow creature.

I can see no stars tonight. The rain seems set and I should be thankful there is a roof over my head. But still I gaze, deep into the darkness, as I remember something else. I did not celebrate Banu's birth with any ceremony, for I was living far from Lucknow, with only Gulzar for company, and, I wonder, how long did the angel wait on that sixth night? And did she, or he, turn away at last in sorrow or in anger? And was my darling's destiny then ill-starred?

I think I see a light in the garden, a candle flickering, a figure carrying it closer. I press my forehead to the glass. Oh my daughter, is it you, my darling, come from who knows where, to thaw your mother's frozen heart? The figure stops, it is so close. But it is not Banu's face I see. It is the reflection of another and I hear another's voice.

'See, marm, a light I've brung to cheer this dismal eve. Come, back beside the fire and let me hide this evil night and pull the drapes.' It is Caroline, and come from duty, not from love.

The silent scream I felt arising breaks full from my throat. 'Noooo!' I beat my head on the window glass several times before she has me in her grasp.

'What is this moil you're maken me?' She shakes me hard but does not stop my moans. 'Cease or I must slap you.'

She pins me to my chair with one strong hand and lifts the other. I slump, defeated, and she stands back, hands on hips, regarding, with narrowed eyes.

'I should call the physician.' But she is not sure, knows from experience that my malady far escapes his powers.

'Bring me my pipe. It knows me better.'

The ignorant say that opium confuses and produces torpor, as with the Turks, who are supposed to sit like statues, mindless, silent. I say the contrary, for I am stimulated, with an excitation that does not eventuate in depression. It may be that in my, unsought, solitude I have the appearance of one in slumber, if with eyes that stare unseeing. Caroline has said as much. She does not see, and no-one does, that inner pageant where I revel, transported from this present gloom, a place more precious than my present life, sometimes more real.

And could they see what I see now, would they believe? Or call it fantasy, a paradise that fools create when mundane matters bear them down and quell their reason. It is true. 'Paradise' comes from the Persian words for walled and garden. Lucknow was famous for its *baghs,* its gardens, it was called 'The City of Gardens'. We lived in Paradise.

7

1787 Lucknow August

'We are going to the Bara Imam-Bara.'

I run into Faiz's chamber where she is resting with baby Charles, now four months old, in a crib beside her bed. She puts a finger to her lips and I move more quietly to look at him. Babies grow quickly, he knows me well and, if awake, would give me that wide smile not of chance but true recognition that brings such joy. Yet I love also to find him like this, in his private world of dreams, his rosebud mouth a little open, his tiny fists half-curled on either side of his head. As I gaze, he frowns and smacks his lips and I think will soon awaken. But his wet nurse will not be far, ready to suckle him when he cries.

'Do come. I do not think it will rain again today.'

The late monsoon rain has been falling in such quantities all morning as to impede one's vision to a few arms lengths beyond the windows and entirely prevent an outing. Now the great puddles, which had formed in every low-lying place, are fast diminishing in clouds of steam that rise to meet the sun's heat and very soon it will be possible to find a dry path.

My sister raises her head from the pillow and lets it fall again with a sigh. 'You must go to the Bara Imam-Bara without me,' she whispers. 'It will be as humid as a steam bath and I am already sick.' She indicates the basin on the floor beside the bed.

'Was some food not to your liking? Perhaps the milk had turned in the heat? You know that I am never much troubled by such -'

'It is not that,' she interrupts. 'Nor due to any malady.' She lays a little stress on the last word.

'Again? So soon?'

My surprise is too great to conceal, I fear it betrays more than a little dismay and, before I can amend this impression, I see tears well in her eyes. I kneel at her bedside, smooth her forehead and attempt to speak as would our mother.

'Hush, hush, all will be well. Allah be praised. Every child is a blessing.'

'Of course.' Now she is impatient with herself and with me. She dries her face and speaks with determination. 'And you must go with my husband and the children also and perhaps call on our mother as you pass as I daresay she will be most pleased to accompany you. I shall go another time.'

***

Crowds throng the Rumi-Gate as we approach and we draw closer together in order to keep sight of one another. To call it a 'gate' is perhaps misleading for it rises as high as many mosques, the surrounding stonework is wrought with more fine detailed ornament than one may see on many palaces or tombs, and its portico is as deep as almost half an entire cupola.

The *ayahs* tighten their grip on their charges' hands and my brother-in-law lifts Hastings to the greater safety of his shoulders. There are stalls selling *limbupani* in bottles with yellow stoppers like lemons, others selling *chai* and fried *channa* in screws of paper. Mary sees a boy selling tiny *jootis* made of coloured paper with gold painted insoles and drags on my hand until I find sufficient coins in my purse to buy a few. I take one of my mother's arms, cousin Gulzar the other.

'It will require a little time to pass through,' I say.

My mother does not like to stand for long but I do not mind for it is a long time since I was here. I saw it once before my widow's confinement, and just after its completion, and am glad to have the opportunity to admire it again at close quarters. 'Is it not a marvel that so many of the populace were involved in the construction?' We are passing through the right hand of the three entrance arches and I have bent my head back as far as it will go in order to admire the

25

concentric tiers of carving. The Rumi-Gate and Bara Imam-Bara were built by order of the Nawab in order to provide employment for the city's population after the famine of 1784 and much of the building was carried out by torchlight at night to hide the shame of those who would normally find such menial work beneath their status.

My mother shakes me and admonishes. 'Stand straight, you look deformed.'

I might demur and wonder at her sense of what is important in these sublime surroundings but instead am instantly transfixed. I had forgotten how my first sighting of the Imam-Bara quite took my breath away. It seems to me of such perfect symmetry and effortless simplicity that it might have emerged without human intervention, its design somehow contained within the brick and limestone laid at its feet.

The side that faces us has at its centre and lowest level three wide arches with scalloped surround and a depth of some twenty feet or more. On top of each are three smaller arched openings with a further four of different design between, all venting a wide shady gallery. Above this the flat roof is walled by slim pillars supporting yet smaller arches between each of which rests a miniature cupola. Viewed together, the several storeys recede with an illusion beyond mere perspective that captivates the eye and leads it inexorably to heaven.

And then we emerge into the glorious garden at the Imam-Bara's heart where the very grass dazzles in its newly-washed brilliance and there are more flowers than I knew existed, let alone can name. There are beds upon beds of closely planted varieties that set off each other's colour and proportions, and, around and between them, and along every bisecting path, row upon row of potted blooms, perhaps for later planting, perhaps to increase the richness of effect. By turns stunned at the complexity of the panorama in its entirety and awed by the perfection of each separate bloom, I think the *malis* must work hard to keep it so. There is one asleep behind a row of potted gladioli, perhaps drugged by the heavy bouquet of perfumes captured by the still warm air, wherein I can detect carnation, rose, marigold and the somewhat rank sweetness of chrysanthemum.

We approach the main building of the House of the Imams itself, where the *tazias* of Husain's mausoleum in Iraq are stored. As one might expect it is the most impressive building of all, especially since it is raised on wide terraces reached by two flights of steps. I hope I shall be able to come here next *Muharram* to participate in the mourning assembly for the deaths of the Prophet's grandson and his family and meanwhile am eager to see again the great chamber where this *majlis* is held.

However, freed from the press of people, our party becomes more unruly. Everyone is in high spirits, enjoying their release from the rain's confinement. My brother-in-law leads the way, bending to hold the hands of Hastings, who wants to walk. My mother and I are a few steps behind, followed by the ayahs and one of the male household servants, whose arms are full of our wraps and umbrellas lest the rain resume. William and Mary race around, their clothes soon splashed with mud from the remaining puddles. Hastings tries to toddle in pursuit but, before he is similarly splattered, is scooped up swiftly by his father. I should have liked to run with the children, and might have but for my mother's restraining presence.

'Look,' she nods her head to where my brother-in-law has stopped near the foot of the first staircase. He is greeting some acquaintance, a man of about his age but even fairer complexion. 'Who is that?' she wonders, clicks her tongue when I show no interest and finds an excuse to join them. 'Come, Hastings, let your father converse freely with this gentleman.' She summons the *ayah* who pulls him protesting from his father's arms, while I lean across to tweak his nose and make him smile.

8

1853 Lower Beeding March

It is a cold wet nose that pushes hard against my hand. It is Silver and his head is also wet from his latest ramblings.

'How come you now? You sense my disturbance and wish to share it?'

He licks my hand and regards me, panting, head askew, one ear cocked.

'Or you want your dinner. Come, let us find Caroline and see what she has kept for you. And then I shall to bed to dream some more and glad I shall be of your company.'

1787 Lucknow August

'Leopold, allow me to introduce my mother- and sister-in-law, this is Herr Leopold Von Wissenburg,' says my brother-in-law. 'He is quite newly arrived from Germany and therefore unaware that one of the world's marvels lies but a few paces from here.'

The German gentleman bows, removes his cap in salute and clicks his heels before he protests. 'I have already admired this beautiful building and admitted that it outshines any of our castles or palaces.'

My brother-in-law inclines his head in acknowledgement with that small smile I love so well. 'Most graciously,' he agrees. 'But I speak not of aesthetic judgments which must always be subjective but of facts and statistics concerning its size and construction. Come and I shall demonstrate.'

My mother and I accompany the two gentlemen up the steps, followed, I turn to make sure, more slowly by the servants and children. Our new acquaintance has a pleasant face and carries himself well, yet without swagger and it is clear that my brother-in-law likes him. His hair is very fair, although, without his cap, I see how thinly it is drawn across his head, his scalp and forehead most cruelly reddened by our tropic sun. We enter the great vaulted hall and everyone lowers their voices in respect.

'Do you see,' whispers my brother-in-law. 'Despite its size – it measures one hundred and sixty four by fifty two feet – there is not a single beam to support the roof which makes it the largest such building in the world, or so it is believed.'

'Extraordinary,' Herr von Wissenburg shakes his head in wonder. 'How is it possible?'

His eyes meet mine, perhaps by chance, but I remember the answer to his question.

'It was done by using the bricks in a special way, we call it *kara dena,*' I tell him. 'That is breaking them in different sizes at different angles and joining them together at these points to interlock them. Then it is covered in concrete, several feet thick I believe…'

'Really, Nur,' my mother interrupts to chide. 'Herr von Wissenburg will think you had a part in its construction!'

'Oh, it is only a description. I do not exactly understand.' I look away, my face hot with confusion and am glad to see William and Mary running to join us.

'Papa, Papa.' They commence tugging at his coattails. 'Take us to the *Bhulbhulaiya.* Please, please.' It is, in fact, only William who manages to pronounce the long word and I doubt if Mary even knows what it is, or will like it if she is taken, but she would follow William anywhere.

This labyrinth of passages, narrow in extreme, wind their way high up inside the building and lead eventually to the rooftop balconies from which there is a splendid view of the whole city. One requires a knowledgeable guide and a lantern, for there are near five hundred identical doorways and many blind alleys and false turns. I did not much like it myself when I visited, but will go again to help with the children when I see that my brother-in-law is of a mind to take them. However, Herr von Wissenburg has refused.

'I fear I have no head for heights,' he apologises. 'But do not let me interfere with your family's enjoyment.'

'Please, please,' the children recommence their pleading.

'Do go,' I am surprised to hear my mother in support. 'Take help,' she indicates the servant. 'We shall look after your friend meanwhile.'

It is resolved, Herr von Wissenburg bows in acquiescence and my brother-in-law offers a final introduction. 'Leopold has not been here long but is already an authority on the city's gardens. I think he has seen them all.'

'Oh, I hardly think so.' It is this new arrival's turn to blush but the moment passes as my mother lifts her hand for him to kiss, which takes him, and me, a little by surprise. I have marvelled before at her quickness to mould to the manners of her companions, which must have helped my father's rapid rise. Today it puts me on my guard, suspicious of her intent. She thinks this man a match for me! As we stroll along the terrace she sets to engage him and appraise his character and credentials.

'Do you find the French or English style of garden the most pleasing?'

Leopold Von Wissenburg tilts his head to one side, considering the dilemma. 'The Padshah Bagh, which as you will know is laid out in the English style, is uncommonly delightful. There is a basin with many fountains that intersects the garden in its whole length and two pretty summerhouses with marble baths.'

'One for the ladies of the household?'

'Indeed, they are connected to the harem which is most spacious and so situated that I understand that the Nawab can view the amusements of the ladies from the colonnade of the palace.'

'Which is perhaps not so very English?' My mother raises an eyebrow. Her von Wissenburg blushes again but she is smiling. 'So you can find no fault with the English style?'

'Oh as to that, I am afraid the effect of the natural beauties of the Padshah Bagh is rather spoiled by the many statues, models of sandstone, which seem to lurk at every corner and produce a most disagreeable impression. But it is only my opinion.' He adds this last quickly, again unsure as to the sensibilities of his audience.

My mother inscrutably pursues her enquiries. 'And the French?'

'The French.' He pauses, considering. 'I have seen the Nasiree Bagh which though small is pleasant enough. But -' he pauses again, as if hesitant to disoblige.

My mother encourages him. 'But?'

'There is a summer house quite overladen with *objets d'art*, that is to say pieces of glass and china, some paintings which are not good, copper plates, all manner of *bagatelles*.' He spreads his hands and looks skyward in a fashion that indicates a degree of despair.

'Yes, yes,' my mother is excited to find him so in sympathy. 'I have seen it myself. It is all quite tasteless.' She looks to me for further confirmation but, seeing none, quickly returns her gaze. I do not care about particulars very much so long as a garden is spacious, sweet-smelling and there is water.

We have reached the great rectangular tank which connects the many smaller channels that criss-cross the garden. My mother sits on its edge and I beside her while our companion stands, as if on guard.

'However,' he continues. 'I do find a very pleasing sympathy between the French *parterres* and the Mughal designs, which tend also to the formal.'

'My opinion entirely,' coos my mother. 'Though I think my husband would insist on a common Persian heritage. Being of Persian origin himself. Which is why my daughters are so fair.'

With this apparent afterthought, she extends a graceful arm to pull me close and demonstrate the fact, but I slip from under its embrace to peer into the water for the gold and silver fish that I saw last time. I feel Herr von Wissenburg's scrutiny yet he does not speak and I do not know if I should take offence. Is his silence what the Europeans call 'ungallant'? Or is he as discomfited as I, in which case I like him the more?

He returns to the surer ground of our immediate surroundings.

'Here at least I find a perfect blend of form and colour that complements and enhances this most beautiful of buildings.'

In case this does not put an end to the conversation I seize on the distant sounds of musicians tuning to provide a diversion.

'I should like to see the performance,' I tell my mother. 'The music master told me about it.'

'A splendid idea,' she takes my arm. 'We shall await my son-in-law and then find our way together to the *baradhari*. Will you not

31

accompany us?' she addresses Herr von Wissenburg. 'You know, my daughter is becoming most proficient on the *sarangi* and her singing approaches the sublime. You must come to my son-in-law's house one day to hear her.'

Ah! She is incorrigible and I am sure he sees through her design. And yet it is pleasant to see him look at me with interest for the first time.

'I have a great partiality for music,' he says. 'My country is enjoying a flowering of the art. But I should like to listen to your country's music which I know to be very different.' He bows slightly in my direction and, of a sudden I am afraid that I may find myself drawn in too soon beyond retreat. I need to leave, to seek my sister, to consult.

'Oh see, it has begun to rain,' I feel some drops on my cheek. 'Perhaps we should go home.'

'It is nothing.' My mother holds me tight.

But then she too feels a splash, which is accompanied by laughter. It is William crept up behind us and, relieved to be thus diverted, I reach into the water and splash him in return. The battle might have continued but for the arrival of my brother-in-law who is carrying Mary, her face buried in his coat sleeve, her shoulders heaving with subdued sobs.

'She fell on the steep steps coming down,' my brother-in-law explains and she turns to us a tear-stained, swollen face. 'Before that,' he continues, 'She was most undeterred by the darkness and the twists and turns.'

I reach out to take her and kiss away her tears. 'I think she is also tired. Perhaps we should go home.'

'We are going to the concert,' my mother reminds me and gestures to Zainab to come and relieve me.

Mary, however, refuses to be removed and clasps her hands more firmly around my neck. 'Nur *chachi* carry me,' she insists and renews her weeping.

'Hush, hush.' I shake her gently and turn to my mother. 'I too am a little tired,' I tell her. 'And should prefer to go home instead.'

She narrows her eyes, unsure as to my true intent, and how therefore she might yet persuade me, but the situation passes rapidly beyond her control.

'Dear *sasurai,* dear mother-in-law,' says my brother-in-law, 'if you would be so good as to escort Nur and the children to my house I should feel free to accompany Leopold and listen to the music. It is a while since I have had such an opportunity.'

'Certainly,' my mother bows her head in acquiescence but then looks up at him and smiles. 'Then perhaps it is time that you host such an occasion in your house.'

'A music party! Indeed I should. I shall.'

'And invite Herr von Wissenburg.'

'Naturally.'

'And Nur will sing.'

A slight frown momentarily furrows my brother-in-law's forehead. He has, I think, now suspected my mother's purpose and he is ever my protector.

'If she wishes,' he says, with a determination that only those who know him well would observe.

9

1787 Lucknow August

'We shall hold a *soiree* next week. I have invited Leopold,' announces my brother-in-law later that day. 'A *soiree* is more intimate and we will not invite anyone from outside the household. I shall engage some musicians, Nur may sing a few pieces as she chooses and I hope that William will also perform a little.'

I select some of my favourite *ghazals* and prevail upon William to accompany me and keep time on the *tabla*.

'You need only practise two hours a day,' I promise him. 'And I shall be so much happier with you beside me. I had hoped your mama might join us but she must still rest. Masterji will play the *sarangi*.'

***

We are partway through the first *ghazal* on the day of the performance when I see Masterji incline his head in my direction and give me the slightest of smiles. I know that he is satisfied, my spirits lift and I find myself able to respond and even play a little with his propositions. Our audience is naturally inclined to be uncritical and at the end is, indeed, enthusiastic.

'Wah,wah!' my brother-in-law claps his appreciation and my mother is not only smiling but, I think, wiping a few tears from her eyes. She stands to go to the back of the room to supervise the provision of refreshments but does not miss the ensuing scene and keeps her eyes upon us. William runs off to eat and accept what compliments come his way, while I am waylaid by Herr von Wissenburg, or Leopold, as he begs me to call him.

'You are too young to be so formal,' he insists. 'Pray tell me more about these songs that you sang so beautifully. I believe they have a special form?'

I tell him as succinctly as I can about the requisite pattern of rhyming couplets and the refrain which is repeated.

'It is difficult to write,' I say. 'Or I find it so.'

Then I hesitate. Should I tell him that the traditional subject is Love, and, more particularly, frustrated love which, if attained, would bring the lover utter fulfilment, even ecstasy? I fear it may not seem appropriate, even though I could go on to explain that the love described may be only spiritual and for God, rather than another human being. Fortunately, Leopold is himself eager to speak and tells me that it sounds quite similar to a European form of poetry, one that is derived from an older Roman source. And then he waves this aside and says that there is a great deal of interest in his country in things Indian, in fact one of their best-known poets has been telling stories in the coffee houses which, he understands, have their source in some of our most illustrious books, the Mahabharata and the Ramayana.

He mispronounces these titles of course but it is not this that I correct.

'But these are Hindu texts, sacred texts,' I explain. 'The *ghazal* is of Islamic origin.'

He is deeply embarrassed and, in consequence, so am I. I hasten to repair the situation.

'There is only one God,' I say. 'It matters not by what name He is called.'

This, of course, is only what I have learned since living in my sister's household but he regards me more closely and I am encouraged. 'You could tell your poet he should read some Persian poetry,' I suggest. 'In fact, you may like to yourself.'

'For that I would have to learn Persian.' He laughs.

'Then you can learn! Many Europeans have learnt.'

'If only I had more time…' He sighs.

His business is his concern and besides, I think our interview long enough. Also, the musicians who will play for the second half of the evening are assembling just behind us and will wish shortly to begin their tuning. I catch my mother's eye, she nods, no doubt in approval of my behaviour, and I find my excuse.

'I must go and assist my mother,' I tell Leopold and quickly take my leave.

***

'How many times has Herr von Wissenburg visited since the musical evening?' My mother is quizzing my sister as, together with Gulzar, we walk down the hill from the Residency grounds to Captain Bazaar, which has lately been constructed by the Frenchman Colonel Martin. We have had word that new goods are expected and are keen to be amongst the first to inspect them. There is already a small stream of other customers ahead of us.

My mother knows that Leopold has come to our house quite a number of times and is convinced that I am the cause, though he keeps company only with my brother-in-law and salutes me only in passing. She thinks that Faiz could glean further facts, indeed is increasingly put out that Faiz refuses to tackle her husband more directly on the subject.

'If my husband thinks this man a suitable match for my sister, I am sure he will find a way of arranging matters,' says Faiz, not for the first time. 'Oh do look!' she points ahead as the river comes into view.

It is full but no longer flooding its banks. A number of boats are tied at the *ghat* and a human chain of porters staggering under their loads leads from them to the white-washed terrace of one-storeyed booths that form the bazaar. From this distance their white rectangular shapes appear not unlike the tented encampment of a small army detachment, but are in fact of more permanent construction.

To me, Faiz has said that my brother-in-law will surely find someone more established, better known, and better looking. I am content to leave matters in others' hands and meanwhile savour this new feeling of an unknown yet, at last, more promising future.

My mother is diverted. 'Perhaps Colonel Martin himself will be there to supervise the display of his merchandise.' She takes Gulzar's arm and draws a little ahead as we approach the entrance to the bazaar.

I do not especially wish to purchase, but am eager to discover whence come the latest wares. We walk past stalls laden with shawls from Kashmir, carpets from Kabul, fine footwear from England, lace and lacquered clocks from France. My mother is fingering some fine porcelain, surely from China.

'One feels that the world is come to us,' I catch Faiz' hand in mine. 'Do you not find it exciting?' We walk on swinging our hands together as when we were children and I begin to hum.

Faiz is smiling at my frivolity but then turns her head to listen more closely and beat time with her free hand. We have reached the porcelain stall.

'That's good,' she says. 'I do not know it. Is it new?'

It is something I am trying to write, I tell her and ask for her assistance.

'Then you can both perform at the music party which my son-in-law promised me.' My mother has missed nothing. 'He did!' she insists as we laugh. 'For the other, by his own account, was merely a family occasion.'

10

1853 Lower Beeding, March

I wake up singing, indeed I think it is my singing that awakens me, for it is earlier than is my habit. I think to surprise Caroline and clamber carefully out of bed to pull the drapes myself. Still the cats are disturbed and frown a little and flatten their ears, before curling up anew and allowing their irritation to subside. Silver, much more forgiving, thumps his tail twice in greeting but his eyes remain closed. For once, I am the only one eager to be up and active.

As Caroline most frequently remarks, the drapes are full of dust and my song is interrupted by a fit of coughing. I wrestle with the casement, which is rarely open, and breathe the still chill air. The sun is warm on my face however, although it is but a week since it overtook the hours of darkness, and, as every year, my spirits rise in consequence. I resume my song and return to bed to await breakfast.

'Lawks a mercy,' Caroline appears at the door, hands to her bosom to still the palpitations of which, once again, I have been the cause.

'I heard that much a'stumbling and a'mumbling I thought thee wust possessed.'

Sometimes I think she manufactures drama for her own diversion finding it over-quiet in my house and am tempted to tease her in return.

'You do not like my singing?'

'So that's what it were.' She shakes her head in apparent mystification, which could be unfeigned. What does she know of the world, of 'furrin parts'?

'Come,' I rally us both. 'What think you to start the spring clean? And to begin by replacing these curtains with their summer cousins?'

A momentary disapproval of my poetic phrasing, (such fancifulness), is overcome by her surprise and satisfaction. It must be several years since I have allowed her to have her will and drag the drapes outside to the garden, there to beat them soundly as they hang defenceless over the washing lines. She shall do the carpets too, I think.

'And I have a mind to order the library, there is a book or two I would find.'

Another task that is much overdue and it is my turn to be surprised, for her enthusiasm abates and she is abashed.

'Ah,' she says and pauses, unwilling to give offence or lose the opportunity. 'I would advise we start the morrer, ma'am, if tis all the same to thee.'

'The morrer.' I ponder, awaiting enlightenment, and then I see. 'I have forgotten the day, have I not?' It is happening more oft of late.

She nods, relieved. 'Indeed tha hast, ma'am. 'Tis Sunday, Palm Sunday, at that.'

'Then I shall go to church!' I am of a sudden delighted at the prospect of a drive through the spring lanes and of seeing my acquaintance at Horsham's Catholic Church. It is months since I was there. 'Make haste and ask James to make ready the cart. And we shall indeed delay the housework until tomorrow. For I doubt not that you wish to go avisiting this afternoon.'

Her already high colour deepens, but she is pleased that I remember. She has but lately taken up with my tenant and gardener, James Budgen, and, though I find him a somewhat shiftless type, I do not doubt that she will soon beat him into shape and I shall wish them well if they proceed to matrimony. She would then not sleep under my roof, but near enough I think.

'In fact, in order not to delay your outing perhaps you may find another to drive me?'

***

The journey to church is not as pleasant as I had anticipated. I guess my old bones take less kindly to the jolting of the pony trap after a winter of near hibernation and the ruts in the lanes have yet to dry and be worn down. Though there are scarcely any leaves to impede them, the sun's rays are still weak and the slight breeze soon chills me despite my wraps. James' neighbour, Albert, is huddled deep into his muffler and coat and we speak little. I am glad to reach St Mary's and to spy my friends, Ann and Michael Howes, preceding me up the church path.

'Helena! Oh I am glad to see you,' says Ann, stopping to embrace me. 'I was just counting the weeks since last you came to church. My, but your cheeks are cold. Still travelling in that old trap I see. Come let us hasten inside.'

I am the recipient of other nods and smiles from amongst the congregation as we walk up the aisle and take our places in the Howes' pew. Across the aisle the Aldridges appear very pleased to see me, while another good friend, Elizabeth Etherton, turns from her seat just in front to greet me. I resolve to come more often. The service gives the comfort of all familiar things and I like to sing the hymns and responses, though I fear my voice is become even more quavery. Father Martin is waiting at the door to greet his flock as we leave.

'Mrs Bennett, a pleasure to have our benefactress with us again to be sure,' he pumps my hand with vigour. His smile is so broad that his plump cheeks almost obscure his eyes and I feel myself beaming in return. 'Allow me to introduce you to recipients of your benevolence. Patrick!' he collars a young man, who had been shepherding his small family past us. 'This is the kind Christian lady without whom you might be living in the workhouse. Mrs Bennett, may I present the O'Connor family, newly of this parish and most recent recipients of our church charity to which you so generously contribute. I found them sleeping in the porch here a week or two since, having no funds to secure a roof over their heads.'

Patrick O'Connor is abashed but bows his head and mumbles his thanks and his wife gives me a wan smile and pushes forward her two small children.

'Say good mornin',' she urges them. 'And thank you kindly ma'am.' But the children only stare and the smallest, a boy, sucks his thumb.

'I thank God I am in a position to be of assistance,' I say and turn away, feeling the children's eyes still upon me. I daresay they have never seen a person of my complexion.

***

I take the cold lunch that Caroline has left me into the library and find that she has made a start on sorting my books. She knows her alphabet and several shelves are accordingly arranged. I search for 'G' but she has not got so far, indeed has been thwarted, I suspect, by the large proportion that are in the Persian or Urdu script. These lie discarded in several untidy piles and I leave them for another day.

I am looking for a book of poems by Goethe for, though I did not know it at the time, this was the German poet of whom Leopold von Wissenburg spoke all those years ago. Strangely, as I had suggested he might, this poet did come to read one of the greatest Persian poets, Hafiz, and was so inspired that he then wrote the '*Diran*', which was amongst his most celebrated work. I find the volume and turn the pages quickly as I scan the verses for something I remember.

> FREEDOM OF SPIRIT
> *Mine be the saddle still to ride*
> *While you in hut or tent abide*
> *And gay I gallop through wilds afar*
> *Naught o'er my bonnet save the star.*
> *The stars were appointed by His voice,*
> *Your guides over land and sea,*
> *That the heart within you may rejoice*
> *And your glance still heavenward be.*

It is re-versified from the Koran and its message gave me comfort when first I read it but the expression I find mundane. No language is so perfect for poetry as Persian. I never mastered its use to a high degree and the *ghazal* I wrote for the party was in English, for Leopold's sake, for my family were assured of his interest in me.

11

1787 Lucknow October

'My husband tells me that Herr von Wissenburg is visiting again today,' Faiz looks up from dandling a toy for baby Charles to reach out to and grasp. He lies in her lap, kicking energetically and I am waiting for my turn to play with him. 'Why do you not join them on some pretext?'

'Did your husband also tell you that?'

She looks away. 'Perhaps. No. He did not. But he is a little puzzled at the gentleman's attitude, having thought him partial to you and he wishes that something would force the matter.'

'Perhaps there is no matter to force and he visits only as your husband's friend, having still a small acquaintanceship in Lucknow. Or perhaps he has some business interests that he wishes to pursue.'

'Hm. Well it is true that today Colonel Martin is also due to visit and he of course has many projects in hand in which a gentleman like Herr von Wissenburg might invest. However,' she decides, 'I shall send you with some token of esteem from me for the Colonel to give Boulone. Some sweetmeats perhaps.'

This is not so wild a scheme since the Colonel's favourite companion is a good friend of Faiz and a little known to me. A short time later, equipped with this pretext, and guided by the sweet smell of tobacco, I find the three gentlemen on the terrace outside my brother-in-law's room. They are reclining, jacketless, on cushions facing out over the Residency gardens, their white shirts bright against the brilliant green lawns and trees, with a hookah set up between them. My brother-in-law draws in his feet a little and indicates that I should share his seat.

'We are discussing the growing trade in indigo in which the Colonel has considerable interests already,' he informs me. 'Leopold appears to wish to become involved and I regret not having the means to do so also.'

Leopold, who has inhaled deeply, offers me the mouthpiece of the pipe, which I pass straight to my brother-in-law. 'I am told that here it is acceptable for ladies also to smoke,' observes Leopold when he again has breath.

Colonel Martin laughs with great good humour. He has a kind face I have always thought, which belies his reputation for sharp business sense and scandalous living. Boulone is far from being his only wife. 'It can be taken as the highest compliment that a lady may pay a man, to share his pipe,' he says. 'But it is not known for this to be the first initiative. Or not in polite company.'

Leopold does not quite understand but he knows he has committed a *faux pas*. My brother-in-law is watching him closely. I keep my gaze fixed between them as if I have no particular interest in the outcome of the debate.

'What the Colonel is trying to say,' my brother-in-law takes it upon himself to explain, 'Is that the lady concerned should have had some encouragement from the gentleman concerned, in other words that there is some understanding between them, some – declared intention to – shall we say - draw closer.'

I feel my face is as scarlet as Leopold's and make my escape as quickly as I may. If there is to be some declaration, I hope that it will be soon. Perhaps Leopold is unsure how to proceed in a society with which he is as yet unfamiliar. Or perhaps he has no desire to draw closer to me. Whatever the case, it is painful to be the subject of such confusion.

***

My embarrassment inspires me to almost finish my lyric.
'It is not mine to give, this heart of mine.
It has its own desires, this heart of mine.
They are mysterious, manifold and deep.

43

I do not know this heart of mine.
Only he can break the spell,
Who holds the key to this heart of mine.
How near is he, the one who knows
How to unlock this heart of mine?'

Next day, Faiz joins me where I am practising in the *sangeet khana*.

'What do you think?' I ask her. It does not sound to me as profound in the singing as when I wrote it at dead of night.

Faiz cocks her head to one side, considering. 'Not bad for a first attempt. Not bad at all. And that need not be an *enjambement* at the end if it is understood as two separate questions. You see?' She repeats the last two lines. 'We can work on it.'

I hug her briefly, eager to begin.

'But he is not near.' She looks at me closely. 'He has left Lucknow. Last night. He is on his way home to Germany. My husband received a note this morning.'

I am dumbstruck.

'It seems one of his children is ill and his wife has summoned him.'

'His wife? Children?'

'You didn't know?'

Her carelessness amazes me, though it is true that my brother-in-law had another wife and family before he met Faiz. In fact, two of his sons visited us not long since. But the situation is different, I feel. Mrs Palmer did not want to accompany her husband to India and appears to live quite happily in London with their two daughters. And their marriage had broken down even before that, when they were living in Martinique. Leopold's wife may have chosen not to accompany him to India, but it is clear that the marriage is not over and that either she expected to join him or that he would return home. In either case, a second wife would not have featured in her reckoning.

'I cannot blame him,' I say at last. 'I am sure our romance existed more in others' eyes than in his own. Or in mine.' I add this with a sudden clarity of vision. 'I do not mind,' I assure her. 'He did not truly touch my heart.'

'Good,' she says. 'So let us finish your *ghazal*. There will be someone else who will.'

***

'Well really,' my mother is outraged at Leopold's defection. 'I do think he owed his friends a little more personal farewell. But, you know, I did find him a little insincere, too ready to ingratiate.'

Faiz and I exchange a look of amusement, which my mother affects not to notice.

'And we shall never pronounce his name again,' she concludes, clamping her lips together in emphasis. 'Now, about this music party, which I do think of the utmost importance. I will not be known as the mother who did not trouble to find her daughter a suitable match and what better way to display dear Nur's best qualities.' She lowers herself with exaggerated difficulty to sit on the carpet where we have lain aside our instruments at her arrival. 'There are few consolations in growing old but seeing one's children well settled is one of them.'

12

1853 Lower Beeding March

I am stiff with old age, having again forgotten that I should no longer kneel, and with great difficulty stand and make my way to the window seat that gives a good view of the front garden, still soaked in the early evening sun. This would have made a fine, if small, music room I think, and I wish I had long ago acquired some instruments and maintained my skill, even had I to play alone. My thoughts drift back to that evening when I had some of the best musicians to accompany me, sitting in a semi-circle around me, all of us cross-legged on the carpetted dais, waiting for that moment when the audience is at last still and our performance can begin.

1787 Lucknow November

My *ghazal* is amended and complete but, despite Faiz's assurances, I fear it will prove insubstantial. The other pieces I have selected are, I hope, not too well known and will therefore encourage less comparison with more expert renditions, besides enjoying the charm of the new. And I am, I remind myself, only to play at the beginning, to whet the appetite, attune the hearing, for the greater delights to come.

Nevertheless, the audience is larger than I expected and some of them are used to the highest standards. There is, to be sure, a large group of family members, my father as well as my mother, most of our neighbours in the Residency, including the Scottish Doctor Blane, Physician to the Nawab, and his wife, who are here as much to support me as for the love of music, although the Doctor was born

46

in India and speaks Persian and Hindustani. Colonel Martin stands at the back in his Company uniform of red jacket with gold frogging and epaulettes. He is chatting to Colonel Antoine Polier, who is a great connoisseur and lover of our culture, has two Indian wives and lives, I understand, entirely like a Mughal noble in either his *haveli* in Lucknow or on his *jagir* near Agra. He certainly has the appearance, being dark-haired with full moustaches carefully curled upward, and a large and impressive presence dressed in deep blue gold-embroidered silk, with jewels flashing in his matching *pagri*. Yet even he, as a good friend of my brother-in-law, will be well-disposed to me, although we have not met.

But there are also strangers, Company friends and colleagues of my brother-in-law, who make very evident their attunement to our culture. Some of them, like Colonel Polier, are entirely dressed in Mughal fashion with long gowns of richly woven silk and matching turbans bound with pearls or sporting peacock feathers. They kick off their embroidered *jootis* to recline on mattresses supported by bolsters covered in red damask. I have not seen these items of furniture before in our house and wonder how much my brother-in-law is expending on the event. Perhaps one may hire or borrow them for, indeed, the household does not possess so many chairs either as are now arranged in rows facing me.

Doctor Blane wears a rather splendid long high-collared blue coat of some light material over straight-cut white cotton trousers, which seems to me a well-judged adaptation to our climate, but then his manner generally is that of quiet confidence, one would like to have him at one's bedside, I always think. Yet other Europeans wear only one or two pieces of Lucknavi clothing, perhaps a *jama*, perhaps a shawl, with their suits or uniforms, which to my eye has more symbolic than aesthetic appeal. One even tops off his hybrid costume with a curious checked cap, while Mrs Blane, whom I have always thought like some elegant wading bird, a heron perhaps, for, though mother of several children, she is thin as a stick, sports some sort of turban of purple silk that sprouts a peacock feather on top of her reddish hair. She manages to catch my eye and smiles in encouragement.

However attractive or otherwise one may find such attire, it is all exceedingly well-meant, that much is clear from the convivial atmosphere which prevails and is not at all diminished when the Nawab-Vizier of Avadh himself enters. Asaf-ud-Daula is an imposing figure, whatever his dress. Tall and powerfully built, he is clean-shaven but for long moustaches which balance the fine upsweep of his imperious eyebrows. He has cause, I think, to be proud since, under him, the city has flourished and been transformed into a great centre of industry and the arts. And our family has cause to be grateful to him for his encouragement of all things Persian; there has been a continuing stream of immigrants who, like my father, have made their fortunes under his benign rule. But tonight he chooses to honour his host and appears to ripples of surprise and acclaim in some sort of British military uniform with much gold frogging and a large three-cornered hat.

'I do believe he is an Admiral!' I overhear the Doctor whisper to his wife as he stands to bow and acknowledge the Nawab's presence.

'I was rather hoping for the bishop's outfit.' Mrs Blane curtseys, peacock feather swaying, smiling behind her fan.

At last people are beginning to settle down and we on the dais are able to hear each other's notes as we tune our instruments. I wait in stillness for the steadying note of the *sarangi* and then I begin to sing my *ghazal* and forget where I am, or in whose company, and become aware only of the words and melody and the interplay with the musicians around me.

'It is not mine to give, this heart of mine.
It has its own desires, this heart of mine.
They are mysterious, manifold and deep.
I do not know this heart of mine.'

I notice a few nods of approval in the audience at this point, but then am lost in the totality of the performance in a way that I have never before experienced.

'I know there is one who can break the spell,
Who holds the key to this heart of mine.
When will he come, the one who knows?
How to unlock this heart of mine?'

Suddenly, and most reluctantly, I become aware of movement in the audience, a shuffling as space is made for some newcomer and others turn to frown at the interruption. I glance in the same direction and see a tall, well-built man in plain and sombre European dress, who is not widely recognised, I guess from questioning looks exchanged in the audience. But Colonel Martin and Colonel Polier greet him warmly and my brother-in-law on the other side of the room acknowledges his arrival with a show of great pleasure.

I regain my composure but not the same miraculous intensity of concentration. Rather, I sing the remainder of the *ghazal* acutely aware of this stranger's gaze fixed upon me, and I develop the impression that I am singing for, and to, him alone.

'One came and smiled but went away.
He did not want this heart of mine.
So still I wait and hope and pray
For the one who will take this heart of mine.
It is not mine to give, this heart of mine.
It is not mine to give, this heart of mine.'

My performance is well-received with various expressions of approval, varying from the formal, though prolonged, hand-clapping of many of the Europeans to the *'wahs'* and kissing of fingertips that we favour. Even Asaf-ud-Daulah is nodding and has raised one hand, palm uppermost in approval, in my direction, so I am much encouraged and the rest of the performance passes off smoothly. I think I convey the essence of each piece with the feeling that it inspires in me and as intended by the composer. I do not look to the back of the hall until I am making my final bows when I see that he has gone. Not knowing when he left, or why, I pass the rest of the evening in turmoil and it is not until the next morning that I am able to raise the subject with my sister.

'Who was the good-looking *firangi* who arrived late and might have destroyed my performance?' I pick up Charles and believe I speak lightly, but of course, Faiz is not so easily fooled and claps her hands.

'I thought I detected an especial interest!' She is triumphant, then quickly reassuring. 'But no one else did, I am sure. Not even our mother, or I should have heard.'

'So who is he?' I persist. 'So good a friend of Colonel Martin and Colonel Polier, yet unknown by so many?'

'His name is Benoit de Boigne, and we have met him some years ago but perhaps, being then a child, you do not remember. Captain de Boigne has lately been much engaged in fighting the Mahrattas' cause against the Rohillas and sundry others, and proved himself most valuable to Mahadji Sindhia. Sindhia is currently marshalling his forces at Gwalior and, if the Captain left our party in a hurry, it was quite likely on some such urgent affairs of state.'

Before I have time to speak Faiz adds: 'I asked my husband, whose business it is of course to have intimate knowledge of such matters.'

Again I open my mouth to speak and again she adds: 'I thought you would want to know and can see I was correct.' She laughs. 'But upon the question of when or whether he may return ...' She shrugs and spreads her hands. 'In fact, I am sad to say that my husband may soon also be required to leave us again, which will at least mean that we receive regular news of events. So, dear sister, I fear we can only wait and see what will occur.' And then she drops the teasing tone and reaches out to touch me. 'But he is most certainly a very suitable match and would be well worth waiting for.'

'I can wait,' I hug Charles to me and go to sit by the window to show him a flock of green parakeets that has just landed noisily in the nearest tamarind tree.

13

1853 Lower Beeding March

Caroline is surprised to find me, as it appears, watching for her. She looks up as she fumbles with the latch of the gate, it is a little swollen after the wet of winter, then, flustered, hastens up the path and around the side of the house to enter by the kitchen door. She is still removing her bonnet when she comes to find me.

'I am not late, surelye. I were most careful to keep track of the church clock's chimes. I will have th'supper to ye in a trice.' She is pushing stray strands of hair into place with the fingers of one hand, her cheeks are flushed, her eyes have an uncommon brightness. I wonder how long before James Budgen declares his hand, perhaps he has already.

'Not late at all,' I assure her. 'I like to sit here. I trust you enjoyed a pleasant afternoon?'

The bright eyes widen. She is not used to such civility. 'I have indeed, thank you, ma'am.' And she hurries to the kitchen before my mood changes. But my memories today are also happy, being of a similar time in my life. I remember the very first occasion he visited. Fortunately, I was in the grounds of the Residency, playing with the children, so it was not hard for us to meet.

1788 Lucknow March

We are lying on the grass at the edge of the shadow cast by the great banyan tree which dominates the lawn in front of the Residency, the dry leaves of the pipal trees, at this season almost bare, falling with a faint clatter to the ground around us. High above, in the hazy blue, kites wheel tirelessly and, at a lower altitude, there is a small paper one also, its string held somewhere by an unseen hand. I am listening to my favourite bird song, the prolonged melodious chiming of the kohl, the greyest and otherwise most unremarkable of birds, claiming attention above the faintly nasal squabbling of the parakeets, constant cawing of crows and background chorus of a myriad smaller birds.

Gulzar has taken Charles inside to sleep and I am amusing the other three children so that they may not disturb Faiz, newly delivered of baby Sarah. It was a difficult birth and Doctor Blane is of the opinion that she should have no more children. We have been playing with bats and ball, William and I, with Mary's occasional assistance in retrieving the ball when it goes astray. Hastings has been happy chasing after Mary and, before that, being swung from two hanging roots, which, tied together, form a makeshift seat. Just now he is sitting on my stomach and hoping I will lift him above me and make him 'fly', another game that he has loved since he was small, of which now, at nearly three years old and sturdy withal, I think I must soon wean him. But Mary is become impatient.

'It's my turn, Nur Auntie.' She grabs my hand and pulls, black curls bouncing under her bonnet, which is somewhat askew. 'Play with me! Hide and seek, you promised!' She pulls again as I do not move. 'You did!'

'It's a baby's game!' William taunts her, swinging his bat provocatively close.

'I did and I will,' I say. 'Only let me catch my breath. William, take care. You must play alone if you do not wish to join us.' Nearly eight years old, I think he is in need of company his own age. 'And Hastings, you are crushing me.' I lift him off, set him beside me and sit up before he can clamber back.

And then we are all distracted by the sound of fast approaching horse's hooves. Chandi also comes galloping towards us from the opposite direction, having abandoned the pursuit of squirrels somewhere amongst the further trees in order to protect us. I stand and squint into the sun as the figure canters closer and see that it is he.

'Call off your dog, Mademoiselle Nur, if you will. I fear he may receive a kicking.'

Chandi comes, reluctant, to sit at my side where I pat and calm him, though he continues to growl as Captain de Boigne swings off his mount, loops the reins round the front of the saddle and walks to join us. The children all instantly attach themselves to my person, awed by the impressive figure. I pick up Hastings, who has begun to whimper.

The great soldier is humming as he bows in greeting, and sweeps his cap low in front of us, revealing a head of close-cropped dark hair. As he straightens, he smiles a little, opens his mouth and, entirely taking me by surprise, sings.

'*I do not know this heart of mine. It has its own desires and they are mysterious, manifold and deep.*' His voice is resonant and deep. 'It was a fine performance, Mademoiselle, and sad I was to be called away before its conclusion. I have found myself unable to clear my mind of this particular song.'

He has a strong, angular face that seems almost hewn from stone, but for the mouth which, close to, has a mildness and mobility that suggests an underlying sensitivity, and for his dark brown eyes where a certain wariness somehow lends me greater confidence.

'You flatter me, Monsieur.'

'I never flatter.' His tone is severe, almost a warning and then it softens.

'You make a pretty sight playing with the children, Mademoiselle. Your sister is lucky to have you as nursemaid.'

'More playmate I think, *Captain de Boigne*.'

He narrows his eyes, surprised, I think, that I know his identity, but soon regains the offensive. 'You are right. You are so young.' He tilts his head to one side and observes me closely. 'Almost a child, one might say.'

I am pondering my next sally, aware that he is playing with me, perhaps testing me, when the horse neighs loudly and stamps a foot. William has left my side and is attempting to touch the horse's head. The Captain leaps to take hold of the reins.

'Come,' he invites William. 'Now you may stroke his muzzle.'

'Now he seems the most docile of pets,' I observe as the horse nuzzles deep in William's small hand.

'A good military horse must be able to change swiftly from ferocity to docility,' the Captain tells us. 'As must a good military man.' He looks at me so closely that, again, I feel I am being tested and assessed.

Fortunately, my brother-in-law just then appears and begins to cross the lawn towards us. The Captain swings both William and Mary up onto the horse's saddle and leads them to meet him, while I carry Hastings, aware that we must give any onlooker the most harmonious of impressions. But my thoughts are in the utmost confusion. I am almost certain that the Captain has sought me out and with the purpose of furthering a relationship with me, which in view of his closeness to my brother-in-law must surely be honourable. I am certainly afraid to lose my charmed existence in my sister's household, but I do not want to be forever the maiden widow-auntie. Gulzar's most apparent sadness is sufficient warning of the dangers of such a state. I want my own life, I decide, my own adventure, and shall take a chance as to whether I also find happiness.

***

'Well,' my brother-in-law views me quizzically when, some time later, he has come back to find us in the Residency grounds and I had watched from a distance as the Captain cantered away. 'I thought Captain de Boigne had come to visit me. It seems not.'

'I believe he came to compliment me on my performance.' I lower my eyes demurely but cannot prevent a smile forming on my lips.

'I see,' muses my brother-in-law. 'For one who is presently so very busy that is generous tribute indeed. Moreover, as he bade me farewell, he indicated that he should like the freedom to visit again. I take it he will be welcome?'

'I am dazzled by the attentions of one so very accomplished, beside whom I feel most insignificant and small,' I say demurely.

He looks at me closely, unsure of my sincerity. Indeed, I am unsure myself for, though my position in the world is of no great note, nor do I possess outstanding beauty of face and form, yet I feel the power of his attraction to me, however inexplicable it may be.

'He is not a man with whom I would trifle,' my brother-in-law observes and I take it as a caution, intended or not. 'You should know that his reputation is most honourable, and deriving not only from his military prowess. His army fights well because he treats them well and pays them on time, which is unusual in these parts as you may know. And so his men even tolerate his reluctance to permit looting and reprisals following victory. Besides,' he adds, 'I feel for him a great affection and trust he will be a lifelong friend.'

***

I was again playing in the Residency grounds with the children when Captain de Boigne paid his next visit, leaving his horse at some distance in care of a *syce*. And Chandi was again most vociferous in his attempt to deter my visitor, first barking at his horse and then circling him growling as he approached me on foot. I was obliged to tap my faithful protector on the nose which, in his view, is a serious rebuke and he has slunk away, leaving me to my own devices and without time to wonder why he was so adamant, only to craft a suitable apology to my visitor.

'I think it is because the children are near. He is their defender.'

The children are now running in front. Actually William is marching, with a makeshift sword on his shoulder, as the Captain has just taught him. William begged to be told more details of the battles he has fought but, on this subject, the Captain seems reticent. I do not know if this is from humility, an unwillingness to revive his doubtless bloody memories, or a desire to spare us from the true horror of war. He now seems preoccupied, as if he is formulating some statement or request. My heart is beating fast at his proximity and perhaps I stumble, for he takes my arm as if to help me over some small obstacle and then softly speaks.

'What think you of this sonnet? The deputy Governor General, John Shore, has rendered it from the Arabic.' He coughs, stops and strikes a pose.

'"*The Dove, whose notes disturb my rest,*
Feels pangs like mine corrode her breast;

Her midnight warblings fill the grove
Whilst I conceal my secret love:
Yet hidden passion fiercer glows
And bursting sighs my griefs disclose..."'

He waves a dismissive hand. 'I thought it the kind of trifle you would appreciate.' And then he speaks very softly indeed so that I am obliged to lean close to hear him. 'Nur, I am tired of only soldiering. I need such light and warmth in my life that only a woman can bring. Will you be true to your name and light up my life?'

I just have time to register surprise that he knows this is the meaning of my name before he wheels away, embarrassed or, perhaps, too proud to plead for long, perhaps both. He gives me no time to reply, walks more quickly ahead and calls back over his shoulder. 'You could do worse, you know. Perhaps I shall have to ask Captain Palmer to give you to me. I have heard him described as like an angel, so surely he would not refuse a friend.'

Then he again stops, turns to wait for me and speaks more seriously. 'I have to go away shortly. There is another battle I must fight. Perhaps it will be the last. God grant I may return here and pursue this our growing intimacy, without which my life now would seem most barren and bereft of value.'

He bows and is gone before I can reply. I see him caress the children briefly and stride off to the house, I imagine to join his friend, though whether to speak further of these matters I do not know. I am standing, still gazing after him, when I hear a voice behind me and notice with a start that it has grown quite dark.

14

1853 Lower Beeding March

'Come, marm, the fire is lit and supper awaiting.'

Caroline helps me stand and leads me to the sitting room. She hovers over me as I swallow a few mouthfuls while gazing into the fire.

'Can you not imagine, in the cracking of the wood and sudden spurts of flame, the musket shots and cannon flares of battle?' I say.

'I wouldn't be knowing, thank the Lord,' says Caroline. 'I only prays to God we never sees in Zussex the troubles there's been in other parts, and that our brave soldiers keep the peace abroad.'

She pauses, considering, I reckon, how best to use this rare moment of confidence and I let pass her comment, knowing our differences on these matters. She is certainly no radical and I do not choose to engage in what would be, I am sure, a fruitless debate.

'Did you know war, marm, where you come from? At close quarters? Wuz that how come you here?'

Where to begin an explanation? 'Only after a fashion.'

Caroline frowns and purses her lips. She is not satisfied.

'And I have heard battle descriptions,' I add. So vivid as to make my blood run cold, my heart cry out with pity and at the waste of life. But that was later. Then I cared only for him.

1788 Lucknow April

'Do you have news?' It is a week or two since my suitor left and my brother-in-law has summoned me to his study.

'The Afghan Ghulam Qadir has captured Aligarh, thanks to an alliance with the traitorous Mughul General Ismail Beg, and is now besieging Agra.'

My brother-in-law is sitting at the fireside, reading a letter to which the broken seal still adheres. A deepened crease between his brows on his normally calm forehead betrays his concern. Aligarh and Agra are on the road to Delhi where sits the old Emperor.

'It is of the first importance to relieve the siege. It is for this that Sindhia has called in all his forces.'

'And the Captain?'

'My correspondent does not say. But I think he must be on his way to join Sindhia. As am I.'

I lean forward, anxious, and open my mouth to quiz him further but find myself spluttering.

March 1853 Lower Beeding

There is chicken broth running down my chin.

'Found a bone? I were that careful.' Caroline leans close to inspect and wipes my bodice with a kitchen cloth.

'Take it away!' I hold my hands in front of my mouth to prevent any further incursions. I do not recognise my voice, it is so shrill.

'Tis good broth, I kept some of the best bits of the bird from dinner to put in it.' She is patient, coaxing. 'Tis the time of year to build your strength. Many's a malady wakes with the spring.'

'No more! No more!' It turns into a chant and I feel myself rocking to and fro in my desperation to be left alone.

Caroline is angry. 'My little brother dursn't show such a temper.' She clatters the spoon in the bowl and retreats loudly grumbling. 'I shall eat it myself. Tis too good to waste. And we'll see whose health suffers.' It is as close to a curse as she dare and she allows the door to bang shut behind her.

April 1788 Lucknow

The door bangs behind me as I run into Faiz' room.

'Did a messenger come?' I demand without preamble. 'I thought I heard a horse.'

She is startled from sleep, her hair loose and tangled, and she raises her hand in mild protest. I clasp both of mine to my breast in mixed penitence and supplication.

'Go and see,' she says. 'You can bring it to me.' And when she has slit open the letter, she reads: 'There has been a battle at Chaksan, near Agra. On the 24th day of this month.'

'And?' I press my nails into my palms, as if a little suffering on my part might yet lessen his.

'Ghulam Qadir and Ismail Beg raised the siege of Agra to confront Sindhia and his commanders and troops, including Captain de Boigne.'

'And then?' My heart is sinking.

'The Captain fought on Sindhia's right hand and withstood Ismail Beg's cavalry but, receiving no support from the Maratha cavalry, had to fall back with heavy losses.'

I sink onto the bed beside her, preparing for the worst.

'Fortunately,' she continues. 'Ismail Beg and Ghulam Qadir have fallen out of alliance, Ghulam Qadir has had to return to defend his own territory and Ismail Beg alone has returned to the siege at Agra.'

'And the Captain himself?' I sit up, determined to be brave.

'Is uninjured, though sorely grieving for his men.'

'Praise be to Allah.'

'But he will surely have to fight again. So there will be more waiting.'

'Yes.'

'So I shall have more of your company.' Faiz puts her arm round my shoulders. 'We shall wait together.'

15

1853 Lower Beeding March

Caroline's arm is around me as she shakes me awake.

'Best be getting thee to bed. Lord knows I'm ready fur mine.'

She almost carries me upstairs, assists me at the commode, washes my hands and face and settles me into my bed. The cats, who have followed us, jump up and take their places one to each side. I daresay Silver will join us at a time of his choosing.

'Thank you, Caroline.' I recall how happy we both were, for different reasons, earlier in the day and wish to restore some harmony. I would say more but am, of a sudden, taken with a fit of the shivers.

'Only doing my duty,' she says stiffly and then she notices. 'Bless me, I think th'as taken a chill on th'ride to church. I'll fetch thee a hot brick.'

While she is gone my teeth begin to chatter beyond my control and the shivering is yet more intense. But it is late to call the doctor.

'Fetch me another quilt,' I hiss between still chattering teeth when Caroline returns and she brings one of green silk from the room that Charles uses on his occasional visits. And will soon use again. The thought gives me some strength and I manage to swallow water from the proffered cup before I start to doze.

June 1788 Lucknow

It is the height of the hot season before the monsoon and the air outside is like a furnace breath, the sun scorches down like a flame. Those who have a *tykhana* spend the daylight hours beneath ground in adequate comfort but artificial light. Our household prefers the solace of shade and water and employs *punkahwallahs* to provide some current of air. I have brought my baby niece to my room to give Faiz some rest and am trying to keep both of us cool by use of my peacock fan. Sarah is mesmerised by its brilliant colours and reaches out to feel the feathers but, as soon as she touches it, I whisk it away, knowing that if I cease moving it she will soon suffer the effects of the heat.

How can they bear it, I wonder, the men of both armies drawn up in opposition on the plains outside Delhi in a battle which must decide the fate of the Empire? Only this morning we received word from a courier and by now the fighting has begun, or perhaps is even finished. I see him astride his horse, sword in one upraised hand, fearlessly repulsing each successive charge. His battalions are famed for standing their ground where other infantry break ranks and run, leaving their flanks exposed. His men are well-drilled, well-paid and proud to fight under his command. But how long can they survive under this relentless sun without even the relief of the air currents enjoyed by the galloping cavalry? I am afraid. How is he?

A knock at the door makes me start. It is Faiz come to take her daughter for her feed. And to give me news.

'He is victorious. The Mughal cavalry are beaten back and entirely put to flight.' Her eyes glow as if she has come from the scene herself. 'Your Captain has made Sindhia the undisputed master of Hindustan. I wonder what Sindhia will do for him. Surely he will now return in glory.' She kisses me swiftly before taking Sarah and leaving me to rest.

For me, these many months pass mostly in the usual comfort and safety of a loving home and only an anxiety as to his whereabouts and well-being remind me that my life is about to change. God willing. Our greatest sorrow is when William leaves us to go to school in England. My brother-in-law comes from Sindhia's camp to take him to Calcutta where he has made arrangements for him to travel in the company of a Company man and his wife who are returning to England. Mary is heart-broken and I am kept busy consoling her and helping with the three younger children. But I miss young William also and certainly share Faiz's sadness that it will be years before we see him again when he will be grown, perhaps much changed, and certainly no longer a child. It is a harsh custom I think, but I also understand that Europeans wish their children to be schooled in their own traditions and I do believe the English schools to be the finest anywhere.

For others less fortunate, not so distant events bring the most appalling terror and outrage. On 10th August Ghulam Qadir returns and, hearing that the eighty year old Emperor has thrown himself on Sindhia's mercy, sacks his palace and gouges out his eyes, which has always seemed to me the worst of injuries that yet does not kill. Terrible to suffer and terrible to inflict. During the next two months, we hear endless stories of the atrocities against the helpless palace inhabitants committed by Qadir's forces when in fruitless search of an imagined immense treasure hoard, while Sindhia waits with his Generals at his capital Gwalior for reinforcements from the south. When these arrive in September, he advances on Delhi and takes the Red Fort without firing a shot. Ghulam Qadir runs away, is captured, mutilated and hanged on a tree by the roadside and Ismail Beg again changes sides.

'Captain de Boigne is now in charge of the Red Fort in Delhi.' My brother-in-law writes. 'But expecting suitable recognition from Sindhia for his immense contribution to the victory, he requested a much larger command. Which however, Sindhia, being afraid to anger his other more senior commanders and split the Mahratta alliance, has refused. Yet have they parted on good terms. He is returning to Lucknow, as am I.'

***

A week passes and my brother-in-law is home yet still the Captain does not come. Longing mixed with apprehension marks my wait for it is not only the great tides of war and peace that at this distance are hard to decipher. I dare not assume he has not changed his mind and what was said in parting he has not reconsidered and retracted. Lest I be too much disappointed, I attempt to detach my feelings from my fate, a stratagem which has served me in the past. On the tenth day my brother-in-law calls me to his study where a fine fire blazes to which I draw near, for I am shivering, despite my Kashmiri shawl.

'See this,' he hands me a letter with barely concealed delight.

'*January 1789,*' I read aloud. '*My esteemed friend, I am but yesterday come to Lucknow. I am presently staying with Colonel Martin and expect shortly to engage with him in a number of business ventures in order to establish some fortune and support a more domestic existence. I beg leave to request your assistance in approaching your father-in-law to ask for his younger daughter's hand in marriage...*' I look up to find my brother-in-law watching me closely.

'Can it be true?' I whisper, still not yet daring to believe my greatest hopes fulfilled.

At this, my dear brother-in-law stands, draws me to my feet, places his hands on my shoulders and looks deep into my eyes. 'Then shall I do as I am asked?' His mouth curves up as ever, not yet in a smile but I think he sees my answer before I can speak.

16

1853 Lower Beeding April

'Mercy me, marm. Tha've been in and out of fever the whole of Holy Week and April is come and Easter Day the morrer.'

It is Caroline, come with a tray and animal entourage. The cats jump up on the bed and knead me energetically, purring all the while. Silver dares to place both paws on the counterpane and licks my face with vigour.

'Silver's been most forlorn and even the cats took fright and stayed downstairs. Doctor's been and gone more than once. We've all done our best to keep you this side of Heaven's gates.'

Should I be glad? Yes, I decide, with some surprise for I would not always have said so. No-one knows what happens to memories in death and there are yet precious ones I would revisit, more vivid and more vital than my present life. So I eat well and then lie back to remember what more I may before making an attempt to get out of bed.

1789 Lucknow March

My father and Captain de Boigne have met. With his renown and my brother-in-law's good opinion there was no serious debate, except on the details of the wedding ceremonies. He prefers a simple form, which reflects, my brother-in-law assures my parents, as much his distaste for personal display as religious scruple. My mother is so overwhelmed at the prospect of so illustrious a son-in-law that she agrees that I should be married from my sister's house.

The day after this meeting I visit her at her home in the *chowk* behind the Imambara to discuss further arrangements. I prefer living in the Residency with its greater space and gardens, but I love to come here also where people live so close together, there is so much activity and everything is much as it has been these past three hundred years or more. Gulzar accompanies me and being veiled, as is appropriate in this quarter, we can privately and at leisure enjoy the sights and sounds in these narrow streets where everyone's workshops and businesses are entirely open to view.

There is a cobbler making leather shoes on a lath, a craftsman hammering silver into fine leaf for cooking, each sheet of which I know requires four hours constant beating. We pass a dark tea shop where several men sit deep inside, drinking and playing chess and a boy runs out past us carrying a tray of teas to deliver elsewhere. Next door is a perfumier's, where two men are intent on filling smaller vials from bottles of brilliantly coloured oils. As I linger here to savour the aromas of rose and jasmine,sandalwood, patchouli and musk, a large black butterfly bumbles in past meand out again soon after, having discovered its error.

There are entire alleys of textile workshops, where men stamp cloth with patterns in blue ink for unseen women to embroider in the *chikan* style for which Lucknow is famous, and shops that sell the finished garments: *kurtas,* jama suits, saris. We pass the *kothis* of courtesans, beneath their high balconies where, later in the day, they will appear to greet their admirers and, if they are particularly renowned, the street will become impassable for the numbers of rich men on their elephants vying for entry.

And there are great merchants' *havelis* of several stories, each with finely carved balconies and doors intricately painted with designs of birds and animals, flowers and fish. Many of these are set back from the busy streets, along even narrower alleys, which abruptly open out into wider residential areas that can take strangers by surprise. At last, we thread our way through a small archway into a passage that leads to my parents' apartments which comprise one wall of a shady courtyard that is blessed with a well and several trees. They are ancient these buildings, the family who lives opposite have lived in the same house for many generations, since Emperor Akbar himself gave it to them two or three hundred years ago, when it had belonged to some French merchants. They still have the deed with his seal and signature.

My mother is jubilant. 'My future son-in-law has refused to accept any *maher*,' she tells me. 'Like your brother-in-law before him. He says that his personal wealth is already sufficient and his expectations greater still. My daughter, you have done well.' She strokes my cheek.

It is plain that we have no need of the services of a *mashata* to extol our virtues the one to the other; to me Captain de Boigne is already the perfect Prince Benazir as conjured in Mir Hasan's *masnavi*. But how does he see me? Does he think me charming as a fairy of the Caucasus mountains or beauteous as a princess? He could surely have his pick of women in any city of the world. It is a mystery.

'I should have liked to welcome him here for the marriage,' she says. 'But he will be much more at his ease in the Residency.'

There is still some disappointment amongst the ladies of my sister's household that he will not visit their quarters and be paraded in front of their peeping eyes, as is so often also the bride's first opportunity to espy the face of her future beloved, so they will have no chance to play the many tricks that are normally visited on the prospective groom. Mary, having already been apprised of these customs, is especially cast down.

'There will be opportunity,' I assure her. 'To you he will not object.'

He sends me an elaborate dress, but it is not brought in any procession and we send him no corresponding garments, nor do our ladies make any ceremonial visit to his abode. On our wedding day, since he has no family to accompany him on his approach, he rides only with Colonel Martin. Newly bathed, I am waiting in seclusion and receive reports through Faiz, who has some system of messaging established.

'He is wearing a green tunic and a red and brocade *shimla* with a sparkling bejewelled *aigrette*,' I hear. 'He looks splendid, truly like a *nau shah*, a king, which on this day is how all should regard him.'

'Then does he ride an elephant?'

'No, only his favourite horse.'

'I must get dressed.' I go into the antechamber and ask: 'Who will assist me?'

There are many who could, but only Faiz and my mother step forward as the others are still unhappy. Gulzar repeats their concern, which I have never understood.

'You should remain wrapped only in a sheet until you are ready to leave the house,' she says. 'Even Faiz followed this custom.'

This is true but my brother-in-law was happy to give my mother a free hand in arranging the ceremonies and feels himself closer, I believe, to our religion than does my future husband.

'I think he would find it most strange if I were not decked in the finery which he has sent,' I say firmly. 'But I will remain without jewellery until later.' This is the compromise that I have agreed with my mother, who now brings my wedding dress.

There is a long-sleeved tunic comprised of tiers of French lace, edged with a thousand tiny pearls, to be worn over pale green silk pyjamas which are made to fit so tightly at the ankle that the lowest part of the legs are left open and two of the ladies have to stitch them once I have them on my person. It is the latest fashion and not one I have yet worn, the inconvenience in my mind outweighing the undoubtedly attractive appearance. On my feet I wear darker green silk *jootis* that are also sewn with pearls.

'He asked advice of Boulone in the design,' says my sister. 'Did he do well?'

She brings the final part of my outfit, a fine *dupatta*, three yards in length, which matches the pyjamas in colour and, like the tunic, is edged with pearls. With my mother's help, she drapes it skilfully over my head and shoulders in such a way that I may easily lower it over my face when appropriate.

My mother wipes her eyes. 'You look beautiful,' she says and there is a ripple of agreement around the room.

'Beautiful Nurauntie.' Mary has so far been charged with amusing her baby sister but now she comes forward and gently touches the lace and pearls.

'He is on his way!' Zainab, who has been keeping watch, calls from the doorway.

Everyone hastens to tidy the room and take their place while I retreat to a corner to keep watch through my veil. Mary, her eyes shining with excitement, stands to one side of the door, Faiz to the other and between them they hold a rope. This is supposed to impede my groom's entry and to be held higher and higher as he attempts to step over it. He appears at the door, almost filling the frame, frowns at the rope but, on seeing Mary, quickly begins to play his part. Naturally, being small, Mary is unable to raise the rope very high, particularly when being tickled under the arms by the Captain.

Once inside the room, he is besieged by all the ladies together attempting to feed him sweetmeats but, towering over them, finds it easy for the most part to foil them. Finally, he charms my mother and Faiz by reversing the onslaught and requiring them to eat *barfi* from his hand. He then bows and is ready to take his leave but, mysteriously, his shoes have disappeared from the threshold where he had removed them. I am suddenly afraid that he will be angry, but it soon becomes clear to all that Mary has hidden them and he allows her to drive a hard bargain in silver coins before she will return them and he can depart. He has not once cast a glance in my direction and I know I must not take affront but appreciate his honouring of our customs. I am proud of him in fact for conducting himself so well.

He has gone to join the menfolk for the feasting and general merry-making. We hear the *naubat* band strike up as he enters one of the two pavilions that has been erected in the Residency grounds. I saw their splendid furnishings yesterday, and know he will be conducted to the seat of honour, which is like a king's throne made of velvet with gold-and silver-brocaded embroidery, at the head of a long table laid with sparkling glass and silver. My mother and sister soon depart to join the female guests to eat in a separate pavilion where they are to be entertained by one of the best bands of *domnis* in the city. Gulzar chooses to stay with me.

'It will bring too many sad memories,' she dismisses my thanks. 'I am content to imagine the proceedings.'

'I wonder what the *domnis* will think to mock today.' We are too far to hear their words.

'I think,' Gulzar pauses, and, to my surprise, a smile of mischief briefly lights her face so that I can see how pretty she must have been on her ill-starred wedding day. 'I think they may very well ridicule English attempts to speak Persian and appreciate our music and dance,' she pauses. 'And perhaps they will cleverly mimic the airs and graces adopted by certain personages in the Residency.'

'Then they may even deride families like ours that curry favour with and inter-marry with the foreigners,' I suggest.

'There will be a point,' Gulzar nods, 'Where Faiz, or someone on her behalf, will have to silence them with generous gratuities before their performance becomes too daring or ribald.'

We both laugh, but my thoughts return to the meaning of this day after which my life will forever change. Am I ready? As much as can be possible. Am I certain I have made the right decision? I could not have refused such an offer. Shall I be happy ever after? It is unlikely. What will the future hold? No-one can tell. Gulzar sees my change of mood and we sit in silence until we hear the music stop.

'It is now time for the marriage contract to be finalised,' she tells me what I already know, but her warning tone seems to suggest that there is yet time for me to change my mind. Very soon after there is a tap at the door and she admits my brother-in-law, who bows to me with great formality.

'I am come as your attorney in the marriage negotiations,' he announces. 'To confirm that you are willing for the ceremony to proceed.'

'I am,' I reply. My voice is steady, my mind is clear, I look him straight in the eyes.

He nods. 'Then you should know that three times the Qazi will say to Captain de Boigne *"I have contracted your marriage with the girl known as Nur Baksh"*, and three times the Captain must confirm his agreement.'

'I understand.'

Then my brother-in-law relaxes his pose, takes my hand and lifts it to his lips, his eyes moist. *'Courage, my sweet bahyne,'* he says. 'May you always be as happy as you are this day.'

Then he leaves us and when the music again starts to play I know that the ceremony is finished and the *qazi* has given his blessing. Soon after, my mother and sister come to deck me in the gold jewellery that my parents have had made for me. There are bangles for my wrists, a heavy and ornate necklace, earrings that hang almost to my shoulders, a jewel in the middle of my forehead and a nose ring to which is attached a chain which Fyze loops across my cheek and pins in my hair. My mother stands back and surveys me critically and makes a number of adjustments before she is satisfied.

'Now you shall meet your husband,' she pronounces at last and the three of them lead me to the ladies' pavilion. *My husband.* I savour the words as I walk and suddenly am almost overcome at my good fortune. Had the Nawab of Pundri not passed on when he did, may his soul rest in peace, I might now be one of his many widows, perhaps living in penury, if not taken on by his successor. I swallow hard, for this is not the time for tears, and keep my eyes cast down for the performance of the *arsi mushaf*.

He approaches swiftly and stands in front of me between my mother and my sister, while Gulzar stands a little behind me. My mother leans to raise my veil sufficient to allow my sister to hold a mirror beneath my gaze, so angled that he may see my face. Since this is not for the first time, as very often it might be according to our traditions, I do not keep my eyes closed until he, exhorted by the ladies, should beg me to open them. Still I find it a moment of most powerful emotion. He holds my gaze so long in his, whether to satisfy himself that it is indeed I beneath the veil or to reassure himself that he has chosen well, that the ladies start to laugh and protest which makes me smile. At this, he nods and steps back out of my sight and I know he will return to the men's tent and I shall not see him again until our departure.

'Now you can join us,' says my mother.

The *domnis* dance and sing in celebration, while Gulzar and I eat a little and then I find myself the centre of attention, surrounded by smiling faces, so much joy and laughter, so much embracing, there is not time enough to greet so many people all showing me such love and appreciation, though I do note dear Mrs Blane in a sari of turquoise silk that well suits her colouring. Too soon the *domnis* change their tune and begin the *babul*, the heart-breaking song of departure and, from this moment, one would imagine there had been a death here not a wedding, as the gathering becomes a place not of joy but of mourning and all the ladies line up to say goodbye and present to me their gifts of money, clothes and jewellery. I cannot hold back my tears as all around me begin to weep and lament as they escort me to a decorated palanquin at the Residency gates. My husband awaits me there, his horse at hand, the male guests crowding behind him. He sweeps me off my feet and lifts me into my seat in the palanquin, his face, close to, betraying impatience or even displeasure.

'What, tears, *madame*?'

There is no time to explain before someone throws an embroidered shawl over the palanquin obscuring my view and I hear the jingle of harness as he mounts his horse. As we set off in procession, I vow to myself that never again will I weep in his presence.

PART II

Marriage

17

1853 Lower Beeding April

'Why tears, marm? Tis a day for gladness. Easter Day and He is risen again. See here, your best bonnet and gown, though you'll not be going to church today, Easter or no. Tis too late now in any case. I took the liberty of leaving you asleeping.'

Caroline is not particularly devout, she never asks to go to church and leave me to a cold lunch. But her tone is uncommonly joyful and I can see from her face that she is most content.

'Then I will also rise and breakfast downstairs. I was only remembering my wedding day.'

She frowns and purses her lips, unable to tell if I am being contrary by design, if not sacrilegious, and I hasten to restore her good temper.

'It is our custom for the bride to weep when she leaves with her new husband.'

I am being most unusually informative, but Caroline chooses rather to express her own opinion than to discover more.

'Bit late if you ask me,' she snorts. 'No use crying over spilt milk.' And then she goes quiet, is clearly making some decision and soon speaks out.

'I'm to be married, marm. James Budgen has asked for my hand. The banns is to be called from next Sunday. He wants us to be married soon as ever.'

I congratulate her and express my pleasure, but she has matters yet on her mind.

'Will I be asking about for another housekeeper, marm? Only see, if I'm to live at James' present house, which is yours I know and which he rents off you, I could easy come up of a morning and see

72

that the girl does her work, make your food and all. And come back of an evening unless it were winter and mebbe then I'd ask James to come and stoke the fires and that. So most in general, t'would be as now, only night-times I'd not be here.'

She needs her earnings it is plain and I agree and will pay the same as now. Privately, I reflect that under her stewardship the cottage rent may now be paid on time. James Budgen may not be the most industrious man and is perhaps too fond of the alehouse, but it is not my place to warn her. What enamoured girl listens to the voice of caution? She would probably think me envious of her youth and future, a sourpuss, a killjoy.

Later, when she has cleared the breakfast tray from the morning room, and I am sitting in shafts of strong spring sunlight that make additional heating unnecessary, I think how settled is her destiny now and how different to mine. For it is certain, or as near certain as may be, that she will live with James in the same village if not the same cottage near her family and lifelong friends until death do them part. When I married, my husband had yet to find a house and it was too short a time before all my expectations were overturned, and many times besides. How different my life would have been if we had remained in Lucknow as he then intended.

1789 Lucknow April

Our first lodging is to be at Colonel Martin's town house by the Gomti. I peer at it from under the shawl covering my palanquin and do not wonder that it has aroused much interest since its construction, for it is large and set in extensive grounds. We approach through a high arched gateway and by drawbridge over a deep moat, which I know must be connected to the river. The *domnis* have arrived before us and are singing songs of welcome in the courtyard. My husband lifts me out of the palanquin and I am escorted into the house by Boulone and the other ladies of Colonel Martin's household, which includes a pretty little Anglo-Indian girl. They wash my feet and take the water away to pour in every corner of the house before removing my veil so that all may see me. The

Colonel presents me with a fine set of pearl jewellery and Boulone and the others with several sets of clothes for everyday wear. I am then taken to the women's quarters to spend the night in seclusion.

The *zenana* is an entirely separate building to the side and set in its own garden. I speak to no-one but Boulone, she taking the place of mother- and sisters-in law who would normally watch over me. My husband has meanwhile progressed to the main building to join his friends and those of my male relations who have followed the procession for more feasting and celebrations.

'You must not be afraid,' Boulone says as she helps me undress after serving me a little food. 'The most important thing is to keep your husband happy and this is quite easily done.'

'But you knew the Colonel well before you became his wife,' I say.

Once my sister had told me how Boulone came to be adopted as a child by Colonel Martin. Her father was a Nawab, grandson of the Vizier to Emperor Aurangzeb, and her mother was a Lucknawi noble woman. Boulone fled the family home when her elder sister was murdered by her father, (for, my sister surmised, refusing to marry the husband of his choice) and she was taken in by a Frenchman. What happened next is unclear, perhaps even in Boulone's own mind, but a few years later, when she was still only nine, this man sold her to the Colonel.

'It is true,' she nods. 'And I knew him to be most fond and caring. For he showed me all the tenderness of a true father, kept me close to him throughout, both in Lucknow and Calcutta, and spared nothing to educate me in a most modest and decent fashion.'

'Did he always mean you to be his wife?' I ask. My sister did not know.

She shrugs. 'Perhaps.' It does not matter. 'When I was eighteen he asked if I wished him to find me a husband but I chose to stay with him. And I always shall.' Then she frowns as the sound of female whispers and laughter pass the room where we are sitting. 'But I had rather he had not taken so many wives.'

***

Next morning I meet her rivals, two of whom are her sisters, Gomany and Animan, who are, I think, a little older. There are also three younger women, besides the little girl who is three years old and called Sally. They all seem to think I am to live with them in the *zenana* and their relations with one another appear quite cordial, with one exception. Boulone is quite careless towards Sally and ignores her attempts to please, whereas she is clearly most fond of her adopted brother James, also known as Zulphikar, whom the general purchased from the boy's drunken father when he was eight years old. Animan sees my surprise and, when Boulone is beyond hearing, tells me.

'Sally is the daughter of a past Resident who refused to acknowledge her and the Colonel has rescued her, as he has all of us. He even pays her mother, who it is said is of bad character, a small pension, although she is not allowed to see her daughter. Boulone is a little jealous. She is afraid that the Colonel will one day prefer Sally to her.'

It is a strange household, quite unlike that of my sister. Some of the Colonel's servants have also been bought or acquired by him when they were very young. There are four Negroes, two eunuchs and a woman who has, I am told, always worn men's clothing and passes for a eunuch. They are all Muslims and there is also a Sikh and several Europeans, including a cook and a Frenchman who organises entertainments and makes fireworks. Then there are several who live elsewhere, including a Spaniard, Joseph Queiros, who is of an old noble family, and two brothers named Qadir who help the Colonel run his other estates and houses. I know I must find my place here if this is what my husband wishes, but it is not what I had expected.

Later that morning, he sends word for me to join him. Boulone and her sisters dress me in a full long skirt of the softest silk, white bordered with crimson and gold, with a matching *ungia* and a crimson veil, sewn with sequins dense as the stars at night and just as dazzling. They escort me, my face covered, from the zenana to the house, across the courtyard, then a piazza and through a large many-sided room, to my husband's apartment.

He is reclining, on a couch by a window, his back to the light, dressed in loose white pyjamas. He stands to receive me, approaches with long swift strides, bows farewell to my companions and closes the door behind them. With both his hands he lifts my veil and, removing it entirely, lets it cascade in a shimmering stream to the marble floor. Then, with one hand below my chin, he raises my face and examines it closely.

'Look at me,' he says and I raise my eyes quickly then look again down.

'Don't be shy.' There is a sharpness in his tone.

I cannot say: '*It is fear and not timidity.*' And this not only because I think he would be vexed, but because I could not give the reason should he ask. I am afraid not of marriage, not of its approaching consummation, but of him. I look up again to meet his gaze and know that I am right to be uneasy. His expression is quizzical, as if he cannot quite recall how events have brought us to this pass and quite without affection, and I think: I must win his love anew. So I smile and am happy to see his face also is transformed.

'Come, *mignonne.*' His voice is gruff, but his expression much more gentle.

He lifts me up and carries me to a bed where, seeing his difficulty, I assist him in removing my clothes. He lies me flat and, leaning on an elbow, lying by my side, inspects me closely, head to toe, as if I am a statue on a marble slab. But, unflinching, I watch him watching me, and when his eyes at last meet mine, he nods gravely, as if satisfied with what he sees, and lowers his mouth to mine.

His lips are softer, fuller than their outward appearance, and do not press on mine so much as caress them, open them and take possession of them so that they act without my willing and dare to explore his own. I would wish to enjoy this sensation longer but his mouth moves to my bosom, which rises to meet his tongue and I arch my back to give him greater purchase. He bestrides me, kneeling, with one arm holds me close, with the other wrests off his shirt and breast to breast, skin to skin, kisses my mouth with increasing fervour. I lose all sense of separation, feel I could drown or melt in this embrace and reach my arms to hold him tightly. He lays me back, rests on one elbow, looses his pyjama with the other hand, parts my legs and enters me.

I knew there would be pain and also blood for my sister warned me, but am, in particular, glad of Boulone's most recent caution.

'Do not recoil,' she said. 'But meet his thrust and if his eyes are open hold his gaze. Cry out if you must, but do not weep. Tears are the enemy of passion.'

He rolls off me, spent, falls on his back beside me and sighs deeply.

'So those dark eyes have depths indeed.'

I am content and might have slept but, with sudden vigour, he takes my hand in his, kisses my fingertips and pulls me up.

'Let us eat.'

He gathers up a gown from where it hangs on a chair and, standing behind me, wraps it close, then frees my hair, lifts it high and bends to kiss the back of my neck, sending a shiver down my backbone. I lean against him and his hands release my hair and cup my breasts, but then he steps back, takes my hand and leads me to an adjacent room where a table is already spread. We dine, he more enthusiastically, I taking but few mouthfuls, looking out over the river where pleasure boats pole slowly downstream towards us, a hazy scene suffused in the pale gold of the setting sun which also bathes my face. He calls for wine, obliges me to take a little and raises his glass.

'You are so fair,' he observes, 'that you might pass for a Mediterranean.'

'You have seen the Mediterranean, sir? And all the places between?'

'And many more beside, I was in Russia and would have gone again but for a chance occurrence. And you must call me Benoit.'

'Benoit,' I pronounce it carefully. 'I should like to hear of your adventures.' I have heard that he was at the court of Queen Catherine and she was much taken with him, so much, some say, that she allowed him to take her.

'Another day. Tell me,' he asks instead, 'Would you cross the Black Water to the Mediterranean and beyond? Are you not afraid?'

'That is a Hindu superstition,' I tell him. 'I will go where you wish.'

He clinks his glass against mine and shortly, as the first stars shine out, we retire to our chamber and throughout the night explore each other's pleasure.

We rise late to find an invitation from the Colonel to join him.

'I must first return to the zenana to dress,' I observe, regarding yesterday's finery heaped upon the floor.

He smiles in answer and throws open a door I had not noticed which leads to another chamber, wherein I see my possessions already part unpacked. 'You may call for assistance. I believe there has been a girl assigned to your care.' Then, seeing my surprise, he steps behind me and holds me close. 'You did not think I would consign you to the harem?'

***

The Colonel's apartment, which also opens off what I now see to be an octagonal room, leads to a great hall that gives onto a balcony, which is built out over the river. He points out that the moat we crossed only two days before, it seems so much longer, extends on three sides of the house, which, together with the river, can thus create an island if the drawbridge is raised.

'For defence,' he explains to me. 'I was attacked severely in '81 by some fleeing troops during Raja Chet Singh's rebellion and was obliged to place two small field-pieces loaded with grapeshot at my doors and was myself armed at the head of my servants. Which reminds me, Benoit, I have found an excellent warehouse for our trade. It is inside an old fort with safe rooms and an armed guard. I will take you to inspect the premises this afternoon. If you wish. But let us finish our tour of the house.'

In one of the larger halls there is a library, housing, the Colonel tells us, four thousand volumes in French or English and five hundred more that I see to be handwritten in Persian. It is an extraordinary number and it soon becomes clear that the General is a collector of other objects also. In another hall there is a great assemblage, one might almost call it a museum, of china and glass ware, Chinese toys, the accessories for a puppet theatre and biological specimens, which include a female skeleton. There are also watches and many new mechanical inventions, air pumps, printing presses, magic lanterns...

The Colonel is surprised, and not a little pleased I think, to see my interest in all such curiosities. I am particularly taken with an 'electrifying machine' of which I have seen pictures in a book belonging to my brother-in-law. He wished but could not afford to send for one from England. I had formed the impression that it was something of a trick or entertainment but Colonel Martin believes it to have most practical applications.

'Do you not know that a countryman of mine thirty years ago succeeded in lighting rooms?' he asks me. 'One day I am sure there will be even better machines with a greater efficiency and effectiveness.' He turns and points to a large metal contraption in one corner. 'And improved steam engines also for I cannot make mine play at all and am thinking I must send for another.'

'Antoine might have advised you,' observes Benoit, 'as he did on other occasions.'

The Colonel sighs. 'Indeed he might. His departure for France is greatly regretted and his company missed on many occasions. Come.' He brightens. 'There is more to see.'

We climb to the roof on which stand two airy pavilions, each housing English telescopes, one of which was designed by a Mr Hershel, of whom I have heard my brother-in-law speak. Thanks to our discussions, I understand the principle of magnification and yet am not at all prepared for the wonder of the experience. Unaided, the view of the city with all its minarets and domes beside the sparkling Gomti possesses enchantment enough. Brought close by telescope, I roam at will through streets and courtyards, and see my fellow inhabitants at their business, quite unaware that I am watching them from afar.

An old man is enjoying a pipe on his verandah in the shade of a neem tree that has grown up through his floor and roof. Two small children are hawking rose petals along a back street and I can see the garden where they might have collected them and a *mali* sits on his haunches weeding a border, while another trims a long row of roses. A group of girls with water pots balanced on their heads walk home along the river bank. Another girl drives a herd of goats and some buffalo wend their own way amongst them. A woman spreads washing over bushes in a patch of wasteground, while another milks her cow. Two men face each other gesticulating as if in argument and yet another sits apart on a crumbling wall, scratching his private parts before spitting a long red stream of betel juice down into the road in front of him, narrowly missing a limping yellow dog.

Even my hearing seems enhanced, perhaps because I can follow the sounds to their sources. Hawkers of all manner of fruits and sweets, vegetables and savouries, a muezzin, a temple conch, the insistent drums of a wedding band, a pig squealing most piteously for two boys have hold of it and are tying it for slaughter.

I turn to my companions. 'Surely this is how God sees the world and watches over us all.'

The Colonel laughs. 'Father Wendel rather saw other uses when I gave him a demonstration.' He sees my confusion and adds. 'He is a Jesuit, a German. And a spy!'

Indeed this is an entirely different aspect to the matter and my husband has just begun to remark its relevance to the conduct of warfare when I exclaim.

'Here comes my brother-in-law!'

I can espy him clearly though he is still far along the approaching road, mounted and drawing closer at a rapid trot. We descend to greet him and I wonder why he is come. It is not, I know, to take me home for yet more ceremonies, as would normally be the case, and can but think he yet wishes to assure himself of my welfare. The Colonel leaves us together and Benoit calls for refreshment in our rooms.

'There is news of Hastings?' He refers to the long-departed but still much-missed Governor General, whose trial by the English Parliament is proceeding.

'It will be a long business, I fear,' sighs my brother-in-law.

'So long as Sir Philip Francis' desire for revenge is unassuaged.' Benoit laughs bitterly. 'There can be no serious case against him.'

'Who knows what they may make appear as crime who know nothing of politicking in this divided continent? You know I loved him well.'

'And you know that I have more than reason to do so also. Without him I might have fought against you or left India on some futile mission.'

'Come, let us speak of more cheerful matters. Nur, *bahyne,* you are well.'

It is most certainly statement and not enquiry. I serve them sherbet and small savouries as they talk of Company affairs and the yet uneasy relations within the Mahratta alliance. When my brother-in-law rises to leave, Benoit clasps his hand in both his own.

'Nur is free to visit you when she wishes,' he says.

'And you must accompany her when you have leisure.' My brother-in-law embraces him.

'But you must come here very soon,' insists my husband as we watch him mount his horse. 'And bring Faiz Begum,' he calls after him as he clatters away across the courtyard.

It makes me very happy to see them on such cordial terms and to anticipate a life with so much pleasant continuity and changes that have, so far, proved only for the better. On an impulse I take Benoit's arm and smile up at him. He looks down at me, a little surprised, and then returns my smile.

18

1853 Lower Beeding April

'How glad I am to find you in good spirits.'

It is Ann and I can tell from her expression that the smile is still upon my face as she pushes past Caroline's restraining bulk and hastens to my side. I direct it at her more particularly.

'You see, Caroline, I do not think an outing would be harmful. I am come,' she explains, 'to take you to dine with us on this most sacred day. Only Caroline thinks it rash. What is your opinion? '

My friend has my best interests at heart. How to tell her I had rather remain here in the company of my memories?

'Tis true she has sat alone all morning and a carriage ride, if well wrapped, might - '

'I shall take the utmost care, Caroline. Pray fetch her bonnet and wraps. Mr Howes is holding the horses.'

***

Michael is sitting in front with Samuel Fuller the coachman, Ann and I are bundled close together inside the carriage. It is indeed good to feel the warmth of the midday sun on my face and to see spring's sure progress after a week indoors. The lambs in the field next to the farm are numerous and some quite large. The leaves of the beech trees are near unfurled and bluebells form a carpet on the ground between clusters of yellow primrose and white anemone. In front of one cottage, two small children huddle around a cat and her tiny kittens. A noisy group of bigger children are playing hopscotch in the lane and jump out of our way. As we pass they all fall silent and stare and one little girl points at me.

'Who's that?' she says loudly.

'It's The Black Princess!' hisses an older girl.

'A Princess? Is she really a Princess?'

Often when I overhear this appellation I feel alienated, estranged from my fellow human beings by no fault but the colour of my skin, which I can do nothing to amend. Today it comes as a welcome reminder of how my dear niece Mary greeted me, on my first visit to my sister's house after my marriage.

1789 Lucknow April

'Auntie! Are you become a princess?' Mary still gazes at the Colonel's carriage in awe when I have descended, for it is a splendid vehicle furnished with carpets and glass windows.

'It belongs to Colonel Martin,' I tell her. 'And he has more than one.'

Little Hastings is impressed by the horses, which sport feathered plumes on their foreheads, red ribbon woven into their manes, and are driven with reins of silk.

'Another day I shall send the carriage to fetch you to visit me. There is a little girl called Sally with whom you might play.' I turn to my mother who has come to meet me. 'And, mother, do come also. And you, Gulzar.'

'I should certainly like to visit the finest house in the city,' says my mother. 'Which I had never expected to do.'

'It is all thanks to my sister and her husband keeping me in their house for all those years.' I hug her. 'And to you, for insisting they hold the *mehfil.*'

***

One hot day, late in the afternoon, my brother-in-law and sister visit us and, together with Colonel Martin and Boulone, we climb to the roof, hoping that the river breezes will dispel our lethargy. Several pleasure boats pass, their occupants clearly enjoying their excursion, their laughter carrying far across the water.

'Oh, I should like to go on such a boat,' I exclaim and then, in case of being thought presumptuous, add hastily. 'One day if it were possible.'

'An excellent idea,' says my sister and Colonel Martin instantly backs the project.

'We shall order one directly.' He departs, calling out directions to Boulone to request a basket of refreshments for our trip.

Within minutes we are settled in a long low boat, poled by a single crewman who stands at the rear on a high platform. Apparently, at this season, the water is too shallow for other propulsion, but, for the same reason, it is slow-flowing and safe to go where we wish. After some consultation, we agree to go first a short distance upstream, in the shadow of the high brick walls and towers that surround the great Macchi Bhavan fort, not long since the home of the Nawab, whose love of all things beautiful is evident in the gardens with which he adorned the approaches to his stronghold. There are beds of pink asters, orange marigolds and purple petunias, others composed entirely of different varieties of rose and potted flowering shrubs besides.

There are few other craft still on the water at this late hour, it is pleasantly cool and the soft steady splash of the oars so agreeable an accompaniment that, as if by accord, we are all silent. I recline on my cushions, trail my fingers through the water and watch pairs of red dragonflies come together and fly apart as if compelled by magnetic forces beyond their control. William had some toy soldiers which acted similarly. Highflying flocks of starlings wheel overhead, swifts dart and dip low across our bows in pursuit of insects, storks and egrets flap lazily upstream to some resting place for the night, while jackdaws race from bank to bank on urgent missions known only to themselves.

At the stone bridge we turn to breast the current across the middle of the river and, once close by the northern bank, our boatman ships his oars and we drift unaided downstream, enjoying views of the

Residency grounds with some of the buildings visible amongst the trees, and a sight of Colonel Martin's house that quite takes my breath away. It rises above the river in a series of elegantly sculpted terraces that appear too delicate to be the work of a human architect or, for that matter, to offer a sufficiently strong habitation for the large numbers of people whom I know to live and work there.

'It is like a fairy palace,' I suggest. 'Seen from this angle.'

'I think it the most beautiful building in Lucknow,' says my sister. 'I should like it to be mine.'

The Colonel smiles, pleased to hear such praise of his creation, but I have already noticed something closer to hand. There is a temple on a small island to which a few hardy worshippers wade cautiously to worship, their clothing knotted high around their waists. It is next to a cluster of rough huts in front of which men and women wash clothing on stones set into the banks, children play in and out of the shallows and a small herd of buffalo noses through the weeds in search of food. Wisps of blue smoke from cooking fires drift skywards between the dwellings, there is a faint sweet smell of burning dung. The whole has more of the appearance of a camp than a village, and is quite unlike the various constructions on the opposite bank in which we are fortunate to make our homes.

'I wonder that those huts withstand the rains,' I observe.

'Oh, they are constantly being dismantled and moved according to the water level,' the Colonel informs me.

'Do you not think it singular,' Boulone entirely changes the subject, 'that we three friends have found us European husbands who are also friends? And they amongst the most distinguished. I wish we could have our portrait taken.'

I follow her gaze and think we do indeed make an appealing group, the men good friends as she has said are we, all relaxed and lounging on the cushions in the boat and in very good spirits.

Faiz is of the same opinion. 'It would make a very pleasant picture,' she agrees.

'Have you seen mine?' Boulone turns to me. 'Which the Colonel had taken together with my brother? People say it is very fine. I will show you one day.'

'Yet it hardly does justice to your beauty,' says the Colonel gallantly and, as she smiles back at him, she does indeed look beautiful. Too often her face is marred by discontent. Later, at supper, when Fyze and my brother-in-law have left, she is much less happy when the Colonel talks with Benoit of his nostalgia for Europe.

'I mean and intend quitting this country in a couple of years,' he says. 'I only wait to hear from Antoine Polier how he is settled. For he was in this country as long as I and has accordingly acquired a constitution for this climate that I fear a European climate may not agree with. Many of my friends who went home advise me to remain where I am, but the greatest number of my friends have gone, though still, I think, I have some good ones left in India. I do not mean among the Blacks.' He adds, then turns quickly to Boulone. 'Amongst whom I do not count my lovely Lise.' He stretches out a hand to caress her briefly. 'For she is whiter than me and has had as good an education as any European. But among all the rest, sincerity, friendship, gratitude, are words not known in their dictionary.'

Despite his thus excepting Boulone, he does not mention taking her with him. He speaks at length, and with most apparent longing, of the 'thousand diversions' that a man may seemingly choose amongst in Europe. 'It is certainly the place where one may enjoy life,' he opines. 'And England most particularly.'

My husband appears thoughtful but says nothing.

***

Many evenings we dine with our host and I thus have frequent opportunity to observe his affection for my husband, both renegades who have thrown in their lot with the victorious British, if of somewhat different national origin. Benoit explains to me that he is himself not French but from Savoy, a small country with its own king, but it is adjacent and, I think, surely similar enough. Since I see the Colonel's delight in his company, and know that we are beholden to our host, very often I retire alone, after eating, to my chamber to enable them to smoke and talk together.

Benoit tells me little of their conversations except that he is making investments in trade in precious stones and metals, besides indigo, Kashmir shawls, silks and spices. Some evenings, I know they also enjoy the entertainment of musicians and dancers for I hear music and the singing and laughter of female voices, whether from the zenana or the town I do not know and dare not ask. On such occasions he does not join me in my bed.

I am writing a new song.

'Love is strange'.

My love is a river that will never cease.
His ebbs and flows in tides like the mighty seas.
Some nights his passion makes bright as a full moon..
Others are quite black when he leaves me all alone.
Sometimes we are as one; others far apart.
So many mysterious changes of heart!
If love cannot grow, can it not stay the same?
I want love I can trust, which never is strange.

Somehow I cannot make it fit into the form of a *ghazal*, but it matters little as I do not think I shall sing it to anyone, least of all him.

***

It is the hottest season and we pass much of the day-time in the lowest of two basements that have been excavated in the river banks. They are agreeably commodious and airy since they are connected to two octagonal towers on the sides, which provide for ventilation. Frames containing green brambles cover the windows, against which fountains play a constant spray as protection against the hot winds outside, thus cooling the air as it enters.

One afternoon, a messenger brings a letter for the Colonel, I think from Captain Polier, certainly from France. Colonel Martin is astonished.

'The King has been compelled to recall the Estates General,' he tells my husband. 'It is one hundred and seventy five years since it met.'

'He is become a democrat?'

'Ha! He is insolvent. And the Assembly has demanded a new constitution.'

When the monsoon begins and the river starts to rise, we move up to the upper basement, where another letter arrives to tell of events that even I know to be extraordinary. The Colonel reads quickly.

'The people of Paris have taken the Bastille!' He exclaims. 'Discharged all the prisoners, taken all the arms, and executed the Governor and Lieutenant Governor who had resisted them. What is more, they were assisted by the French guards and not opposed by German and Swiss troops stationed near. The King is at his palace of Versailles awaiting a massacre of the Royal Family, the court, the ministers and all connected with them, while the aristocrats and clergy in the Assembly declare themselves sincerely converted to the justice of voting by ordinary persons.'

'It is no time to return,' observes Benoit.

'No, indeed.'

Much relieved, Boulone takes me roaming the upper halls. In a separate room there is a vast quantity of cream silk collapsed in swathes around a large basket together with a quantity of ropes. In one corner there is some sort of large brazier.

'It is the balloon which by means of hot air the Colonel made ascend over Lucknow some years back,' she tells me.

'I remember hearing tell of the experiment,' I reply. 'I believe I was in Delhi with my parents at the time.'

'He intends constructing one large enough to carry up several persons,' she continues. 'And the Nawab wishes one capable of carrying twenty armed men.'

'For what purpose?'

'Oh, to give some advantage in battle I suppose.'

She is losing interest, and ready to move on, when we hear a step behind us.

'At great risk to the men concerned.' It is Benoit. 'Although the Nawab had no concern on this aspect of the matter. I was present at the discussion. And there have been other displays besides, in Calcutta, France, and even in my home town, Chambery.'

'Boulone is taking me to see her portrait,' I tell him. 'Will you come too?'

He shakes his head. 'I came to tell you I shall be out this evening. There is some Company event I must attend. You may amuse yourself with Boulone or ask for dinner in our apartment.' He kisses my hand, bows to us both and departs.

The Colonel has many fine portraits and other paintings in his collection. There are views of this house and several of different places as seen from a boat on a river journey between Lucknow and Calcutta and a collection of sketches of Calcutta itself. There are eleven by Mr Zoffany, in several of which the Colonel himself appears. There is one painted at a cockfight, which was attended by several Europeans, of whom I think I know one or two, and the Nawab himself with some of his courtiers. Another shows the Colonel pointing at a picture of this house standing between two other European gentlemen who are seated.

'I think you will recognise Colonel Polier?' Boulone points to the moustachioed figure on the left. 'He was often in this house before his return to France. I do not know the other.'

'I believe it is Mr Wombwell,' I say, peering at the smooth, somewhat full-faced, gentleman and recognising his small mouth and rather tight expression. 'He was the Company Accountant and is also recently departed for England. I do not know the man seated on the far side of the table.' But then I look more closely and exclaim with great delight.

'Why, it is Mr Zoffany himself!'

'Yes indeed.' Boulone is not much interested. 'He lived here for quite some time before he left for England.'

'He painted my brother-in-law and his family some years back,' I tell her eagerly, 'And I am also in the group, though on the periphery and in profile.' But she is not listening and very soon she stops and points.

'There I am.'

She is fishing, wearing a long brocaded cloak, with her brother, aged perhaps ten years, looking up at her and a pastoral scene behind. She looks queenly, pensive as in life, her gaze is on something beyond the frame. It is an arresting composition which I survey at length.

'The Colonel cares for you most particularly,' I say at last. Surely it is both true and what she wishes to believe.

'Perhaps,' she replies, with a faint smile. 'Do you know, we are soon to take Mr Zoffany's son into the household. He did not take his *bibi* with him to Europe.' She pauses and looks at me, again with that ambiguous smile, perhaps expecting to have shocked me, punctured what she may see as my complacency. Then, abrupt as ever, she changes tack.

'Enough of paintings. Do you return with me?''

'Shortly,' I tell her. 'There are several yet I should like to examine.' But I also wish to ponder the sense of unease that has again crept upon me, as Boulone intended.

***

'The enemy of enduring passion, Time clips the wings of love.
By habit dulled, days like each other, Time clips the wings of love.
First rapture dazzles. So blinded and crazed, new lovers do not see
The awaiting cruel awakening. Time clips the wings of love.
I flew careless in your arms, amongst the stars, touched heaven's gate.
Bewitched by kisses, how to believe Time clips the wings of love?
I have learnt ecstasy, known perfect bliss. Now all I feel is doubt.
And lying alone, I think it is true: Time clips the wings of love.'

'Why so melancholy?'

I did not hear Benoit enter my chamber and turn to him quickly. His tone is curt, a small frown creases his forehead, he is displeased. I put away my instrument and hasten to greet him.

'It is but a classical theme, of which I saw a painting. By Mr Zoffany. When Boulone took me to see her portrait. It seemed a fit subject for a *ghazal*.'

I fear I speak too quickly, as if protesting my innocence of some crime but his expression changes, though the frown remains, so then I think how best to cheer him. I take his hand and lead him to the window seat, kneel behind him and gently massage his shoulders.

'The shipment has arrived?'

He has been supervising the unloading of cargo at the warehouse and I know there had been some delay, and a need for especial scrutiny lest the goods be of inferior quality or less in quantity than had been promised. I like to pay attention to his activities and find them of considerable interest, perhaps more so than he.

He sighs. 'In some disarray. Some of the cases were broken open, whether by thieves or careless handling I do not know.'

'But all is there?'

'I believe so.' He breathes in deeply, raises one shoulder to trap my hand and turns to kiss it. 'There is magic in your hands.' He guides me round to sit in his lap, my back towards him, and begins to kiss my neck. When he speaks, I feel his every breath.

'I would have asked Mr Zoffany to paint you, were he still here.' He slides his hands up under my tunic. 'Or both of us together,' he murmurs, and blows a little in my ear.

'In what position?' I wriggle back closer against him.

'Mmm.' He tugs at the string that holds my *ungia* closed until he has my breasts bare in his hands. 'Perhaps like this?'

'Perhaps.'

'Or this.' He loosens the string of my pyjama and takes them off, pulls me around so that I face him and wraps my legs around his waist.

'That feels good,' I agree.

'This might feel better yet.' He raises my tunic and opens the front of his breeches. 'And make the best portrait?' He lifts me and brings me down upon him.

'Then perhaps it is as well that Mr Zoffany is not here?'

'I think we would request that Mr Zoffany leave us and return after some while.'

'That would be better.' I hold him close.

And yet I am a little melancholy.

19

1853 Horsham April

'Helena, if your face mirrors your mind your mood has changed.'

It is Ann, concerned for my welfare as ever. I am sitting with her and Michael in their comfortable sitting room after a very large and lengthy lunch.

'I found you in most cheerful a condition. Does our company so reduce your spirits?'

'Oh I am perhaps a little tired after such an excellent repast.' I did try to eat well in appreciation of my hosts.

'I gather you slept most of the journey,' Michael observes. 'I daresay 'tis all in the process of healing.'

'Or proof of continued ill health,' retorts his wife. 'I wish you would consider removing back to Horsham, Helena, so that your friends can keep closer watch on you.'

She has said this on several occasions during the past two years since I insisted on returning to Lower Beeding and each time I have resisted.

'If you still do not wish to sell nor live in lodgings, we might find an entire house for rental.' Michael joins this latest foray, prompted by a frown from his wife.

'I am concerned that you will spend your nights alone after Caroline is wed.' Ann clicks her tongue and shakes her head.

'I have promised Caroline continuing employment,' I object, but, knowing that this cannot be entirely persuasive, marshall more arguments. 'And I so love the countryside in these light months of the year. And what of Silver and the cats?'

My friends exchange glances. They have no particular fondness for animals but have experienced the strength of my feelings on this score.

'Perhaps we might delay until the autumn.' Michael looks for his wife's approval.

She purses her lips. 'Let us talk to Charles again when he is here.'

To this I do agree, while maintaining the suspicion that my son is in communication with the Howes on other occasions between his visits. But I shall not move, most particularly not into another's household. I wish to follow my own habits and be beholden to none.

When I take my leave I press the Howes' hands. 'You are very kind. But I have preferred to live in my own establishment for almost the entirety of my adult life, believing it the best remedy for other less avoidable ailments.'

Which was the conclusion I had reached when I was attempting to explain to my mother my lack of contentment so soon after marriage. Indeed, I may have used almost these very words and, though I had then less evidence, I believe I had more confidence that my prescription would prove the solution. For I had not then discovered how far one's own choices may be determined by events far beyond one's sway. I thought I should be happy if only I could have my own home. And, alone in the carriage on the return journey to Lower Beeding, I return to that scene and become again my so much younger self.

1789 Lucknow August

I am gazing out at the Gomti, presently in full flood. 'I should prefer to keep my own establishment, Mother, however grand my present accommodation. And however welcoming our host.'

My mother is visiting me in our apartments in Colonel Martin's house where she had thought me so well settled, and I await her further objections, knowing her ever able to find counter-arguments to suit her purpose. But this time she keeps her peace, while fixing me with quizzical regard.

'So that is why your cheeks have paled and your eyes lost their sparkle. I had thought it due to your recent underwater mode of living, if not to a change in your state of health.' She adds this last with a frown and some suspicion.

'Mother, I promised you ...'

'Hmph.'

She asked me on so many occasions *whether there is yet any indication that she may expect again to be made a grandmother'*, that I promised to inform her at the very earliest opportunity if only she would cease her enquiries. Evidently she does not quite have confidence in my holding to our bargain. Nevertheless, she lets go the matter and again surprises me with her next assertion.

'I was myself very much more content when we moved from Delhi and my brother-in-law's house,' she says. 'I do not say this as a general rule but have no doubt that there are circumstances in which a separate household is to be preferred.' She pauses, thoughtful. 'Why do you not speak to your husband and discover what is his intent? It may be that he is himself considering the acquisition of a house.'

'Oh I could not. For surely he will inform me when he so wishes.'

She looks at me and I think divines my apprehension of arousing his anger.

'Then shall I speak to my son-in-law?' she asks, and raising her voice a little, adds: 'For surely I have some duty where the welfare of my daughter is at question.'

'Oh no!' I am aghast. 'You must not.' My horror increases when I hear a step at the door, and I am instantly suspicious that she had heard him approaching.

He crosses the room in a few paces, bows to my mother and kisses her hand. I smile to see her blush. I have observed on other occasions how she enjoys this gallantry, which is generally lacking in our menfolk.

'Of what would you speak, dear *madame*? What ails my wife?' He glances at me quickly, eyes narrowed, questioning, but I cannot discern his temper.

'Is it not the custom in your own country for the newly married to set up their own household?' She makes her enquiry in disinterested fashion, as if it is quite by the bye.

'I understand your purpose entirely, *sasurai*.' He places an emphasis on the last word. It is the first time I have heard him use it. He is not put out of humour. 'I have considered the matter myself and being now more settled in this city, being persuaded that I can make a living here, I shall indeed make enquiries, with greater speed if my wife is of similar inclination. I had thought her rather partial to the company of the ladies of this household, Boulone in particular, but, if this advantage is outweighed by other considerations, then there is no reason to delay. I shall ask Colonel Martin, who owns many properties in Lucknow as you will be aware.'

***

Mr Wombwell's house is still vacant,' he informs me later that same day. 'We may move as soon as you wish and view it beforehand if you wish. Don Queiros will make all the arrangements.'

It is only a *bangla* of a single storey, its tiled roof supported by plain wooden columns, and it is not large at all, having perhaps eight rooms opening off a central courtyard with a small tank in the centre. But it is set at some height above the river, with a shady and airy verandah on three sides that gives unobstructed views up and downstream and of the mostly wooded land on the northern bank. Also it is near, one might say part of, the Residency compound whither I shall be able to walk to visit my sister. I wander alone around the dusty rooms, thinking how I shall improve them with bright hangings and carpets, and return to where Benoit is sitting on the verandah in conversation with Don Queiros. The latter stands to greet me and, bowing, indicates that I should take his seat. Of all the Europeans I have met, he is the most courteous, I do not know if it is due to his Iberian origins, or, more likely, to his noble lineage. I glance quickly at Benoit to see if this is also his wish and he seems not averse. Don Queiros pulls up a third chair.

'I was telling the Captain that Mr Ozias Humphreys was a guest here of Mr Wombwell for some months a few years ago. I believe you must have seen some of his work at Colonel Martin's?' He smiles at me, I fancy with some admiration. 'I have heard that you have shown a good deal of interest in the collections there.'

'Oh, but I fear I cannot recognise individual artists.' I say quickly. 'I only took a particular interest in Mr Zoffany because he painted my brother-in-law and his family.'

'And a very fine picture it is too,' Benoit interjects. 'Which includes the figure of my wife.' He turns to me. 'Joseph tells me that Mr Humphreys made some sketches whilst he was here of the nearby buildings and such like and on one occasion saw a most fearsome sight. Tell her, Joseph.' His eyes have taken on a strange glitter.

'Oh it is not something I should like to tell a lady,' protests Don Queiros. 'It is too sad to imagine.'

'Only now that my curiosity is so aroused I feel you must.' I am sorry to embarrass him but determined to meet my husband's unkind challenge.

'Well then...' He speaks slowly, with reluctance. 'Mr Humphreys was sitting outside here one day eating supper, looking out across the river, when he – saw a wolf seize a child.' The last few words are expressed so swiftly I almost think I have misheard.

I daresay my face betrays the horror and pity that would surely be experienced by all but the most calloused souls. But I do not openly lament an event which, it seems to me, may sadly not have been as exotic to the child's family as it appeared to Mr Humphreys.

'That would surely be the worst imaginable sight for any parent to behold,' I say calmly, and pause before adding: 'And terrible too to be the helpless observer from afar. But I wonder if one could not prevent a recurrence? Perhaps by the erection of some sort of barricade around each group of dwellings in order to give some protection from the wild creatures of the forest? One that may easily be moved as need be.'

My audience exchanges looks of surprise. Don Queiros is the first to speak, while my husband regards me with, I believe, new interest.

'I imagine it would,' says Don Queiros. 'I will ask the Colonel who, as you know, is not averse to acts of charity.'

'See to it on my account if you will,' my husband intervenes abruptly. 'One's home should be a place of safety and security. And so,' his voice softens as he turns to me. 'What think you of our proposed dwelling?'

'I like it.'

In truth, I should like anywhere that gave me my first home of my own.

1853 Lower Beeding April

I am so eager to open my front door when the carriage stops at my gate that I do not wait for Samuel to hand me down. But I have need of his assistance in turning the key, which is stiff, and am grateful that he accompanies me inside. I let him lead him to the library where he helps me remove my outer wraps and settles me on the window seat.

'Thank you, Samuel. It is good to be home.'

He is never inclined to unnecessary comment but my heartfelt utterance has struck some chord of sympathy, which he feels the need to express.

'Every mortal man and woman they needs a place to call their own,' he observes. 'And the longer one resides in such a place the more one is loath to leave.'

He falls silent and might remain so but I am of a sudden struck by a recognition of how very long I have resided here.

'I have lived here half my life.'

'More'n forty year,' he nods. 'And if I might say so, a handsome woman you wuz in them there days.'

I wish I could repay the compliment but cannot recall seeing him then. I think I observed little in those days beyond the small circle of my solitude. Instead I confide my dearest wish. 'I hope I may die here.'

'God willing.' He makes no attempt to divert me from thoughts that most, particularly younger, persons call morbid, whilst feeling a mortal fear of the death that awaits us all.

'God willing, indeed. Thank you, Samuel. You are most kind.' I press a silver coin into his palm and close his hand over it with both of mine.

'Good evening, Ma'am. God bless.' He touches his cap and leaves me, I guess he supposes, to enjoy further eschatological contemplation.

But I am in no mood to explore my ending. Today my soul is as young as it was then, at the beginning, in that first home of my own.

20

1789 Lucknow September

'Claude says we may extend the house as we wish,' Benoit informs me one evening shortly after our removal to our new abode. 'I say, let us wait to see what are our requirements.'

The Colonel is come to pass the evening and I have joined them some half hour after his arrival. He smiles at me and spreads his hands to indicate his agreement. Benoit meanwhile is regarding me closely, perhaps merely to ascertain my approval, but I wonder if he makes reference to future offspring. He has never spoken of the matter but after three months of marriage many women have conceived.

'Perhaps one day we might add a second storey.' I shrug, but then imagine it more fully. 'With perhaps a pavilion on the top and, oh, I should like a telescope, if it were possible.' I stop, embarrassed at my exuberance, for I see their smiles.

'Do not make it too grand,' cautions the Colonel 'Or the Nawab will want it.'

'Even though he has but recently moved to a new palace?" This is the Daulat Khana, which has been constructed on the far side of the Great Imambara.

'He will never be satisfied.' The Colonel shakes his head and addresses us both. 'Have you not heard that he has been demolishing the Emperor Akbar's old palace in the Allahabad fort and transporting the stones here? Whether to rebuild the whole in this city or merely to utilise them in some new construction -'

He breaks off and looks up as a servant enters to announce a visitor. It is Mirza Abu Taleb Khan, a member of the Nawab's court and old acquaintance of my parents, come to pay his respects to my husband or perhaps myself, as I do not think they have met previously. Uncertain of my status in this company, I reach for my veil to cover my head.

'No no, child,' he raises a hand in protest and then addresses us all, doffing his velvet headpiece with a sweeping bow. '*As Salam Alaikum,*'

'*As Salam Alaik,*' Benoit responds as both he and Colonel Martin rise to greet the newcomer.

'Long be your life,' Abu Taleb tells him, though, I realise, he can only be the elder by a few years and am not sure if this is a compliment or an affectation on Abu Taleb's part. He is dressed rather splendidly in green and orange patterned silk and he has lately acquired a full though carefully trimmed beard which lends his face greater authority. 'May you be fortunate.' He touches his cap to his forehead before replacing it

My husband bows and indicates that all should be seated. '*Masakum Allah Bilkhair.*'

'May God make the evening favourable to you also,' Abu Taleb returns the courtesy before turning to the Colonel. 'How is your health?'

'I pray for the best. And actively pursue my own remedy.'

'So I hear!' Abu Taleb appears to wince. 'It is one which does great credit to your strength of character and endurance.'

It is evident that he and the Colonel enjoy cordial relations and it soon becomes apparent that they agree on some matters concerning the Nawab.

'We were debating how long the Daulat Khana will satisfy the Nawab's desire for ever more splendid lodgings and belongings.' Colonel Martin claps Abu Taleb on the back. 'What say you?'

'It is a very fine palace in the design of which I believe you played no inconsiderable a part.' Abu Taleb raises one hand, palm uppermost to indicate his admiration. 'It is my opinion that you have given us the best of European design yet so adapted to suit the needs of a court such as ours. And we have some splendid gardens with fountains and tanks and waterways connected to the river. I hope that I may enjoy living there for many more years.'

The Colonel is visibly gratified and bows to acknowledge the compliment. 'However...' he prompts.

'However, it is sadly true that Asaf-ud-Daula has a most restless nature and an acquisitive soul and is constantly taking people's property with no compensation nor redress. He orders the demolition of houses for the sake only of the bricks that he may use them elsewhere, thereby leaving the residents homeless. And often without even the opportunity to first carry away their furniture.'

'In truth,' Colonel Martin concludes. 'He is a vainglorious, trivial fellow, mostly drunken and engaged in various perversions and he expends millions on amassing worthless trifles for which he has no use. Particularly from Europe.'

I am surprised to hear these two gentlemen thus criticise the Nawab, who has long since been the Colonel's employer as supervisor of his arsenal, and pleased to find my husband more circumspect.

'Some, perhaps a considerable proportion, of which trifles I believe you may have put in his way?' His tone is arch.

'We do business, *mon ami*.' Colonel Martin waves away any suggestion of wrong-doing.

'And perhaps there is some degree of seriousness behind the frivolity?' Benoit continues. 'I heard that he established a most amicable relationship with Governor Hastings when the latter visited Lucknow, based upon the discovery of common interests in the problems of administration. Tax collection in particular, the adequacy of income and ability to meet one's expenses being a problem besetting most leaders, both military and civilian. It is not easy, I think, ruling over people.'

Abu Taleb is nodding but the Colonel speaks first.

'Well, *mon cher*, I must surely take your word on that. My own experience of command being of small measure in comparison to your own.'

My husband makes a dismissive gesture and turns to me. 'Perhaps you would prepare a pipe for our guests?'

'Would you not prefer -?' I begin, but break off as I see his face darken.

I have but recently learnt the skill as part of my mother's body of instruction on the running of a household, but am a little concerned at the increasing frequency with which he makes this request, though perhaps tonight, since we have not eaten, it is only tobacco that he intends to smoke. I rephrase my enquiry.

'Will you eat dinner now or later?'

'What is our menu today?'

'Sadiq, the *rakabdar,* is making *murgh zafrani* and *galawat kebabs.* That is,' I hasten to explain as I have found Benoit's knowledge of our gastronomy to be limited. 'That is, saffron chicken and kid goat –'

'Yes, yes,' he interrupts. 'And?'

'I have myself prepared one of my mother's vegetable dishes which you have in the past enjoyed. From aubergines and –'

'*Dhungare baigan!*' It is now Abu Taleb who interrupts me with clasped hands raised as in near ecstasy. 'Your mother has prepared it for me. And a most perfect dish it is from her hands. Although quite simple in its ingredients and method, I believe?' He looks to me and I nod. 'But all the better for that. Really you know there is no need for extravagance, such as wrapping food in gold and silver, which is quite tasteless and used solely for its effect. And as for these clever transformations and representations of one food in another, which I believe one could call *trompes d'oeil?*' He appeals to the other two members of his audience, 'Whereby every dish whether bread or rice, vegetable or meat, sweet or savoury is in fact made of sugar. Even the pickles. Yes! What say you to that, my French friends? Or of a *khichri* which is not composed of rice and lentils as one would expect but of almonds cut as rice shapes and pistachio nuts as lentils. Would you ask a man to expend the short hours of his precious life in such labours?'

'Surely it is no wonder that a man who is a chef should want to improve his craft to the utmost of his ability and thereby reap the rewards of pleasing his employer?' Benoit objects.

'This is true,' concedes Abu Taleb. 'But I would insist that the pleasure of food should consist in its taste rather than in its appearance and that the two should not be at odds with each other. Although in truth the *nut khichri* I described is a most delicious confection.'

'And I should like to see,' the Colonel adds, 'But not consume, the wondrous pies of Hyderabad which, prepared by a chef from our own fair city, when opened, release a number of small birds that then fly away!'

I have not heard of this before and should like to question him further but Benoit intervenes. 'Come, all this talk of food will make you too hungry to delay eating, my friends. Let us enjoy a pipe together while Nur supervises a dinner that will certainly satisfy your palates and perhaps also please the eye.' He escorts me to the doorway and whispers. 'Is there some most especial dish that you can make or order and which can be prepared within perhaps one hour?'

We were to have eaten plain rice which is sometimes desirable as a complement to the rich diversity of other dishes. But Lucknow is known for its great variety of *pulaos*, which, in the opinion of its citizens, are much to be preferred to the more strongly flavoured *biryanis* favoured in Delhi.

'There is one *pulao* about which I could instruct Sadiq but I should have to send for young lamb, freshly slaughtered.'

'Do so.'

'And one is supposed to use some silver leaf although it is optional.'

'Buy it. Gold if you prefer. And tell one of the boys to see to the pipe.'

Light-hearted, I hasten to the kitchens, keen to fulfil my tasks knowing my husband to be pleased with me. I feel that I am his partner, his equal, or, at the very least, his trusted lieutenant in this most important matter of serving our guests.

Sadiq has no great reputation but he has proved himself an able accomplice whether as teacher or pupil, and I like him. He has a noble profile with a high sloping forehead, a fine-boned nose and neat moustaches. He is near middle age, surely a little older than my husband and I have wondered at his apparent lack of family. He is not fazed by the last minute addition to the menu, in fact, he is eager to attempt this new dish. Together we rehearse the list of ingredients.

'Onions, garlic, ginger, green cardamon pods, cinnamon stick, cloves, peppercorn, bay leaf. Rice, ghee, yoghurt, milk, saffron threads, keora water, silver leaf ...'

21

1853 Lower Beeding April

'I've made you a nice rice pudding for your supper, being as you've had your dinner and I dursay a fine dinner too, better nor I could contrive though I tries my best, I do hope you knows that.'

I did not hear Caroline return nor come into the study where I have been dreaming. She puts a tray down beside me and stands back, her hands clasped against her ample stomach, her face flushed from her endeavours. I regard her offering, a steaming bowl of milky slop with a shiny scarlet centre, the whole of which emits a strong and nauseating sweetness.

'I took the liberty of judging your fancy from words you wuz saying in your sleep,' she continues. 'Anycase, it seemed a fair idea though I've not all the ingredients you wuz mentioning. Nutmeg I have but not them other spices, as I'm thinking they must be. Mebbe we could send for some from Brighthelmstone or even Lunnon. But it looked a bit plain so I added the strawberry preserve. And sugar of course. Will I help you? It's very hot.'

'Thank you, Caroline.' I hope my expression does not betray my disgust.

Cooking is not Caroline's strongest suit, but normally the food she produces is palatable. I am not sure how much of this I shall succeed in swallowing and delay the attempt, hoping that my cats will come to my assistance.

'I will wait for it to cool and call you when I have finished. You are most kind to prepare something special in so short a time.'

Which is the compliment my husband paid me after I had swiftly organised that successful meal, and which I thought indicated his growing esteem, a good opinion I would be glad to nurture through all the years together. It is hard to live without approval, without love. I shall henceforth be kind to Caroline.

1789 Lucknow September

'At such short notice! Our guests were most impressed.'

My husband takes my hand and raises it to his lips. We are reclining side by side in my bed. *'"The most exquisite flavouring!"* Claude said. *"A pulao which even the Nawab's kitchens would be proud to produce."* That from Abu Taleb whom one might expect to be less easily impressed.'

'There is no more noble occupation than to be a good host,' I affirm. 'And it gives me pleasure to please others.'

At this he turns towards me, a quizzical tilt to his mouth, an eyebrow raised, perhaps testing my sincerity. If so, he is satisfied for his expression of an instant softens and he reaches an arm over me and draws me close.

'Ah *mignonne*.' He kisses my lips. 'I am glad of it for you surely please me.'

My heart swells with joy and my body moulds to his with a sudden passion that, I think, surprises us both. I feel I could be the equal of this extraordinary man, as necessary to him as he to me, and it seems to me that he responds in like manner. We fall asleep, still in close embrace.

I wake while it is yet dark and finding him still beside me and not retired to his own chamber, lie motionless, rejoicing in a swelling certainty that I am pregnant, which I know to be not rational, but which I believe I can already feel in my breasts and in my womb. Of a sudden he begins to moan, thrashes his limbs free of the bed covers and sits up with a shout.

'What ails you?' I grasp his hand.

His eyes stare, his expression is distraught, but he is entirely unaware of his present situation and remains in the thrall of his sleeping dreams. After some moments he shakes his head, sighs deeply and falls back on the bed. I pull up the covers again and am glad to see he sleeps in peace.

Our new harmony endures through the following days, extending into some weeks. He spends much time at my side, if smoking somewhat in excess and finding slight diversion in business matters, in which Colonel Martin is most assiduous, frequently visiting to propose new ventures.

'Tell me why,' I venture after one such occasion when we are sitting together on a window seat where I have brought him a pipe. 'If Colonel Martin is a Company man he is so much involved in his own affairs. Does he not have duties also?'

My husband laughs. 'He has long contrived to allow the one to benefit the other, whilst not to the extent that he may be accused of wrong-doing. He works hard, he has many talents. And he knows when to be generous with his gifts and to whom.'

'I wonder that my brother-in-law and he became close. He would seem a somewhat risky associate for the Governor's representative.'

'He has been in Lucknow a long time. Together they have seen many changes.' He sucks on the pipe and speaks while holding his breath. 'Do you know why Governor Hastings made your brother-in-law his representative here?'

'Because he trusted him?'

He exhales. 'Because he had suspended the Residency, blaming former Residents for much of the misrule in Avadh, for exploiting and corrupting the Nawab. Captain Palmer was appointed to report on the conduct of the staff of the Residency in the same year that our predecessor in this house -'

'Mr Wombwell?'

He nods. 'Mr Wombwell was appointed to order the Residency accounts, the previous Resident having been unwilling or incapable of keeping any.'

'I did wonder on occasion why my brother-in-law was not himself appointed Resident.'

My husband sucks deeply on the pipe and holds the smoke in his mouth a long while before exhaling. 'Company politics, I daresay. Hastings, though Governor, was constantly outvoted by a particular clique on the Council in Calcutta, which would not now occur for the English Parliament changed the law a few years since. Claude, by the by, has very good reason to be grateful to your brother-in-law for enabling him to remain in Lucknow and pursue his various interests.

He wrote to Hastings requesting Claude not be transferred to active service, pleading his ill health and advancing years.'

I have yet another question but at this point my husband puts down his pipe and looks sideways at me, sardonic. 'Shall you write a history of these events?' he asks then leans towards me, buries his face in my bosom and begins to worry at the strings of my *ungia* with his teeth. I feign disinterest.

'I wonder that you are so very well-informed, not being a Company man yourself. What brought you to Lucknow at that time? Or should I not ask?'

He has succeeded in uncovering my bosom and is nibbling experimentally at first one nipple and then the other as if to compare the effect. 'You may ask,' he traces a finger slowly around and between my breasts, 'But I may not tell.' He sucks one breast deep into his mouth and mumbles 'On the other hand...' He transfers his attentions to the other as I move under him and begin to unbutton his breeches. 'Have you so soon lost interest in my history?' He tugs at my pyjama. 'Why, I was here as a student, tasked to learn languages.' He begins to caress me, his fingers more insistent with each succeeding word. 'Persian, Urdu, and to improve my Russian.'

I try to stop his mouth with kisses, to pull him close to me but he laughs and continues to tease. 'I was going back to Russia. Don't you want to know why?' He puts his mouth very close to my ear and blows softly. 'I was going to be a spy. A secret agent.' He blows again. 'Can you guess for whom?'

At this juncture I do not care in the slightest and say the first thing that comes into my head. 'The English.'

He chuckles and nods. 'Clever girl, my clever little girl.' He is very pleased with me.

***

But there are not many more such occasions. My husband becomes steadily more morose and distant, does not often wish to make love and I wonder if it is the effect of too much opium.

106

Boulone, who visits more than once a week, soon intuits my unease and offers another opinion.

'Perhaps it is the pox,' she surmises. 'The Colonel has suffered in a similar fashion for many years.'

I do not of course entirely trust Boulone, knowing her to be more than a little jealous of my status, and I would never ask her whether my husband had disported himself with any of the women in the Colonel's household, whether before or after our marriage, and might thereby have acquired the infection. But there is no one else with whom I can discuss such matters.

'As you know, I am without child as are we all in his household.' She looks at me closely but I will not tell her yet of what I am now almost certain.

'Of course,' she continues, 'the Colonel also has had other problems affecting the same organ, of stones causing obstruction, for which he has treated himself in a most painful way.' I see a wistfulness cross her face and understand how much her archness and abrasive manner may conceal her own suffering and disappointment and, indeed, her affection for the Colonel. But my sympathy for her is short-lived as she voices my next fear.

'More likely your husband suffers only from *ennui* after a life so filled with action and danger,' she pronounces, with some satisfaction and perhaps a little malice. 'He is bored.'

I think she is correct in her conclusion and, the longer I consider, the less surprise I find in it. Naturally I had rather be the source of sufficient comfort and diversion for my beloved, but I cannot be associated with his unhappiness and loss of manhood, even though it be by force of circumstance and not my fault. And so, when one day a messenger arrives, I can find it in me to rejoice.

My husband comes into my chamber holding a letter. 'It is from Sindhia,' he says. 'He wishes me to rejoin him and would reinstate me on my terms. I shall not be required to fight the English and my troops will be regularly paid.'

'You are glad?'

'I shall be master of ten battalions of infantry with cavalry and artillery officered by Europeans.' He can barely contain his pride but maintains a neutral expression, in deference perhaps to my supposed dismay.

'That is great preferment indeed and shows how great is his need and estimation of your services.'

He allows himself a fleeting smile of self-congratulation that I think is tinged with incredulity. 'With the rank and income of General.' He can scarcely believe the turn in his fortune, but is plainly ready to embrace it.

I go to him, bend and touch his feet. 'It is your just reward.'

He raises me and, hands on my shoulders, regards me closely. 'I do not have long to prepare,' he says. 'I must leave in a few days for Mattra. But I will send for you when my circumstances are resolved. Unless you prefer to remain here.'

'Where my husband goes I would go,' I tell him and I think he is well satisfied.

PART III

Motherhood

22

1853 Lower Beeding April

It will be one of those spring days that comes as a messenger from summer to remind us that it follows not far behind. I know this as soon as I throw up the sash and lean out to inhale the dizzying spectrum of a hundred different aromas. The first rose flush of dawn fades even as I gaze into a deepening golden haze, which permeates the vapours rising from the damp earth of the night. But the air itself is still and there is not a sound, nor movement of which I am aware. The birds themselves have not woken, perhaps dazed by the unseasonal warmth of the morning, or awake but awed into silence by its glory.

'Shall we go out, Silver?' I whisper and he pricks his ears the better to hear. It is he to whom I am indebted for this rare delight, he who woke me with an insistent and somewhat wet paw laid on the crook of my arm, causing some brief dream which I have already forgotten. He stands beside me now, his front feet on the window sill, sniffing at the scene with such discerning attention that, not for the first time, I envy his canine sensibilities. I stroke his head, which is also damp. He has been out already.

'Out?'

He has heard aright and, with a joyful yelp, lowers his paws and trots to the door, head turning to ascertain that I follow.

'Hush,' I caution. 'Let us not wake the household.'

I do not mean the cats, who have but briefly stirred, their ability to sleep being a trait I have also sometimes wished that I possessed. I mean only Caroline, for she would surely chide and try to prevent such rash behaviour on the part of one so recently sick. And in the majority of circumstances she would be right. And I would not expect one as young as she to understand how I could gladly trade however many days that may yet be allotted to me for this chance to partake just once more of the world's perfection.

We pass swiftly down the garden path where I see how near to flowering are my lilies-of-the-valley, tiny shining white heads piercing their green leaf sheaths. I shall return later and kneel to absorb their wondrous fragrance, as also those less singular of the bluebells, tulips and narcissi that now overshadow the fading daffodils (I must tell James to cut their heads). Many times have I wondered why it is only the sensations of sight that we can exactly recall, where memories of smell and sound, touch and taste are only of recognition and we require their sources to be present. This morning I think I understand God's purpose: it is so that we may be continually astonished by the wonders of his creation.

We turn left on the lane and take the first path across a field in which today there is a fine herd of Jerseys, pulling tirelessly at the grass or ruminatively chewing. They raise their heads at our appearance and I reach for Silver's collar. If it were sheep he would require more restraint, but cows, being of more stolid a disposition, present less of a temptation. To my surprise, however, he growls and for an instant I think that I have unwittingly caused him pain. But then I see a distant shape emerge from the woods at the top of the field. It is a man and it becomes apparent that he carries a gun across one shoulder.

Despite the felt hat pulled low over his head, I recognise my gardener at thirty yards. No doubt that he has been a'poaching. I do not need Silver's excitement to alert me to the sack slung over the young man's shoulder, but I think that there are sufficient rabbits in the area for every man, even if these may have been taken in another's land. Some warreners are unreasonable by my reckoning, for who can say where a rabbit might choose to surface or make his principal abode? And I remember that James will soon find more cause to stay home at night. He tips his hat with the end of his gun.

'Glorious morning, Missus Bennett madam.'

'It is indeed, James. Too good to stay abed. I pray it will be as fine for your wedding day for which do accept my best wishes and congratulations.'

He lowers his gaze to the ground as the visible portion of his face flushes a deep red. 'I thank you, ma'am, I thank you.' And then some thought causes him to recover his confidence and he looks me straight in the eye.

'Take care where you walk, ma'am. There's new squatters in the forest, come I knows not whence. Irish may be, come to seek work in the heathland restoration. Down near the brook I seed their hovels. Best beware, keep th' dog close.'

'Why thank you, James, I shall heed your words.' I am touched at his consideration, it is more than I had expected of him.

I have reached the edge of the forest, release the impatient Silver and he is gone, disappearing with a flick of his feathery tail into the dense undergrowth. I shall not see him again unless I whistle, and I do not follow for I wish to skirt the wood today and remain in the warm sunlight. Not far along, my nostrils begin to sting with the acrid smell of burning bracken, the smoke from which I now see coiling a short distance inside the forest. James' squatters I think and, peering more closely, I see them huddled round their fire, a family group I think, perhaps five or six of them, some very small.

'Good morning!' I raise my walking stick in greeting.

Their faces turn towards me, white in the gloom. It is too far to read their expression but they make no further movement, unless it be to shrink even closer to the fire's protection. They are more afraid than I, perhaps have no legitimate business and fear being moved on by the parish authorities and that I shall be the reporting agent. I resolve to return on another occasion with some provisions. I am not concerned for my safety, even if I held my life to be of any value. What should I fear, I, who at the tender age of eighteen, lived where marauding bands made seasonal sport of pillage and murder?

I wander on, looking up at the trees lining my path, the tall horse chestnuts of which the wide five-fingered leaves are always the first to spread, the sycamore and silver birch shaking out their finery, the ash at last bursting its tight black buds and the high and mighty oaks still awaiting the sure arrival of spring. In the roots of one such ancient denizen I spy a favourite mossy hollow where I like to lie and gaze into the forest canopy. The rooks are building high this year, which is said to be a sign of a good summer, and I watch them fuss around last year's nests making refurbishments and perhaps improvements while listening to their incessant commentary. It always recalls to me the crows of my youth, crows being there as common as rooks are here. In the early morning, when the survivors of the night trumpet their triumph, the crows are always the first and the most loud. We used to hear them often in those far away woods and forests, when we made camp on that long journey to Koil.

1789 Lucknow October

'*I am given a jagir by my Lord Sindhia, the rents from which will form a large part of my income. It is at Koil, near Aligarh,*' my husband writes from his headquarters at Mattra. '*I confess I had rather be paid in harder currency but must be glad I have the means to pay my troops.*'

I understand his logic for I have heard him many times discuss the evils and inefficiencies of this Mughal custom of giving land rather than gold to their officials, land whose residents then find themselves at the mercy of a new master, who in turn may still not be free of demands for further tribute from his Nawab.

'It is not easy being a *jagirdar* unless one is of entirely unsympathetic disposition,' is Colonel Martin's opinion. 'Better for the governing Nawab to lease the land direct to the farmer, who would more gladly pay a fixed rent and better care for his land, knowing his profits now his own.'

'*I had rather make this our home at least until I can order its affairs,*' my husband continues. '*I shall join you when I can and meanwhile ask Joseph to go soon and make things ready for you. He has business in that part of the country for Colonel Martin. I know you will make a good and orderly establishment but suggest you bring a female companion. Do I recall some unattached cousin in your sister's household whom you might request to accompany you?*'

He speaks, of course, of Gulzar and I am unpersuaded, despite my fondness for her, her temperament being so dissimilar to my own, but my mother disagrees.

'She has lived in similar circumstances when in her late father's house,' she tells me. 'She will know how to speak with the peasants and I think be glad to be of assistance to you. I too shall be happy to think you have the added protection of her company. I would come with you myself if I were able.'

When I tell my mother that I am with child she doubles her delegation. 'You shall take Zainab,' she insists. 'I will speak with Faiz.'

Colonel Martin and Mr Queiros between them provision our train and lend vehicles and bearers until such time as I may acquire our own. Zainab, who has abandoned her usual plain white garb for one of brilliant blue which suits her well, insists on riding in an open *bahail* with Sadiq so that she may oversee the whole and ensure that we are not tricked or robbed by our companions. Several of these carry muskets, the others staves to ward off wild animals or bandits. Two men are mounted to scout the surrounds and way ahead. And so our party sets off with many tears but promises of a visit from Faiz and family around Holi time next year.

'I fancy we may also spend some time in Gwalior,' she sighs. 'I trust it is not entirely uncivilised.'

She does not envy me my rural exile, she can imagine no place preferable to Lucknow, but my spirits soar once we have left the city limits. I have not made such a journey since I was a child and visited my grandparents in Delhi. We travel along roads lined with poplar, eucalyptus and casuarina, through forests of pipal, banyan and tamarind. I see rich green groves of mango, islands of swaying date palms and clearings where patient buffalo pull ploughs to prepare the ground for sowing with wheat, millet and corn and all the vegetables that city dwellers expect to find in the bazaars at their convenience.

Gulzar peers as eagerly from the other side of the *rath,* her eyes bright, face constantly alight with smiles as she exclaims and draws my attention to something she has seen. I am glad to have been the cause of this adventure and know now I shall be grateful for her company and her care. Our journey will take many days and I have begun to feel that sickness which is the proof of my condition and, although she has never been blessed with child herself, Gulzar tends me with calm experience as I guess she did my sister before I joined the household.

We sleep on straw mattresses in a canvas tent with adjacent bathing room and insist Zainab share our comfort, but she is also our invaluable go-between with the other servants. I grow accustomed to the outdoor life and, as I sip my early morning tea, love to watch the world awake and smell the sweet cooking fires of sugar cane, when the heads of the long grass are still silver with dew.

One night our train encamps in the shelter of an ancient fortress, the top storey of which has long since fallen in, and the corner towers become vantage points only for pigeons and crows and homes for bats which, as dusk falls, stream from each in a dense and long procession. In the surrounding walls there are rough arched apertures where remaining fragments of detail hint at their former more intricate design. I imagine veiled women watching through fine carved grilles, waiting for their men to return from battle, and, when in vain, when they did not, or when only their bloodied bodies were carried in, see them proudly descending and ordering their own funeral pyres be lit. It is a Hindu custom and one which so appals the English that they try to prevent it. Not long ago, I reflect, I might have fancied myself capable of such sacrifice were my husband to perish, rather than return to a life without him. But, now I am carrying a child, I reckon I have reason enough, if not obligation, to survive.

23

1789 Koil November

Our house is situated on the outskirts of the town of Aligarh near a small walled village whose inhabitants cease their activities to watch our arrival. A few children run excitedly alongside, some dogs bark at the hooves of the horses but otherwise there is silence and a singular lack of expression on the faces of the people.

'They do not welcome us,' I observe. 'Do you think them hostile?'

'More likely afraid of our intent,' Gulzar replies. 'And resigned to discovering the nature of their new overlord.'

'I am sure they will find my husband a kinder master than they have known.'

The main building of our residence is fortified, having a high parapet round the roof with embrasures for guns. A flight of steps leads to the entrance and, to my great delight, Don Queiros emerges to greet us. I had not known he would await us and am very relieved to see a familiar and friendly face so far from home.

'It was a hunting lodge, a simple square stone construction of two stories, not intended for permanent residence,' he says as he conducts Gulzar and I through the length of the building. 'But as you see, it has been enlarged through these linking courtyards. There are stables and other outbuildings for the animals, a surrounding garden and a good supply of water from a deep step well, which has never been known to run dry. That you share with the villagers. The lands they farm are your domain as far as one may see in every direction. Come, you must be fatigued, I have ordered refreshment in your chambers.'

'You are very considerate, Don Queiros, it is more than I expect.'

'It is my duty,' he replies with a bow to us both. 'And my pleasure also.' He is a kind man.

We have been assigned a suite of rooms that enclose a small shady courtyard containing a secluded bathing tank and a few pots of somewhat dry pelargoniums. I water these immediately from the tank and am eager to instigate other improvements. Everywhere is recently swept and washed and the furnishings are clean if faded. It is no worse than my previous habitation when first we took occupation, only larger and giving greater scope.

'You should rest,' insists Gulzar after we have eaten. 'Zainab and I shall make a full survey.' She returns later. 'We shall make a fine home here for the General to return to,' she announces, standing hands on hips, as if ready to begin the renovations at this instant.

I laugh at her. 'How should I do without you?'

We rejoin Don Queiros for an evening meal, which is of good fresh ingredients but a little plain in taste.

'You will wish to send for additional condiments,' Don Queiros apologises. 'And I think will find what you require in Aligarh which is but a quarter hour's ride, though not a city worth visiting in its recently besieged state.'

'Recently?' I am a little alarmed, but Don Queiros is reassuring.

'Last year. By the Mahrattas, to divert the forces besieging Agra. Since only this past month Koil Fort is held by a Mahratta leader who has just agreed alliance with Sindhia.'

'Small wonder then if the people do not trust us.'

Gulzar shrugs. 'We must do what we can to improve our relations.'

'You are right.' I turn back to Don Queiros. 'You have arranged everything most conveniently. I thank you again. We expected to occupy our tents for some time yet. I hope we may continue to enjoy the pleasure of your company.'

He inclines his head in acknowledgement of the compliment. 'I am requested by the Colonel to ensure before I leave that you are established with an adequate complement of staff, and am much assisted in this matter by a cousin of the Qadir brothers who lives most conveniently close. I recommend that you make him your chief overseer. His name is Mahmud. I will introduce you tomorrow. And there is a Brahmin of some standing in the village, one Mohanlal

117

Das, who is skilled in accountancy and appears as honest as it is reasonable to expect. But it will be wise if you learn to exercise your own authority so far as you are able and, indeed, most rewarding, for the output of the land currently stands far below what it should be. Mahmud reckons it may be as little as one half so you will soon see the benefits of better management.'

I am gratified to discover such high expectations of me and wonder what conversations may have taken place between my husband, the Colonel and Don Queiros.

'I understand you have other business in this direction on the Colonel's account?'

'It is on your husband's and my own account also,' Don Queiros corrects me. 'Perhaps you know nothing of it, for I know that the Colonel has only recently been engaged in correspondence with your husband on the venture. We are together forming a Society to trade in piece goods and I am tasked to visit the *aurangs* which produce the cloth and contract with the weavers in return for some advance payment for their sustenance until delivery of the goods. The Colonel believes we may strike a good bargain since the capital of most of our European rivals is currently tied up in indigo production.' Don Queiros laughs. 'And I daresay he is right. He is surely the most successful entrepreneur of all his peers and never one to miss an opportunity.' He laughs again. 'And he pays most close attention to every detail even when he delegates a task to another. I have received two further letters giving me yet more instructions since I arrived here. I must not buy too early in case the price of cotton falls and I must keep close check on the quality produced or we shall not be able to sell at a price that will make the whole enterprise worthwhile. It seems another trader has failed to sell his cloth in England and might be forced to try his luck in Portugal. And then I must beware the *gomasta*, the middle man... but surely I tire you with such superfluous information.'

'And where are these *aurangs*?' Gulzar is listening also with avid interest.

'In the north of Avadh, near the foothills leading to Naini Tal. I must leave in a few days but I shall return this way. I am to escort the baggage train back to Lucknow, indeed I may employ its capacity in transporting my purchases if I have made any.'

My husband visits some days after Don Queiros' departure and is well pleased with the conditions in which he finds us living. He made love to me most urgently on his arrival and now reclines on my bed, newly bathed and clad in pyjamas, with his head in my lap and pipe in hand. He is amused when I recount Don Queiros' descriptions.

'Claude forgets that, before entering his employ, Joseph ran an auction house in Calcutta and besides has his own investment to protect. I too have received letters from Claude,' he says. 'Which, in the same breath as congratulating me on my new position, urged me to engage in this trading enterprise for which he has lent me half a *lakh* on the strength of my expected future wealth. So you must certainly turn a profit here at the very earliest opportunity or we shall have his agents at our heels.' Clearly he jests for he is most relaxed and at ease.

'What did he say to you of your new position?' I ask, knowing him likely to keep it private, tending always to modesty where his own accomplishments are concerned.

He reaches for his discarded jacket and hands it to me. 'You may read for yourself,' he says. 'The letters are in the inner pocket.'

I find and unfold a number of sheets closely written with a neat small script and read aloud. '*You cannot fail to be a great man in the history of India,*' writes the Colonel. '*The balance of power will be held by you.*' I look up, questioning what I guess may be a friend's hyperbole but see my husband nod.

'Sindhia is invited to govern as Shah Alam's regent, the Emperor being, as you know, old and now blind and his government weak.' He takes a pull of the pipe. 'And I am Sindhia's chief deputy.'

'You are yet more elevated than I had understood.' I lift and kiss his free hand and read on. '*What distinction to see the Mogul Emperors at your feet, princes and princesses seeking your friendship and God knows what more.*' I look up and shake my head. 'It is extraordinary and most wonderful.'

It is indeed hard to believe, not least because this powerful man lies here with me. And I am to have his child. I must tell him very soon.

My husband smiles. 'Yet it is in the very next sentence that he outlines his project and, though I know him well, this struck me as

119

most extraordinary! But I am grateful that he has shown me opportunity where I would not know to look. It is time I paid attention to material security, for who knows how long this preferment may continue.'

I believe he means that it is time now that he is become a husband and man of property and think how much more he will feel his responsibility when he knows he is also to be a father. I am on the point of telling him when he reaches up to caress my breasts through my gown. 'You have increased in size, do you not think? Perhaps I should take a closer look to make sure.'

He sits up and bestrides me, parts the front of my gown and lifts my breasts out of the opening where, pushed together and upwards, they certainly look very much fuller than they were. I take his hands and lay them on my belly.

'This too is larger, if yet too slight to notice.'

He moves off me in great haste, as if I am afire, and throws his arms wide with loud exclamation.

'At last! A son to take my name!'

Then he kisses my hand and, crouching low, lays his head on my belly as if to hear his child speak.

24

1853 Lower Beeding April

I awake with Silver's paws planted on my belly and his tongue licking my face. My outer garments are damp from the moss, which had seemed dry when I lay me down, and the tree trunk is hard against my spine. Silver's tail begins to wag as I sit up straight and push him off me.

'I am not yet dead, my faithful friend.' I stroke his head. 'The proof being that I am hungry.' With the necessary assistance of my stick I heave myself to my feet and brush down my dress. 'What say you we hasten home and see what Caroline might give us to break our fast? A little kidney perhaps?'

And yet I linger along the hedgerow to pick a nosegay of purple vetch and dog violets, yellow toadflax and celandines and wild pansies all gathered in a surround of feathery cow parsley. I know most of these will drop within hours but shall have them in my chamber a short while to remind me of this heaven-sent morning.

'If this fine weather persists,' I tell Silver, 'summer's flowers will this year bloom before those of spring are gone.'

Being assured of my welfare, however, he has again deserted me for the wilder delights of the wood, and reappears only as I walk back along the lane to my house. I hear voices from some distance, and a young girl's wailing, and I realise how late must be the hour from the shortness of the shadows of the trees on either side. It is, I guess, mid-morning, and I have been out much longer than I intended. Caroline's voice makes itself heard above the others.

'Start where last you set eyes on her,' she is counselling. 'I'm thinking she did not heed your warnings, which would be most like her. And stay together, mind.'

Evidently she speaks to James but now I hear another man's voice mumble, perhaps in some dissent, for Caroline's tone becomes yet more insistent.

'It's my opinion, Albert, you never knows what those furriners would be doing if they found yous on your own. Oh stop thy wailing, Mary, and be of use. Run up and see if the missus' rings are lying on her dresser. I'm a wondering if she wuz wearing them, which would be an attraction to anyone of ill intention. Never mind the bells on her toes.' She laughs most unkindly and her voice now takes dramatic emphasis. 'I jest about the bells, but I reckon them rings might well be worth the trouble of slitting her throat.'

At this I hear a gasp from Mary followed by a muffled whimpering. I am not wearing my rings apart from the one around my neck, though I often do and it is true they are of some value. I fear it is time to make my entry for I have reached my garden gate. I walk up the path alone to meet the storm, while Silver sneaks under the hedge and disappears round the back of the house.

I am a little saddened, if not surprised, to note that Caroline's face betrays more guilt as she wonders how much I have overheard, than relief at my appearance. Moreover, her expression quickly turns to anger.

'Where in heaven wuz you, marm? Worrying us all sick without ever a word of your intentions.'

'Am I to leave written word of my whereabouts?' I enquire. 'I was up too early to inform you in person.' My tone has been mild but becomes more pointed. 'I wished to take advantage of this beautiful morning. Instead of lying in my bed.' But then I relent, for I would not after all expect her to long ignore my absence. 'Look,' I give her my bouquet. 'I have picked these flowers to bring spring into the house.' Please fetch my purse,' I add more softly and turn to the others. 'I am sorry that I caused this upset to you all,' I tell them and when Caroline returns, give James and Albert each a silver coin and three pennies to Mary. To Caroline I shall make recompense later; in fact I have already thought that I shall make her a generous gift to assist in her wedding preparations.

'I should like to take some breakfast in the orchard,' I tell her now and make my way to my favoured sitting place.

There is a bench in a sheltered corner against the old flint wall, which faces southwards and is therefore often warm. It has a table positioned near where I sometimes take my meals, but it is the first time this year I have come here and the wood is still a little damp and the seat covered with last year's fallen leaves. Before me, on a slight downward slope, are the fruit trees, planted when first I came here and to my design. They produce apples for eating and cooking, pears, plums and damsons, which serve to make pickles and preserves to feed us through all the seasons.

But it is watching them flower and fruit that has been my chief delight. As I expected, the buds on the pear tree are fast unfurling; by the end of the day there will be clusters of full flowers opened on the tree tops. Soon they will form so dense a blanket of white blossom that, from this vantage, the grass beneath will be hidden from view and I shall fancy I am above the clouds and quite out of sight of the house. Now, I can see Caroline approaching with a tray that she sets in front of me.

'There's but new baked bread, a morsel of cheese and damson preserve,' she says. 'For soon enough it will be time to dine. And the milk is watered, for Mary is only just gone to fetch us fresh.'

She jerks her head in the direction of the farm along the lane where Mary can be seen crossing the field on the far side of the orchard, a pretty sight in her bonnet and light gown, a pail dangling carelessly from one hand. She is skipping, no doubt delighted to be away from her chores, a slight figure that I fear will thicken all too soon under the weight of increasing work. It reminds me suddenly of another young girl, who worked for me once, long ago in my other life. I had quite forgotten her and wonder if I can recall her name.

1789 Koil November

'Preethi is going to the well,' observes Gulzar, pointing from my chamber window to the retreating figure of one of the girls who assists in the house.

She is very young and small, yet is balancing a brass *kumbh* on her head. When she is older she will carry two or even three such pots and they will be larger. She stops to caress a calf whose mother is grazing beside the path and continues on her way with a small skip that betrays her still childish nature.

'Let us go too.' I have been wanting to visit the well for we had none such in Lucknow, the Gomti serving all our needs.

'Now?' Gulzar is embroidering a border on a fine woollen shawl. I could never find the patience for such work but, in all her leisure time, she has developed a skill which, to my eye, is as good as that of any who make their living by such work. I have been composing a *ghazal,* but idly.

'It is too fine a day to rest indoors.' I put down my *sarangi.*

Gulzar laughs and folds the shawl away into a basket. 'Come then.'

I go to invite Zainab and find her in the courtyard outside the kitchen helping Sadiq roll *mathiya.* There are rows of them laid out to dry in the sun. She is laughing loudly at something he has just said and makes some rejoinder which amuses him. She is wearing a red patterned pyjama suit today, her head is uncovered and I see for the first time that she has coloured her once grey hair a glossy black. It makes her look years younger. She and Sadiq fall silent and look up as I draw near and I do believe she has drawn a faint line of *kohl* round her eyes.

'Gulzar and I are going to the well. Won't you accompany us?' For the first time I wonder at her lack of a husband, and, seeing her glance sideways at Sadiq, as if to gather his opinion, think that she may have found one. They make a handsome couple. She does not want to leave her work.

Outside our compound I take a deep breath and look up into the high blue sky, which betokens the approaching cold season. The air however is warm with the slightest breeze that caresses my face and raises my veil. I feel carefree as a child and, like Preethi, stop to stroke the buffalo calf.

We ask directions to the well, for it is not immediately apparent, being covered by a square pavilion-like structure having elegant arches and carvings around the entrance. It is very much larger than I had imagined, perhaps thirty yards along each side, and of inestimable depth, consisting of successively lower levels each reached by a further flight of steps that give access to ledges round the edges upon which it is wide enough to walk. There are also recesses in which one could safely sit and smaller ones where I imagine one might place lamps. The whole gives the impression more of an underground palace, not unlike the lower chambers of Colonel Martin's house, but so much larger and deeper and without separating floors, only the great open chasm into which rain falls and underground water wells up.

We descend one staircase and, sitting most carefully, peer further into the cavern, where it is just possible to discern the far off glint of water.

'I guess it is near its highest point at this season,' I observe. 'Though clearly there is room for more.'

'It is bigger than the one I knew,' says Gulzar. 'And since the level will often be much lower, even deeper than presently appears.'

'I should not like to have to collect water in the hot season. In fact I should be feared to descend so far. And it is no place for a child.'

Gulzar laughs. 'My sisters and I used to race up and down the steps of the one near our house,' she says. 'And think it great sport. Listen!'

She puts a finger to her lips and leans forward, a smile on her face. I lean also, though more cautiously, and hear laughter and girlish voices echo from far below. As we listen, it grows louder and two small figures begin to emerge from the gloom. It is Preethi, together with another girl, climbing the stairs, both carefully balancing full *kumbhs* on their heads. When the girls see us watching them they are struck dumb, the smiles gone from their faces, and, when they pass us, in response to our greeting, only nod and veil their faces with the free end of their saris. Which may signify modesty and respect, but perhaps also some resentment that we have intruded on their private enjoyment.

Mahmud, the overseer, is squatting on a low wall in the courtyard when we return, alternately smoothing his full moustache and cracking his knuckles. He jumps to his feet and salaams. He has an open honest face and it is easy to see that he is troubled.

'I cannot work with the Brahmin,' he says at once. 'He never has more than two thirds of the money due to the General and says it is all he has been able to collect. '

'You do not think he speaks the truth?'

125

Mahmud spreads his hands and raises his eyes to the sky. 'Who can say? I cannot oversee his every move and he does not go to every village but requires the headman to bring him the money. Who may himself take a proportion.'

I cannot oversee Mahmud's movements either, though I have trusted him from the beginning. 'I must await my husband's return,' I tell him. 'Perhaps he will form a solution.'

***

Benoit has again ridden from Mattra to pay a short visit and I am telling him of my relations with our servants and the village.

'It is hard having charge of another's destiny,' he says.

'And I feel my superior position is undeserved, yet confess I should not like to exchange it.'

'Indeed!' He laughs but instantly grows serious. 'Remember that and you will be a just master. And, if they are well treated, remember also that most people prefer to be in someone else's charge.'

He speaks from great experience and yet I doubt. 'I should prefer to maintain some freedom in my movements.'

'I too! And I did not say all people.' He kisses my fingertips. 'And even the lowliest servant should retain some time and place where he can be his own master.'

'Upon Mahmud's advice, I have encouraged the reintroduction of the growing of cash crops such as cotton and double cropping on land which has lately been left fallow between seasons,' I tell him. 'We have offered loans to purchase seed where necessary and Mahmud is overseeing sales in the *ganj* to ensure the farmers receive a fair price.'

Benoit nods. 'And that is the other requirement for the successful wielding of power,' 'Trusting one's subordinates and allowing them their sphere of influence. But I must speak to Mahmud some more about the collection of revenue, for good principles require method and system to be effective and efficient and this Brahmin will need to employ a small army of deputies to encompass the whole area.'

He calls Gulzar to join us on a walk around the village where he is much impressed by the well and says a French king of old would have been glad to discover such a way of accessing water to supply the wondrous fountains in his palace gardens which, sadly, were mostly dry. On the way back, we notice much coming and going between houses and that people are wearing what is surely their finest apparel, whether saris, *kurtas* or pyjamas. There is a general air of merriment.

'A wedding?' I wonder aloud. But then I see a group of women together preparing trays of *dias* and remember. 'Of course, it is Diwali. I should tell Sadiq to prepare and send some food. My mother always exchanged sweets with our neighbours even though it is a Hindu festival.'

'So did mine,' says Gulzar. 'In the Avadh countryside all are proud to light *dias* to celebrate Lord Rama's victory over evil, for it was his domain. And I think,' she adds, a little slyly, 'That Sadiq and Zainab have been busy on some such preparations for some time.'

'Go with them to distribute these gifts if you will,' my husband addresses her. 'It will look well without overwhelming their festivities by our presence.'

I wish we could join the celebrations but, as soon as we are alone, Benoit takes me by the hand and leads me to the window seat. I think he wants to make love, for he has not as yet, but he sits beside me and reaches a small box from his tunic.

'I did not give you one upon our marriage,' he says. 'Although it is our custom. But now you are to be the mother of my child, it is right that the world should know you as my wife.'

He opens the box and takes out a ring of gold, which is wide and heavy and bears an intricate raised pattern of leaves and flowers. When he slides it onto the third finger of my left hand I am overwhelmed with emotion and lean to kiss his lips. He puts one arm round my shoulders in an uncommonly companionable fashion while I hold my hand up the better to admire my wedding ring.

'I have written to my father informing him of my marriage and the expected birth,' he says. It is the first time he has spoken to me of his family.

'Will he be glad?' I am sure I am not the daughter-in-law he would have wished for.

'I wish my mother were still alive,' he sighs. 'She long since ceased expecting a grandchild of me. Or indeed anything of me, even to see me again. And I daresay my father is amazed that I am alive after so many years of absence and finds it hard to imagine what I have become.'

'You will surely wish to take our child to visit his grandfather and other family when he is a little grown,' I speak with more equanimity than I feel. 'And there is no necessity for me to accompany you.'

He frowns. 'Who knows when it will be advisable to return to Europe? And I do not imagine I shall be free to leave my position with Sindhia for quite some time.' What he says is no guide to his feelings on my proposal, but it affords me some relief nonetheless.

'What do you have to do for him? I should like to be able to imagine what you do when you are away from me.'

'I am entrusted to raise, equip and train ten battalions which together will form a brigade, what Sindhia calls a *campo*. I have two already and there is a Frenchman, Lestineau, who is bringing us one more.'

'So you must find still seven. Is it difficult?'

'To find the men in time of war, no. The expectation of regular pay and hope of plunder are attractive. Since I do not allow the latter, I must ensure the former, which is why the good management of this *jagir* is essential.' He taps my shoulder for emphasis.

'And these battalions will be clad in English uniform?'

'The majority,' he nods. 'Seven will be composed of Talingas wielding muskets and bayonets and wearing English cloth. But three, you will be interested to hear, will be Persian, being Pathans, armed with swords and shields. All, however, will be drilled according to the English system, which is very much more orderly than the native system and depends on obedience to central command. In fact,' he sighs. 'I have heard Sindhia's wild horsemen likened to a pack of wolves. They are certainly more interested in conquest than subsequent administration of lands so obtained. And this region has known so much pillage.'

'How many men make up a battalion?'

'Seven hundred and fifty.'

'But you cannot command so many! Seven, eight thousand?'

He laughs and draws me closer. 'No indeed, and I am most fortunate to have recruited European officers to do so, some of whom I know well.'

'And there is cavalry?'

'Certainly. We are raising five hundred. In fact, I have been in communication with your father to seek his assistance on that matter. In all, with sixty cannon and five hundred irregulars to look after the camp we shall have an army of almost ten thousand.'

I embrace him. 'Both my mother and my father will be most appreciative of this preferment. I had not expected it. Have you told your father of your recent elevation and increased responsibilities?'

He shakes his head. 'They know nothing of India. It would mean little. And he did not want me to be a soldier.'

'What then?'

He is silent awhile, but then sighs and continues. 'My father had me down for a lawyer. Which at seventeen was a dull prospect, or so I thought. For him it would have been advancement, having less education himself. He was a furrier, a successful merchant. Now I think I understand him and doubt if I should want my son to be a soldier either, but that is all I would become. I signed up first with an Irish brigade. And they called me Bennett for they could not say Benoit. But never did I dream when I enlisted that it could lead me here!'

This time he remains silent and I do not disturb him, for this is more than he has ever confided. Finally he rouses. 'The present is more precious than the past. And the future most pressing.'

'But while you are here you must rest.' I reach to stroke his brow and allow my hand to slide down his neck beneath his shirt. He stiffens and pulls slightly away.

'No, we must not.'

'I think it is safe.' I have asked Zainab for her opinion.

'You must not lose this child. Be so good as to call for a pipe.'

'Then let me sing for you. I have completed a new piece.'

I fetch my instrument and sit at a little distance on a mat facing him, while he quietly smokes.

'*My life runs to the world's demands; my love is greater than I knew.*

My love rules over the world's domains; my love is greater than I knew.

He arbitrates as nations war; my love is greater than I knew.

Let emperors beg his favour and princes bend their knee.

Let him prosper but keep him safe; let him return to me.

Let not my life be incomplete; my love is greater than I knew.'

It is the first time I have sung it all through and I repeat it several times making small changes, by which time I think he is asleep. Yet when I cease, he opens his eyes, puts down his pipe and raises his hands palms upwards.

'Wah wah.'

And then he calls me to him.

26

1853 Lower Beeding April

My ring is worn thin, the pattern flattened and barely visible. I wear it close to my heart on a ribbon round my neck for it does not fit my old crooked finger. I often fetch it out and hold it when I am alone as now, seen only by the eyes of God. I put it away as I notice Caroline struggling back up the slope and wonder why she comes, for it is too early for dinner. When she is nearer I see she carries a letter and my heart beats faster for I do not receive many. She arrives and holds it out.

It is from Charles. I see instantly from the handwriting. I crack the sealing wax and unfold the sheet. Caroline still stands beside me, very likely from curiosity; perhaps, I shall be charitable, in case I need to send an urgent reply or succour in the case of bad news. I read quickly.

'My son is coming at the end of next month and will stay for a week. Can we be ready for him?'

My question is rhetorical but Caroline has bitten her lip and is, most uncharacteristically, wondering how to express herself. Then I remember. This is precisely the time when she is to be married. I think quickly.

'Perhaps you could suggest someone to take your place for a week or two? Perhaps Mary could manage alone for a short time if you schooled her a little?'

'I will speak with her, Ma'am, that I will, thank you Ma'am.' Her relief is most apparent. 'Meanwhiles, we will surely make the house spick and span for the Count.'

'Splendid. I do wish him to see me at my most presentable for he will surely be again after me to move from this house.'

131

'I'll start on them curtains this very afternoon,' she promises and I reflect that, since she is surely to remain in the vicinity, she will now be as keen as I to prevent such a removal.

'And I will sort the books. Perhaps also this afternoon.'

Our pact agreed, she leaves me to my reflections, which she must imagine to be pleasantly anticipatory. How could a visit from one's son be other than a happy occasion? She has yet to learn how twisted the human heart can become through time and circumstance, how much old griefs can sour the sweetest present. Of a sudden I am shaken by a violent shiver. It is early in the year and a small cloud has crept up to obscure the still weak sun. There were just such mornings in Koil, if earlier in the year, when the rising sun still took several hours to cast any warmth.

1790 Koil February

'Faiz has written,' I tell Gulzar when she joins me in my chamber for breakfast one chill morning. 'From Gwalior.' I am wrapped in a shawl yet cannot subdue a shiver as I speak. 'Let us both eat in my bed where we may keep each other warm.'

Gulzar slips in beside me. 'There are insufficient carpets on the walls and floors in this place. For next winter we shall be better prepared.' She huddles closer. 'What does she say?'

I scan the letter quickly. 'They are coming to visit next month...she longs to see us again...she cannot believe it is nearly a year since my marriage, *"and yet it seems an age. I do not pretend to comprehend the correspondence of our perceptions with actuality."* But she can tell from how the children are grown. How I long to see them! Oh no! She was interrupted and now she says the visit must be postponed.'

''For what reason?'

I read on quickly then look up and smile at Gulzar with relief, 'It is only for a few days. They should be here by the sixteenth.' I read on. 'There is likely to be war she says, but not in Avadh. In Mysore. Tipu Sultan prepares to invade his neighbours, and the Company fears his French connections.'

132

'But why does that delay their travel?' Gulzar frowns.

'I don't – oh, I see. There is urgent need of funding, all the Residences must contribute and my brother-in-law must importune them. Including, she says, *'our dear Nawab. One wonders sometimes why the English remain if they find it so hard to turn a profit. But I am of course most glad that they do or how should we survive?'* I pass the letter to Gulzar to read for herself. 'And she sends you her loving greetings. And tells me to keep all cows and other animals from her chamber!'

Gulzar laughs. 'She is not a country lover!'

'And she never travels light,' I add. 'I fear she will bring half her household! Do you think we have bedding and accommodation enough?'

***

One day shortly thereafter, Gulzar and I are sorting out mattresses and bedcovers when we hear horses approaching at a gallop and come to a halt in the outer courtyard. A few minutes later in strides Benoit, still removing his helmet. He stops at a distance, erect and unsmiling, more an emissary on official business than a husband returning home. He notes the disarray with a tilt of his head and a rise of an eyebrow.

'We are preparing for my sister's visit,' I explain. 'Which we now expect on the sixteenth.'

He continues to look grave and indicates that he wishes me to withdraw with him to our quarters.

'I shall not be here,' he says as soon as we are alone. 'I shortly begin to move my troops, though they are but recently mustered and provisioned. This is extremely private information you understand? Do not divulge it to anyone, even your cousin.'

My eyes do not leave his face, which is tense and lined with grime from the journey. I long to make him undress and help him to a bath, but he holds himself rigid and apart as if already preparing to take his leave.

'So there will be war here as also in Mysore. This I heard from Faiz,' I explain.

It seems I have contrived somehow to make no connection in my mind between his distant preparation of an army and their engagement in battle. Now I see all too clearly the prospect of his injury or worse.

'But you are well prepared?'

He shrugs. 'Much also depends on the enemy and their shifting alliances, which we endeavour to influence through threats and promises as we may.' He pauses. 'After your sister's visit you must leave here immediately for it will not be safe. Who knows what roaming bands there may be, whether following victory or defeat and my estate may prove a target.'

I nod, my eyes fixed on his face.

'Since this is sooner than we discussed you must say it is on account of the baby, which indeed is reason enough. I have arranged for adequate accommodation in Agra fort. Of course,' he looks at me closely. 'You could return to Lucknow or go with your sister to Gwalior where I hear she may stay for some time.'

'I wish to remain as close to you as possible. I shall go to Agra fort as you have suggested.' I take his hand. 'Do you stay overnight? Then let me prepare a bath.'

He kisses my hand and, for the first time, smiles. 'I am dusty indeed for a lady's chambers.'

***

'Colonel Martin has sent you a gift.' My brother-in-law hands me a package soon after their arrival. 'I understand it can be hand-held and will need no special mounting.'

Mary helps me unwrap what we discover to be a small telescope.

'How very kind! I shall write to him,' I declare. 'And tell him how I enjoy spying on my neighbours!'

Mary requires Gulzar to give her lessons in needlework for, she says, this is a necessary part of an English lady's accomplishments.

'And I certainly cannot look to Mama for instruction,' she says with newly adult archness.

'There will be time enough for you to become a lady when you go to school in England.' Faiz sighs deeply. 'Which will be only too soon.'

But, in the event, Mary is scarcely in the house, being so taken with all the animals, in particular two new bullock calves whom she watches suckle from their mothers with close attention and delight. She makes firm friends with Preethi and I also engage Preethi's friend Sita to help care for little Charles and Sarah. Hastings spends much of his day pursuing imaginary enemies with makeshift swords and lances and says he is a General with ten thousand troops at his command. We all have many happy days together, despite our regret at my husband's absence, and my sister even compares our rustic simplicity favourably with her own domestic situation.

'If there are amusements in Gwalior city I do not see them, for we live entirely on a high precipice, a very long and very steep drive from the town.'

'For which reason it is very safe.' My brother-in-law smiles. 'It is in fact the second largest fort in all of India and Sindhia is glad to have secured it. But it houses also palaces that were once of great beauty, Hindu palaces, where music and dancing flourished and there is-'

'Unfortunately your brother-in-law speaks of a time three hundred years past,' my sister interrupts. 'Since when the lovely palaces have been prisons and places of execution for unwanted relations of the Mughul Royal family. Where once hung swings for the relaxation of the Queens then swung the corpse of Aurangzeb's brother.' She breaks off her complaint to join in our laughter.

She does however allow its superiority to Koil Fort, to view which Faiz, Hastings and I accompany my brother-in-law one day. It is a short and easy drive and the fort itself is raised only a little above the surrounding plain. Hastings is very excited to be taken by his father to greet the Commander, while my sister and I remain outside and regard the fortress across its wide moat, whence the damage wrought by recent cannon and fire is clearly visible.

'My husband says that it has long been regarded as an enviable stronghold,' she says. 'And the Emperors Akbar and Jehangir both visited for hunting. Imagine such illustrious visitors to such a backward place.' She raises her eyebrows.

'I like it here,' I defend my new home.

My sister laughs and hugs me briefly. 'You would like anywhere in the world if it were by the side of your new husband,' she says. 'Let us hope that he and Sindhia will soon restore order and that you may return here. And that my husband will soon receive a permanent posting for I am already tired of our travels.'

One day my brother-in-law receives more news.

'Company troops are preparing to march out from Madras to engage with Tipu's army,' he tells us. 'And Sindhia has offered to help the English. Fortunately, I do not think the offer will be accepted, but I have alerted Benoit for it would mean Sindhia's forces fighting on a second front.'

'Which would put my husband in greater danger?'

My brother-in-law purses his lips in part agreement. 'It might certainly make the enemy more confident. But do not be too afraid,' he hastens to assure me. 'For your husband's army is far superior in numbers and in prowess. All will be well, God willing.'

27

1853 Lower Beeding April

'All will be well, God willing.' Evidently I have spoken the words aloud for I hear Caroline agreeing with me even as I open my eyes.

'Indeed, Ma'am. Trust in the Lord, His will be done.'

She has brought me luncheon upon a tray and is perspiring from the effort in the noonday sun but seems to bear no grudge.

'Caroline,' my mind is now relocated in the present. 'Do you recall seeing a telescope when cleaning in the house?' She does not comprehend. 'A spyglass? I once had one in my possession. It crossed my thoughts just now and would give me pleasure if I had it to hand.'

'There's a fine view across the meadow, right enough, though whether t'would benefit from great enlargement I would not know. Perhaps in the attic, marm, there's trunks there in which I could explore.'

'It is no task for so fine a day.' I know well what is in one of them and it is not for others' eyes. 'Perhaps you might ask James to fetch them down some time for me to sort. They have lain there unexamined these many years. I wonder in what state we may find their contents. My spyglass may be broken. It has certainly travelled far and been packed and unpacked many times.'

1790 Agra April

'Did you yet find my telescope? I pray it is not broken.' We are unpacking our trunks and laying out our possessions.

'I wrapped it in a shawl,' says Gulzar, running her hands through the clothes in one trunk and locating it. 'Here,' she hands it to me. 'I wonder how long before we may repack?' Her tone is wistful. She did not wish to leave Koil.

'There is more space here than I expected. And it is but three days travel, perhaps two when I am less encumbered.'

We have been allotted an apartment overlooking a large courtyard where there is a very big and deep tank in which Shah Jehan used to fish with his favourite wife, Mumtaz, each standing at opposite ends on a balcony. These buildings once housed the Emperor's *zenana* and, though now mostly empty, there are other families living here, perhaps those of other military men, for a large part of the fort is inaccessible to us, being used entirely for military purposes

We soon discover that, without leaving our building, we can walk along a long white marble terrace that looks onto the Jumuna River and sit in the shade of the Emperor's pavilion

'We shall spend all the hottest hours here,' I determine. 'Where the grilles filter the light and air. You can sew and I shall play. I am going to compose some music to accompany some of the poems in that book of new Urdu poetry by Lucknavi poets that Faiz brought me. And when I tire of this, or you of listening, I shall take my telescope from one vantage point to another and examine the view. Oh look!'

It is only at this point that I see why this was also Shah Jehan's chosen vantage point for, slightly to the right and on the opposite side of the river, rises Mumtaz' mausoleum, the exquisite Taj Mahal.

'Was there ever a construction of such sublime shape and proportions? And it is already over one hundred years old. How I should like to visit it.'

Gulzar comes to stand beside me. 'Shah Jehan himself never visited it in its completion, only viewing it from afar.'

'From this very place. In which case I suppose it easy to imagine worse prisons.'

'But perhaps not a worse state of mind, knowing it was his own son who imprisoned him.'

'No indeed. That is hard to imagine.' Without conscious intention I clasp my hand to my belly and Gulzar misconstrues.

'Come,' she is brisk. 'Let us go down and see if Sadiq and Zainab have prepared a meal. And then while you rest, I shall make enquiries amongst our neighbours for suitable cleaners and laundry persons.'

It is a strange existence, living next to what must once have been the most luxurious royal apartments, the walls now stripped of their gold and silver, the silken curtains ripped from their hooks, the coloured glass in the *jalis* broken or entirely missing. And though we see very few people, yet we hear constantly the distant noises of the military quarter; of soldiers drilling, cartwheels rumbling, the stamping of horses' hooves and hammering in the foundries, all in a frenzy of preparation for whatever wars lie ahead.

***

One morning Zainab comes to help me dress. 'I must find other help before the baby comes,' she says and then flushes most extraordinarily, sits down suddenly on a corner of the bed where I am resting and draws her veil low over her face. Gulzar is in the room adjacent.

'Zainab, you are ill?' I touch her shoulder.'What ails you?'

'Oh Nur Begum, what will become of me?' She commences to rock herself and beat her head against her palms in most uncharacteristic distress. 'Of us?'

I begin to understand. 'Tell me? Perhaps there is some remedy, some assistance I can give?'

'Ah! Ah!' Zainab cries again and Gulzar comes running in. She is more direct. 'Cease disturbing your mistress,' her tone is sharp. 'What is the matter? Quiet now or you must take your leave.'

Zainab, who was indeed about to recommence her wailing, unveils her face, looks at me only and makes confession. She is to have a baby, some three months after mine. Sadiq is happy at the news but has neither funds for marriage nor alternative accommodation.

We enquire as to whether we may extend our apartment into neighbouring rooms and, though I write to my husband to request his authority, do not await his reply. Gulzar found Zainab's approach too brazen, but we do not wish to lose either her or Sadiq from our household and I am happy for them both.

'We are much indebted to you, Nur Begum,' Zainab says when I tell her of the plans. 'I never expected to be blessed with my own child.'

We have a small celebratory meal on the terrace once all is arranged.

***

Benoit replies in the first week of May. '*You must make what arrangements for your comfort you think best,*' he writes. '*For who knows how much time may pass before I can attend to such matters myself. I have been working from dawn til midnight these many weeks. We set out two days hence.*' He tells me of the grand parade he held of his assembled troops, designed to instil pride and sense of comradeship in their combined strength. '*I had them march before the white cross of Savoy and have written to my father to tell him so.*'

I am concerned for my husband's health under such burdens, besides his safety in any battles, and feel the more so, as my own condition advances and the heat intensifies. We receive news weekly and, in June, Ismail Beg is again the traitor and has induced the Rajput rulers of Jaipur and Jodhpur to assist in attacking the Emperor's supporters. Benoit is gone to crush them, together with one of Sindhia's best generals, '*a Brahmin whom I respect and trust though must take care not to make jealous by signs of Sindhia's preferment*'. They are encamped near Patan, a fortified town which, he says, has never yet been taken and, though he does not say so clearly, appear outnumbered and outgunned, despite Jaipur having later thought it prudent to withdraw in order that his lands be not devastated.

I take my binoculars to my customary perch in the pavilion and gaze at the Taj Mahal. Shah Jehan built it after Mumtaz had died giving birth to their fourteenth child and he still loved her so much after so many years. Which fact is more remarkable I cannot decide.

Suddenly I feel a strong spasm of pain, far more than the frequent minor pains to which, of late, I have become accustomed, and hasten back to my chamber.

'We have just received another message,' Gulzar greets me.

I lie on my bed and open the note with trembling hands. 'He is victorious! These four days since. The Almighty be praised.'

My labour lasts a long night until, as the first light disturbs the birds at the dawning of the twenty-fifth day of the month of June in the year 1790 she is born, long and pale, with a headful of black hair and the darkest of dark eyes.

'She is beautiful,' says Gulzar.

Zainab wraps her, gives her to me and continues to attend to me. Gulzar sits on the bed beside me and shows me how to touch my daughter's cheek with my breast so that she turns her head, finds it with her mouth and begins to suck successfully at once which seems to me a miracle.

'What shall we call her? Until the General is here to decide.'

Gulzar reaches to touch one tiny hand that curls instantly around her finger. She regards intently the small and still somewhat squashed red face. 'Banu,' she says at last. 'Princess. Little lady.'

'Banu,' I echo. 'Baby Banu. Beautiful Banu. My beautiful baby Banu.'

1853 Lower Beeding April

Tears choke my throat and I stand too swiftly, knocking the tray and its contents to the ground. Stumbling to the house, I fall into a chair in the nearest room, which is the library. Caroline has heard me and comes running.

'Quickly, I need my pipe.'

'Mercy me, and you wuz so well. Tis not wise, not - ' She breaks off, silenced by my glare. She had been emboldened, I guess, by my late good humour but sees she is defeated, sighs and retreats to do as she is bid.

While I wait, my eyes fall on the piles of books that, it seems an age since, she took from their shelves, the better to dust and clean.

The 'furrin' ones are nearest and on top of one pile I spy the volume Faiz gave me and take it up, thinking its poetry may calm my troubled soul. But, as I open it, a sheaf of cuttings fall into my lap. The first is dated 24th June 1790 from the *Calcutta Gazette*. I remember Gulzar reading it to me as I nursed my week old daughter and read it now for the first time in many many years.

'THE BATTLE OF PATAN

The troops of Ismail Beg and his Rajput associates were drawn up outside their stronghold of Patan opposing the forces of General de Boigne and the Maratha Confederacy. For three weeks nothing had changed. Let the General himself tell the story...'

Which is of an extraordinary victory over a far more numerous and well-armed enemy which resulted in his taking twelve thousand prisoners of war, to whom he gave a safeguard to conduct them to the other side of the Jumna, and possession of the town of Patan which, its fortifications being very strong, was never taken before. *'Our victory is astonishing,'* Benoit wrote. *'Gained by a handful of men over such a number. They had two guns to our one. My officers have behaved well; to them I am a great deal indebted for the fortunes of the day.'* The cuttings fall to my lap. How strange and far away these events, how long ago. Can there be any still alive who recall them?

Caroline has meanwhile brought my pipe and as I draw its smoke into my lungs I hear long dead Gulzar's voice speak to me across the years.

28

1790 Agra July

'There is another account in the same paper.' Gulzar has turned to an inside page. 'Which praises his *'conspicuous courage and judgment. He spent the whole battle on horseback directing the troops.''*

'How conspicuous *he* must have been to the enemy,' I observe. 'Thank heavens for his merciful preservation and that it is over.'

Gulzar has become very quiet. She is still reading and a line of concern divides her brows.

'What? Tell me.'

She bites her lip. 'Sindhia has ordered him now to invade Jodhpur.'

***

By August Zainab and Gulzar have given up their attempt to make me employ a wet nurse. Why would I not wish to feed my baby myself? I have no other pastime and her presence is my sole joy. The more she fills my life, the less I can dwell on her father's circumstances, so different to our own. We receive regular reports as before, in the first of which he sends a brief sealed note for me with his blessings to his daughter and hopes that my health may soon be restored. He adds that he is heading for Ajmer, *'thinking it advisable first to take this massive fort lest our enemy regroup behind us.'*

'I am quite recovered,' I reply, *'Having mercifully been spared any of the complications which can arise. I spend much of the day on the terrace with our daughter enjoying what breezes there may be, (we have had little rain), and telling her of her father's great exploits. You would*

not credit how one so young can appear to attend one's every word and she has also begun to smile. We all pray for your success in this new campaign. May the Almighty keep you safe. Your loving wife, Nur.'

Two weeks later we hear that, finding Ajmer impregnable, his strategy is changed. *'A few large stones rolled down must carry everything before them,'* he writes. *'The noise they make in rolling I can compare to nothing but thunder. I have therefore left two thousand cavalry and infantry to turn the blockade into a siege. At this point, the Rajah of Jodhpur, offered Ajmer to me to a distance of fifty kos around but I have refused and continue towards Jodhpur as Sindhia has bid.'*

***

While we await further news, our household is preoccupied by the safe delivery of Zainab's baby, also a girl whom she names Razia, and it is only afterwards, when the fighting is over, that we read of my husband's next complete victory over the Rajputs at Merta, a walled city thirty miles east of Ajmer. Gulzar and I are lying on a couch, with Banu between us discovering her fingers and her toes, as I read aloud the dispatches.

'Greatly shamed by their defeat at Patan, the Rajputs issued a call to arms of all Rathors between fourteen and sixty years old that could hold a sword. Thirty thousand assembled at Merta....' I skim some paragraphs before continuing.

' "De Boigne knew that, at Patan, but for darkness he could have inflicted much more damage. So now he decided upon a surprise pre-dawn attack while the enemy still slept. Waking from an opium-assisted sleep on the 20th September, their chiefs, finding their camp in chaos, called four thousand followers, drank opium together and rode forth wrapped around with shawls of yellow silk, the sure token of victory or death. One of the French officers took it upon himself to engage and found his battalion encircled, but de Boigne swiftly reformed his troops into a hollow square and the Rathors met instead rows of bayonets and gaping guns, upon which they flung themselves again and again until only fifteen were left. "Remember Patan!" they cried and even they then found the death which they despised and sought.'

144

Gulzar looks at me in silence as we both imagine the bloody scenes. Just then Banu laughs, quite distinctly and for the first time. One foot in mouth she eyes us slyly, expecting our acclaim, which naturally she receives before I return to the news reports.

'Look, this is from another's pen. Let us see what further light it sheds on my gallant husband's deeds.'

Indeed, it gives him every credit for the victory, surely more than he would claim himself. He showed foresight and *'incomparable presence of mind'*. *'This great victory is solely to be attributed to the coolness and intrepidity of our general in making so complete a disposition of his forces in time to repel the rapid charge of the most courageous cavalry in the world.'*

'You must be very proud,' Gulzar says as I put all the reports aside.

I pick up a silver bell and dangle it just out of Banu's reach. 'In truth,' I reply, 'I find it too great an achievement to comprehend, knowing nothing of warfare and my days so very differently spent.'

Banu flails her arms and legs in some excitement and at length by chance makes contact and the bell ring. For a moment she stops her kicking, then resumes and again the bell is rung.

I laugh. 'Clever girl! How I wish your papa were here to see you now.' I lift her up to hold her close and whisper in her ear. 'But we must not wish him home again until his task is done.'

1853 Lower Beeding April

My arms are empty, clasping only my own bony frame and there are tears in my eyes, but my hysteria is passed. Caroline has brought my pipe and left it near, finding me dreaming without its aid. I pick up the cuttings that have slipped to the floor. Correspondents in the *Calcutta Chronicle* of 14th October 1790 were fulsome in their praise. After the Battle of Merta, Benoit's army was dubbed the *Chiria Fauj*. The flying army. For they had shown how much greater than hitherto believed possible was the power of the infantry, if properly deployed. *'De Boigne has shown such ability and courage that the corps seemed to act as if they thought themselves invulnerable,'* says one. And another: *'General de Boigne's history will immortalise his name, and add celebrity to the European character.'*

After all these years, once again I feel astonishment at these public proofs of my husband's stature and achievement, which surely I was then too young to comprehend. Perhaps I also felt a little pride, to be his wife, but mostly I think what I felt was relief that he might soon come home to me. It was in December that Jodhpur sued for peace and on the last day of the month I received a message to return to Koil. I reach for my pipe, light it and inhale deeply, wishing to be returned to those happy days.

1790 Agra December

'We are to return to Koil,' I am breathless from my haste to give Gulzar the news. 'My husband is to make it his headquarters.'

She is playing with Razia while Zainab sorts some linen. 'Praise be to Allah!' she exclaims and sets down her charge. 'I shall begin to pack this instant. Zainab, tell Sadiq he should begin to close the kitchen. Let us all make haste.'

But Zainab does not quickly acquiesce. She leaves us with a troubled expression and, returning shortly after with Sadiq, begs to remain in Agra, finding life here greatly superior to that in Koil. Perhaps they think of future opportunities also and though I shall regret their loss, I do not blame them for harbouring ambitions beyond my service. I also regret not having visited the Taj Mahal, having expected that my husband would one day come and we would go together.

***

So many of the villages through which we pass are in a sorry state. Always subject to raids from bandits, they have now endured a drought and many fields are bare. The country is not yet a desert, however, and trees still line the road to shade the buffalo and the twitching horses, whose curved Arab ears turn back and forth, whether the better to hear or to repel flies I have never been able to fathom. The roads are emptier than is usual. But we do pass the occasional cart of people and produce drawn by one or two bullocks, their horns decked as ever with marigolds and with tinsel around their ears, though their passengers appear in far from festive mood and regard us unsmiling or avoid our glance altogether.

The road into Aligarh is more potholed than I remember and many buildings are incomplete. It is hard to say if they are half demolished or still under construction, yet most are inhabited, their residents appearing oblivious to the inconveniences of their accommodation. I watch one strong young woman, her sari hitched high enough to reveal her muscular calves, washing down the courtyard of one such, a row of recently washed copper pots gleaming in the sun, and reflect how much easier would be her task if dust did not continually blow in through the holes in the walls.

As we enter our own domain the countryside becomes greener, and it seems our village has planted crops as every year, no doubt thanks to the well. Chickens scatter and dogs race out to meet us but the people are subdued, the women have covered their heads and all peer cautiously until, on seeing who approaches, they greet us warmly with great show of friendliness and cheer. On our arrival we hear that Aligarh town has again, and only a matter of weeks since, suffered attack.

'Since September the Fort had been entrusted to one of Lord Sindhia's relatives,' Mahmud tells us. 'There was word of raids by parties of Sikhs into another part of the region when suddenly they changed route and sacked our town. The people are much relieved to have the General and his army return, for it was he who, after much bloodshed on both sides, succeeded in repelling the assailants.'

I think it a little strange that Benoit has not informed us of this but know that he must have been confident of our safety. He is presently absent on some mission and we have a few days to settle ourselves before his return. Mahmud has engaged another chef and Preethi and Sita come calling and offer their services as nursemaids. Banu is strong now and almost sitting, so I can trust her sometimes to their care and, henceforth, she sees more of the village than I know and, being so fair, doubtless receives much attention as she progresses.

Benoit arrives in mid-January, accompanied most impressively by a bodyguard of Persian cavalry. Hearing horses, I run to greet him, leaving Banu inside with Gulzar. He swings from his horse, bows and kisses my hand. I am a little abashed to have such an audience, and the Captain of his escort is particularly bold and smiles at me directly. Then I see who it is.

'Father!' I run to him as he dismounts and strides towards me, arms outstretched. He is more grizzled, there is grey in his moustaches, but he looks fit for his fifty years and most clearly enjoying his new position. It is good to feel his arms about me.

'I had no idea of your appointment. My mother's letters are filled with domestic detail.'

'I doubt she observed it herself,' he laughs. 'She has been all the time at your sister's house while Major Palmer was in Europe. And I was happy to surprise you.'

Benoit has been watching with indulgence but now grows impatient. He summons Mahmud who is hovering in the background, waiting to oblige as he may.

'Pray conduct the Captain to his chamber and make all other necessary arrangements,' he says and bows to my father. 'We shall meet later.'

He takes my hand and strides into the house. 'You wish to meet your daughter?' I enquire as we reach our apartment.

'When I am bathed,' he says and roughly pulls me close. 'And when I have had you.'

***

We are reclining, Benoit somewhat awkwardly dandling a complaining Banu, when my father knocks and enters. His face lights up as he spies his latest grandchild and she bestows on him her widest smile as he takes her in his arms. When finally he sets her on a mat, she sits as straight and unaided as if she has been doing it for weeks, regarding us with such a look of triumph that Benoit laughs.

'I did not know a baby could be so wise,' he says. 'And pretty too.'

I look from my daughter to her father and back again and know it is a moment I never shall forget.

29

1853 Lower Beeding April

I can feel the weight of Banu in my arms when I picked her up and kissed her and almost smell her sweet baby smell. I can sense her father's presence watching us quite seriously and my father smiling broadly on one side. But the faces of my lost loved ones begin to fade the more closely I attempt to examine them. They have all left me. They are gone and I am alone, so alone. I clasp my hands to my breast, half in prayer, half to control my grief and not again alert attention. I close my eyes.

Almighty God, have pity on me. Holy Mary, Mother of Jesus, show me how I may bear my sorrow as you have done before. I interlace my fingers and press my palms tightly together. *Do not forsake me.* Loosening my grasp, I breathe in deeply and lower my hands to my lap. As I open my eyes I am dazzled by a shaft of light that emanates from the ring on the third finger of my right hand, from the very heart of the blood red garnet stone in its centre.

1791 Koil February

'See what I have found for you.'

Benoit pulls from his pocket a small box that is covered in red velvet. He has just now returned from yet another mission to find me in our apartments. Banu is asleep in her crib beside me.

It is a ring, a delicate gold ring that holds a flower constructed of finely cut garnets and pearls.

'As beautiful as Banu,' he says, and as I reach to kiss him, adds: 'And you.'

We make love in the greatest contentment and afterwards he sleeps peacefully in my arms until Banu begins to stir and he watches me feed her.

'I shall now be in Koil much of the time,' he tells me. 'I am to form another two brigades and discover this to be a good place whence I can exercise control. There is space for a cantonment between here and the Fort, which will also bring benefits of commerce and trade to our region.'

'And make it safe from invasion?'

He nods. 'Although it will be some time before our enemy has regained his strength, there are marauders in plenty. By the by, I have received news from Claude. He has left Lucknow for Calcutta whence he proceeds to Madras to join Governor Cornwallis as his aide.'

'I thought him long unfit for active service.'

Benoit shrugs. 'I do not know exactly what his duties may entail but still am much impressed, I do confess. Nor do I know if he volunteered or was invited. I do know he has been busy all year raising backing for the Company's campaign against Tipu and provided one hundred and six horses of which forty he paid for himself, others coming from the Nawab's stables.'

'Then he continues to prosper, the Colonel.'

My husband does not immediately agree. 'He surely still has many resources,' he says at last. 'But as to ready money for the purchase of the horses, he borrowed sixteen thousand Rupees from the Resident, the need for which surprises me.' He frowns and wondering, I guess, how well fare their joint enterprises.

'Perhaps it has to do with the rate of interest he must pay compared to that which he would forgo on other moneys,' I suggest, as much to cheer him as from conviction.

Benoit stares at me a moment then claps his hands once or twice in approval. 'That is a most likely explanation indeed, and perhaps one of the reasons Claude is as rich as he is.'

***

As Banu begins to crawl, I become certain that I am again expecting a child. My sickness persists longer than with Banu and I am glad of so many eager helping hands. She learns to walk before her first birthday, tottering between doting grandfather and aunt with the two girls often at hand to catch her when she falls. My father has time on his hands when not out travelling in the district with my husband, but Benoit is busy from morning til night assembling his second battalion and appointing some European commanders.

It is a great responsibility and, at the end of the day, sometimes it is only his pipe which can relax him. He has little time for me or his daughter, although he likes to watch me feed her and is regretful when I stop doing so on account of the expected child. He is quite sure this is a boy and Gulzar supports him with some story about the shape of my belly and the way I walk, which is of course nonsense as my father points out, while bouncing Banu on his knee.

'I have been most blessed with my two daughters,' he says, loud enough for my husband to hear.

But I do pray it will be a boy, for I know Benoit will otherwise be disappointed, and it is true that my experience of this baby is very different. If not nauseous I am overly fatigued, the more so as the hot weather continues and we still have little rain. Preethi tells me she has to go down two whole further levels of stairs and platforms to fetch water, which she has never had to do before.

Benoit is concerned for my health, even more perhaps for that of his expected son, and in May conspires with my mother to come and stay. She is glad to be reunited with her husband and daughter and to make the acquaintance of her granddaughter. She does not, however, like Koil, where it has indeed become less comfortable in its current dry and dusty condition. Before long, and expecting the arrival of the monsoon which will make travel difficult, she has arranged for me to go with her to Delhi to stay with my Uncle Ali and Aunt Zohra. It is against my wishes but I am out-manoeuvred by medical arguments.

'It is one point on which I must admit the superiority of Delhi over Lucknow,' says my mother. 'For not all the best physicians have left the city and the one who cared for our family, including myself when I gave birth to you girls, is the best in India. Which is to say the world. You would be crazy not to have his expertise at your disposal.' And she taps her head for emphasis.

'I shall come to you before the birth,' Benoit promises. 'Between Dasshera and Diwali when my work here will be well underway.'

1791 Delhi July

I have not seen Delhi with an adult's eye and might have found it less impressive than in my memory, but when we drive past the famed Red Fort I find it huge beyond imagining; it quite dwarfs the fort at Agra. Its great red outer walls loom immensely high, stretch a mile in every direction and are fortified with many bastions, while the entrance gates appear so thick that surely no elephant nor other battering ram could ever force them. Inside, I know, there must be palaces and pleasure domes, built as a fitting setting for the Emperors when at the zenith of their power. Now the fort houses old, blind Shah Alam and his family and he is only there because Mahadji Sindhia, a Hindu, wills it so.

In the next few months we visit other sights of Delhi's wondrous past.

'Long gone,' my aunt says sadly.

The Shalimar Gardens are a mile in circumference and cost Shah Jehan several lakh rupees over a period of nine years to construct, which one would not now credit. All the buildings are in ruins, the canals and fountains dry, but it is yet a pleasant expanse of walkways circling ponds and lakes that are shaded by tall neem and banyan, mango, sisam and jamun trees and massed shrubs, whence can be heard the chorus of a myriad unseen birds. Still my aunt sighs.

'When I was a girl I remember coming here to see the flowers,' she says. 'Bed after bed of geraniums, poinsettias, antirrhinums, dahlias, sweet peas and you could not believe how many varieties of rose there were. Now it is all neglected and run wild.' She points, disgusted, at some struggling marigolds in a flowerbed so overgrown its outline is scarcely visible.

My mother nods, she too remembers. 'Each year in spring there was a flower festival with every garden in the city vying to outdo the others and a parade of huge fans made all of flowers and, in the evening, songs and dances and entertainment of all kinds.'

'You think Lucknow a city of gardens, you should have seen this,' says my aunt. 'It was paradise.'

'*Paeri daeza,*' echoes my mother, strangely disinclined to argue with her sister-in-law.

However inferior the present state of the gardens may be to the past, Banu is entranced. She has never seen so large an open space where she is allowed her freedom. We sit upon the heat-scorched, uncut grass in the waving shade of a palm tree and watch her toddle from us as far as she dares, then turn to spy us secretly over one shoulder before venturing further.

***

Benoit comes, as he promised, at the end of October when I can walk only with great discomfort.

'I have hired a horse carriage,' he says on the first morning. 'It is not large but we can take Gulzar as well as Banu if you wish. I have a great fancy to see the Jantar Mantar of which I have read.'

But dear Gulzar says she is preoccupied, I see she is sewing a tiny garment, and I am happy to enjoy an outing with only my husband and child.

The Jantar Mantar is a garden of giant stone geometric shapes designed to read the heavens. Most can be scaled by long flights of steps, the better, I imagine, to chart the movements of the planets, but I am in no condition to explore and find instead a shady bench upon which to sit. Banu wants to climb all the stairs and I am much amused to watch the great commander of men follow his tiny daughter and do as he is bid. She has quickly learned to say 'Papa' as if the better to enslave him. The sweet sound of her childish voice echoes from wall to wall, now far, now close, and has almost lulled me to sleep when I hear it.

'Mama! '

Do I imagine it? For it is the first time she has said it. I hear it again.

'Mama, Mama!'

30

1853 Lower Beeding May

'Ma'am? Ma'am?'

It is not my daughter. It is Mary Piper, newly promoted and come to stay to learn my ways for when Caroline herself is absent, a girl so shy she swallows her words to make her presence less in evidence. She stands beside me, eyes cast down, hands twisting in her pinafore.

'Ms Gold'ne's'gone out for th'aft'noon, ma'am,' she says, bobbing a curtsey, which I like. 'She said t'see what needs tha has, t'make myself useful, and p'raps she'll stay away th'night an' I'm to call her if needs be.' For her it is a very long speech and she is quite out of breath.

I vow not to intimidate this meek creature. Hitherto I have had little to do with her, beyond passing pleasantries if she be cleaning near me.

'My needs are few enough and none as now,' I tell her. 'Though stay,' for she is almost gone a'bobbing off. 'Does the sun still shine? Is the day still fine?'

She eyes me quickly, frowns, then again looks down. I think she searches my questions for darker meanings, for she has doubtless heard that I am strange. 'I b'lieve it does, ma'am, it is.'

'Then I should be much obliged if you would assist me to a garden seat and bring me some refreshment. I would take some air again for who knows what tomorrow may bring.'

'Oh yes'm, f'sure'm.' She almost looks me in the eye in her relief at my request so easily met, and we proceed most companionably to a sheltered corner against the west wall of the house where I have watched the sunset more times than I can reckon. There is no breeze, but the sun is low and losing strength.

'And best bring a shawl or I may take another chill and cause Caroline more trouble.'

'*Ne'er cast a clout 'til may is out.*' Mary colours sharply and bobs a small curtsey, as if to beg excuse for her untoward outspokenness. 'M'Gran says.'

'Do you know, I believe she is right,' I say as if it is the first time I have heard this wisdom. 'Then what say you we take a turn and then return indoors and sit me in the window seat.'

Her arm is warm 'neath mine and I am curiously glad of her company and seek to prolong it when she is about to leave me in my seat.

'Where did you say Caroline has gone?'

Oh, how carefully she responds, for fear of saying wrong, for she has not said. She regards her feet. 'T'see'bout weddin' celebrations?'

'Of course, what else! Thank you, Mary. I shall call if there is anything else.'

Mary looks up with a thankful smile and off she skips, abruptly slowing her pace to a sedate walk as, I guess, she remembers her new responsibilities while Caroline is away organising her marriage. It is a long time since I lived in the midst of celebrations, I reflect; in fact since I had any event worth celebrating. I daresay the greatest such occasion followed the birth of my second child, a boy, which threw our household instantly into a state of high excitement.

'A son! A son!'

The words echoed from room to room and into the streets beyond. News spread so quickly there, we lived close to our neighbours, but I guess some messenger was sent to the Fort.

1791 Delhi November

Benoit comes from his lodging in the fort, takes his new born baby in his arms and inspects him closely as if afraid there be some error.

'Is he not very small?' he enquires.

Certainly, he looks small in the arms of his tall father, but it has been a long and rather difficult birth for which our son's largeness was principally responsible.

He hands him back and watches in continuing amazement as the tiny mouth latches hungrily to my breast. 'We must celebrate our good fortune,' he decides. 'I shall speak to your mother to arrange what ceremony she will.'

My uncle's house is old and in a congested part of Chandni Chowk but it is large, much larger than its neighbours. In truth it is too large for everyday use, especially in the cold of winter when it is difficult to heat the high-ceilinged spaces. But it is of elegant design and, when freshly swept with newly laundered white sheets on the floors, able to accommodate a hundred guests and more with ease.

By coincidence the *chhathi* day is also Diwali. We call our son Ali after his great uncle who, childless, is delighted and sacrifices two goats as is appropriate at the birth of a boy. My mother and Gulzar help me to bathe myself and Ali and we all dress in new clothes. My mother and aunt, custodians of the family's particular rituals, lead the proceedings. They wrap Ali in a green silk cloth, lie him on a cushion surrounded by a garland of marigolds, and bid Benoit and me to sit cross-legged in front of him. Banu sneaks onto my lap and together, the three of us light a large *dia* which stands behind a small pile of green moong beans. The other ladies join in prayers, which variously ask the blessings of the Almighty for the health and good fortune of this child and promise to bring him up in the love of God. Ali is unwrapped and the moong beans wrapped in the green cloth.

'One day you must scatter them in a river which will join the ocean and thus the whole world,' my aunt tells us with great solemnity.

She and my uncle have called in extra cooks and there are packets of sweetmeats for all their friends and neighbours. Benoit gives a purse of *annas* to distribute to the poor of the neighbourhood and has engaged a troop of *domnis* to sing and dance for the assembled party after they have feasted. This entertainment will continue all night for, as they present their gifts, many of the guests tell me that they will remain to keep vigil with the household and at dawn go to the mosque to make offerings and give thanks.

And then the ladies assemble and lead me, carrying Ali, outside into the courtyard to perform '*taare dikhana*'.

'Look at the stars,' I whisper in his ear, 'And know that your angel is watching over you,' and, I pray silently, has written a favourable fate for you. It is a fine clear night but as I lift Ali higher in front of me, bursts of brilliant coloured light fill the sky, which somewhat obscure the stars. My aunt says this is highly auspicious.

'You see, the whole of Delhi, indeed India, celebrates with you.'

***

Benoit stays a week more. One day he brings me a gift, my third ring, fashioned of precious opal and turquoise.

'I hope it pleases you.' He regards me with uncommon diffidence. 'It is Persian turquoise, which I thought appropriate.'

'It is beautiful.' I finger it gently, touched as much by his desire to please me as the gift itself.

The day before he is due to return to his duties at Koil, he receives a letter from Colonel Martin, who is still embroiled in the protracted war against Tipu Sultan in Mysore and for once, therefore, in more danger than my husband.

'Perhaps he is not involved in actual skirmishes,' my husband reflects. 'He says he has been engaged in some reconnoitring and provisioning.'

'At which I daresay he is most efficient,' I observe.

'And he has found time for the collection of botanical specimens,' my husband is still reading. 'He has found "*a sort of long grass which the cattle are voraciously fond of, which is of so strong an aromatic and pungent taste that the flesh of the animals, as also the milk and butter, have a very strong scent of it*". Well! I confess I have never stopped to take such note when on my campaigns!'

***

As the winter rains end and spring begins, pots of lilies and hollyhocks appear on every rooftop and, defying my aunt's disparagement, the public gardens revive somewhat, with their channels and basins full of water and the scent of frangipani filling the air. Benoit comes to take us back to Agra where he must stay awhile to supervise the armouring of his new battalions. My father chooses to return to Lucknow with my mother, thus leaving my aunt and uncle altogether bereft. Banu cries too when the time is come to wave farewell but, in the way of small children, is soon distracted by the new experiences of travel, the horses, bullock carts and novelty of sleeping several nights under canvas. My husband rides ahead, while Gulzar and I combine our efforts to keep both children content.

Along the way we receive news of the final victory over Tipu Sultan at Seringapatam on 6th February. Colonel Martin is at the peace talks in Governor Cornwallis' tented headquarters, which, he writes, *'appears more like the various departments of a great office of state,'* and still has time for his botanical collection. *'I have discovered another most useful plant which Tipu's father had planted around the fort and I have named "Mysore thorn". It makes an excellent fence, and I shall ensure that specimens are brought north with me on our return which I pray may be soon.'*

1792 Agra March

Gulzar and I are glad to regain our previous accommodation and to re-employ Zainab and Sadiq, whose daughter, Razia, now makes a fine playmate for Banu. They run around constantly and we must keep a careful eye that they go not near the big water tank. Benoit is rarely in the house in daylight hours and often travelling between here and the growing cantonment in Aligarh. We do not speak much of his activities, for he is tired at night and the children take my attention in the morning. Sometimes he sits with us while he reads his correspondence, which includes letters from my brother-in-law.

He is reading one, written on 6th February, as we take breakfast one morning. Banu is sitting in my lap and I am attempting to feed her a mixture of rice and milk for which she does not much care. My husband looks up.

'He says to "*give my love to the Begum and kiss the young Baron for me.*"' I laugh but then, as I take up another spoonful of rice, cannot repress a sigh. 'I hope we may see them again soon.'

'Would you like to return to Lucknow?' Benoit asks, so quickly that I spill the rice on Banu, which makes her squirm and protest. 'Since your sister is again living there?'

'My answer is the same as it has ever been,' I reply, perhaps a little shortly, as I wipe the mess from Banu's clothing. 'I wish to remain near you. It would be fine if somehow we could all meet. I do not say it is possible.'

I think my tone surprises him, as indeed it does me, but he does not comment, so I say nothing more.

***

We receive a second letter from my brother-in-law, written on the 29th February, which informs us that Governor Cornwallis '*has told me to accompany Sindhia to Pune, so that I look on myself as fairly off. I do not know when I may return.*' Benoit remains silent for some time and I break off feeding Ali and hold him over my shoulder.

'Is it not a sign of the Governor's trust?'

'Indeed,' he nods. 'And, perhaps, imminent promotion. When no doubt the increase in income will be most welcome since he will have two children to support in England, now that your niece is on her way there also.'

'Mary has left Lucknow? I did not know. I must write to my mother. She will be very distressed that Faiz and her family will again soon be far removed from her.'

***

I am again feeding Ali when another letter arrives from Colonel Martin. He had written it on 27th February, the day after peace talks with Tipu Sultan were completed according to which, as well as paying three crore and thirty lakhs of rupees in reparations, he is to cede half his kingdom to the British.

'Does it not seem excessive?'

Benoit only frowns and looks uneasy, and I am so much absorbed in domestic detail that I pay little heed, even when a third letter comes, this one from my brother-in-law. Banu and Razia are taking turns pushing each other around the room in a small handcart that Sadiq has fashioned while yet again I am feeding Ali. Benoit enters, holding the letter, and sits in an easy chair that we have acquired especially for him. He appears about to speak when Razia falls out of the cart and begins to wail, and he shouts for Zainab to take both girls away.

'Major Palmer says to make his affectionate salaams to his sister the Begum,' he says but then falls silent.

Ali has fallen asleep so I rock him a little and put him in his cot, go to my husband and stand behind his chair.

'You are anxious,' I say and start to massage his temples. I part expect him to take my hand and pull me to his lap as he has so often before, but he jerks his head away and my hands fall to my side. I retreat to the window seat where I hope that, the light being behind me, my expression will not be visible, while I can see his face more clearly. 'You have had bad news?'

He rouses, throws me a glance that seems apologetic, and hesitates before he speaks. 'He thinks Sindhia unwise to prepare for more war. Which is what I am in effect assisting him to do.'

I see his quandary and guess that his sympathies begin to be at odds with his loyalty. 'The British do not own India.'

'No indeed, and yet there is such flux that who knows where the balance may next tip.' He falls silent, brooding once again and then seems to come to a decision. 'I should prefer for you and the children to return to Lucknow shortly,' he says. 'Where you will certainly be safer, whatever Sindhia may do, and may pay some attention to my businesses, at least until the Colonel, the Lieutenant-Colonel I should say, may return.'

I had not expected this at all and turn to look out of the window so that he may not see how I am affected. I cannot argue with his reasoning, I shall again be near my mother, which will please her greatly, and I am glad he values my stewardship of his affairs. And yet ...

'I feel the need of air,' I say. 'I would go to the terrace for a while. You may call for Zainab's assistance if Ali wakes.'

In solitude, a state that is now so rare, I stare across the river to Mumtaz' mausoleum that still I have not seen close, nor now perhaps ever shall. The sun is setting and the white marble gleams gold then pink which fades to grey until the stars shine out and restore its white perfection.

31

1853 Lower Beeding May

'Ma'am?' Mary's soft voice rouses me to find that it has grown quite dark.

'Oh Mary, do light the lamps.' I try to sound cheerful. 'Sleep takes one often and unawares when one is old.'

She hastens to do as she is bid and I see that a fire is already well established. 'It made that much cracklin''n'spittin' I feared t'would wake you,' she says. 'Supper's ready, ma'am. Shall I fetch it?'

Mary's chicken broth is very good and very welcome. Taken with a little bread I think it quite sufficient for my ancient body's needs. I think I always could survive on very little, giving my mother occasional concern, most especially when I heard from Faiz on my return to Lucknow.

1792 Lucknow April

Faiz and family have already left for Pune but a letter from her awaits me at my mother's apartments. I settle Ali in a rocking crib on the verandah, where there is some breeze and Banu is playing with some pots purloined from the kitchen. Since my mother and Gulzar are watching over the children, I go to my old chamber and throw myself on my bed.

'*My dear sister,*' writes Faiz, '*I am desolate not to be there to welcome you and my dear niece and nephew. The tides of war and peace continue to determine our fortunes and I fear this time we may remain away from my beloved Lucknow for some time. It is too cruel that this is exactly when you return and there is especial reason why I would wish to be with you.*

Be brave, my dear, for I know you are more sentimental than I. My husband has heard that your husband has taken a mistress, or to speak more truly, has had a girl given to him in appreciation of his military services. Her name is Mihr-un-Nissa, that is all I know. Our thoughts are with you. Be patient, I am sure de Boigne loves you and you alone ...'

I cast down her letter, cover my face with a pillow and weep. I know I should not be surprised, for he is often away from me and, during so many years as a soldier, surely accustomed to finding women wherever he went. Perhaps I had thought our relations so close that he would have made confession to me, rather than allowing me to find out as I may. Certainly I feel betrayed, with the growing conviction that he sent me here in order to give free reign to his new love. And I cannot bear to imagine him with another, which thought redoubles my tears as I twist and turn and beat the pillows in anger and in anguish, falling at last into an exhausted sleep.

'Come, child, your son is hungry.' It is my mother bearing a furious, red-faced Ali and some refreshment for me. 'I have tried to pacify him this half hour past thinking you in need of rest,' she continues. 'Of course if you would only have a wet nurse...' she breaks off a plaint that commenced in Koil and continued in Delhi. 'Oh my dear, are you ill?'

I sit up to take Ali, push my dishevelled hair from my face and hand her Faiz's letter. My mother scans it, sighs and sits on the bed, reaches to adjust the pillows behind me and strokes my cheek.

'Your sister is right,' she says at last. 'Do not distress yourself.'

'That is easy to say, Mother.'

A glint appears in her eye which I know well and still fear. 'You think you are the first wife to be betrayed?'

'Of course not.' My reply is instant, unthinking, and then I see her face. 'Even you?'

'Of course.' Her voice is brisk. 'Your father is a soldier and has always been a handsome man. He still is.'

There is an emphasis on the last two words that can only mean one thing.

'And he still...' I cannot finish.

'How long was he at Koil before my arrival?' The question evidently holds its own answer, for she sits back satisfied that she has made her point and, I guess, will show me no more sympathy. But then she leans forward again.

'Do not let others see your distress,' she says. 'Eat, drink and keep yourself well. You have become too thin.' She strokes Ali's head. 'While Ali grows fat.' Her tone becomes more confidential, serious. 'And do not reproach the General when he returns. Be as sweet as ever you have been and he will remember why he chose you as his wife.' She stands, smoothes down her clothing and turns to go from the room. Yet she is not done, for at the doorway she turns. 'And do not always have Ali at your breast.'

'Oh little one.' Ali's eyes are open, though unfocussed, as he feeds and I look deep into them, trying to read his soul. 'Will you too break your wife's heart?' A tiny frown creases his forehead and I bend to kiss it away. 'Don't worry,' I whisper. 'I shall not stop feeding you, at least until your Papa returns and who knows when that may be.'

***

'Don Queiros. I am very happy to meet you again.'

We have met as appointed in a message received two days after my arrival. I am indeed glad to see his handsome, gentle face which quite resembles my brother-in-law's, I think, for Don Queiros is also dark-haired and clean-shaven and his expression is always calm and clear, the reflection of an honest and sincere disposition. His eyes are darker and his skin is, I notice now, of much the same hue as mine, or at least as my children's. I wonder briefly if Ali might look like him when he is grown. He has, as requested by my husband, found me a house, which is on the river bank and not far from my mother's house.

'You are very kind to find me so pleasant a residence,' I tell him. 'And I recognise your thoughtfulness in seeking one with an airy upper floor. Only,' I gesture at the tiny courtyard. 'I cannot keep our cattle and other animals here and would have my husband's property under my supervision, rather than leave them at Colonel Martin's house.' Thus far,

I believe I am following my husband's expressed wishes. 'There are twenty two bullocks so we have need of more space for them.'

'I see.' Don Queiros nods. 'So, I shall look for a property altogether larger. And I think it must be a little further from the city.'

'But do not trouble yourself on my personal account,' I insist. 'I do not wish any but the simplest accommodation for myself and my cousin and the children.' I do not want to take any more of Benoit's money than is necessary and wish I had my own fortune at my disposal.

Don Queiros hesitates before speaking. 'Your husband has expressed most explicitly his instruction that you be not too economical, having charge of his two dear children, who should not be exposed to the danger of too close lodging, and to avoid buildings covered with tiles which can be extremely hot, as you may know.'

'I am glad to hear it.' Indeed it does make me feel a little less desolate and abandoned. 'However, I am confident that you may find a place that will meet all these requirements, Don Queiros, whilst nevertheless not incurring very large expenses.'

He looks at me closely to see if I speak my clear intentions. 'Very well,' he agrees at last. 'And I shall be sure to inform your husband that it was your wish to be frugal and not squander his resources that has been my guide. And I may add that he is most fortunate to have such a wife, for very many, in my experience of such matters, are of the opposite tendency.'

'Oh dear,' I raise my hands to my head. 'Suddenly I feel quite faint.'

'You must sit.' He guides me to a nearby bench. 'Rest your head on your lap,' he says, sitting beside and continuing to support me. 'I will send for some refreshment.'

'Please stay. I feel a little better already, thank you.'

It is true. What I do not say is that this is in large measure due to his comforting concern and the regard for me which he has made so plain. It is always sweet to be admired, how much more so in my present state. I raise my head but am still a little giddy and lean closer to him so that I may rest it on his shoulder. He gently strokes my hair which makes me think how long it seems since I was the object of such tenderness. It is tempting to prolong the sensation, to confide my sadness and enjoy his sympathy. But I must not and he is married with a wife and eight children living near.

'Don Queiros,' I take his hand in mine and sit upright. 'You have always been so very kind to me, to us.'

He kisses my hand, releases it and stands, offering me his arm that I might do the same. 'I should also say,' he adds, 'That it would surely be the General's wish that you should also take good care of your health which does not appear at present to be of the best.'

***

When it is time to move our animals to my new accommodation I pay a visit to Boulone where I am much on my guard, being unsure as to what confidences my husband may have shared with Colonel Martin. She says how thin and pale I have become, but is too full of her own sadness at his long absence to enquire into my own. She does not support his determination to serve the Company at his age and with his fortune already well established.

'He wants to be made a General,' she says with some bitterness and a little derision. 'He has wanted it for a long time. And certainly not for the additional salary it might bring. Why does he care what the English think of him? If he must fight for someone, let it be an Indian prince like your husband.'

'It is not so simple,' I murmur, knowing she expresses more her own unhappiness than any particular conviction. As I go home I count myself lucky that I have an independent household and two beautiful children besides the help and company of a mother and loving cousin. At home, I write to my sister with a cheerful account of my new circumstances.

'The estate is just outside the city on the banks of the Gomti, having quite extensive grounds. The house itself is a little in need of repair and was never grand, but elegant in its proportions and surrounded by a raised terrace. It has two floors, with a parapet around the roof and a chattri where I shall like to sit sometimes and admire the view. So my dearest sister, I feel myself to be well settled and much too busy with the children to be lonely. Oh, and I almost forgot. All along the wall of the parapet there is a line of pineapple shapes fashioned of green glazed pottery, which may sound quixotic but are most charming to behold. I wish you could come and see for yourself.'

My letter is scarce sent when I receive disquieting news through Don Queiros. Benoit is now at Ulwar, some fifty cos from Delhi, having remained with the first brigade while the second proceeds to join Sindhia at Pune. He has been very ill with a dysentery which has killed some of his men. Why does he not call for me? Surely *she* will not be at his sickbed.

'You may go to him if he calls you,' says my mother. 'And leave the children with me, now that Ali is not dependent on your milk.'

'Oh I should not care to do so,' I say.

'But you would if that is what he asks,' she says, and this is true.

My sister, who is not yet arrived in Pune, does not seem to have heard of Benoit's illness and expects to meet up with him there. '*Let us hope that you also may be able to join him with the children and we shall once again be all together.*'

'Perhaps that was my husband's intent before he became too ill to travel.' I say to my mother after she has read my sister's letter. 'Faiz seems to have no fears for her safety or that of her children, despite Sindhia's warlike intentions.'

***

At the end of the monsoon Faiz writes from Pune with the highly confidential news that Sindhia is hoping to make alliance with the ruler there, the Peshwa, and be in a stronger position to demand of the Company a fixed share of the Mughul tribute. He even hopes to bring together the Sikhs, which might enable the restoration of the Imperial throne to one of the Hindu religion, '*himself, I daresay*'. However, there are divisions as ever in the alliance, one General Holkar in particular becoming jealous of Benoit's successes.

'What will be your husband's role in all this?' wonders Gulzar when I have finished reading.

I cannot imagine. Why does he not at least write to me?

'Perhaps you will be together again soon.' She reads my thoughts and a shiver runs up my spine which cannot be due to the temperature.

32

1853 Lower Beeding May

The fire has died away and the room become chill. I am shivering and would summon Mary but decide it is time for bed, stand with some difficulty and walk to the door. As I reach the hall, I hear soft snoring from the small room under the front eaves and resolve to ascend the stairs unaided. Mary is young and, mercifully, as yet unused to long hours of labour. I wonder if I shall sleep without my pipe, which I should have asked for, and think to read awhile instead. I return to the library and pick a volume of poetry which I know well though have not read these many years.

Installed in my bed, nightcap low over my face to keep at bay the vapours of the night, I search for an example of a *vasokht,* a form of Urdu poetry which had its origins in Lucknow and which has suddenly come to my mind. In such poems, in verses of six lines, a lover proclaims his love, describes her but then reveals that she is unfaithful. He is at first hurt and angry but then tells the beloved that he has become enamoured of another woman, whose imaginary beauty he praises at length to make his true love jealous and entice her to return to him, when there is a joyful reconciliation. I tried to write one myself during that first long year when my lover remained far from me, sometimes in the arms of another woman.

1792 Lucknow November

I have been trying all day to write a *vasokht,* thinking it might help purge my feelings of rejection and loss. Proclaiming my love is easy, but even to pretend I have found a new lover to make him jealous, I find impossible. Finally, I give up and realise that what is running through my head instead is some form of *ghazal*. Then it comes to me quickly.

My lover took my life, I shall take no other love.
My lover breaks my heart, I shall take no other love.
My lover takes another love, another tells me when.
My love is far away, I shall take no other love.

He sent me to another place so he could take his love.
Others smile and tell me to take another love.
But time goes by, my eyes are dry, and still my heart is full.
I love him yet and ever will, I'll take no other love.

My love writes he is ill, how could I take another love.
He calls me, not the other, knows I have no other love.
My heart while beating can yet mend, I need no other love.
I shall give my life again and take no other love.

I wish to set my new piece to music while it is yet fresh in my mind. The children are playing on the verandah with Gulzar but, as soon as she hears the first notes of my instrument, Banu comes a'running and sits in my lap.

'Banu play,' she says and plucks at a string with one tiny finger. 'Ow,' she says. 'String cut Banu's finger.'

'You are too young, my darling. How old are you?'

'Two. And alf.'

'That's right and you must be much older to play. Maybe five.' I know this will impress her as an impossibly distant age but, seeing her face fall in disappointment, hasten to make amends. 'Mama buy you *janjar*, so that you can dance and make music at the same time. Like you saw when you were with Grandmother that day and the ladies wore little silver bells round their ankles that jangled as they danced.'

'And people will say *wahwah*?'

I laugh and hug her. 'They will if you dance nicely.'

She scrambles to her feet and runs to the chest of toys on the verandah, whence she returns with Ali's silver baby rattle jingling in her hand. 'Mama play, Banu dance.'

Oh, how my children distract me from my sadness, the whole day long, and I have no time nor reason to complain.

169

'Ali's not a baby anymore,' says Banu later, or perhaps on another day.

He has just taken his first tottering steps from my arms to Gulzar's and is very pleased with himself and about to set off on the return

'He will be one year old next week,' I remind Gulzar.

'We should have some celebration.'

'It is usual,' I agree. 'You are right. We shall have a small party.'

'Banu dance for Ali party,' Banu announces and off she whirls, a tiny dervish shaking her bells, little pigtails flying out.... What moment could be more precious than this? How much my husband misses, without even knowing that he does. His loss is greater than mine.

'You must dance for Papa when he comes,' I call to her. 'He will think you very pretty and clever.'

1853 Lower Beeding May

I awake before five o'clock in the morning, for Mary has not thought to draw my curtains, no more did I. I should not mind to see the dawn except that I have slept badly, and my mind is still troubled without quite understanding why. I know I was dreaming of that long period of separation but cannot quite recall how it was ended and believe I may discover with the help of my old pipe. When Mary comes at last, fresh-faced from her good sleep, to see about my breakfast I tell her I wish to spend the morning in my bed. And it is time that she learn how to prepare my pipe for just such occasions.

'Yes ma'am, f'sure ma'am, I'll do my best ma'am.'

Free of Caroline's carping and disapproval about it being a waste of a fine spring morning, only the cats are offended and take off in high dudgeon when they see the pipe arrive. Silver is already off in his own world to explore as the fancy takes him, at no-one's beck nor call. I name the parts of the pipe, demonstrate how to crumble the tobacco and opium into the top piece, to fill the base with water, secure the pieces together and attach the long pipe to the side. Finally, I light the charcoal.

'You see it is easy,' I tell her. 'You can leave me now. When the charcoal is hot I will place it on top of the tobacco mix. Thank you, Mary.'

Alone, I begin to recall events that were unclear to me at the time, and most unwelcome, for spring does not always bring good news. It can be a fresh beginning of strife and warfare when kings bestride their horses, rally their armies and set out once more to kill. And keep their commanders even longer from their families, who wonder when they will ever see them again if they have not, as in Ali's case, forgotten them entirely.

1793 Lucknow March

Banu is being difficult. She will not dress as I have chosen nor eat what has been prepared. No game or toy distracts her and, when I track her to a favourite hiding place behind a curtain, she strikes me before bursting into tears. I hold her wrists for she would strike me again, but at last she weakens and lets me take her in my arms.

'Why does not Papa come to see us,' she sobs. 'You said he would come when the spring is here and the cold weather gone.'

I am quite sure I said only that he *might* come, though it is true that, wishing her to retain something of her father in her memory, I have surely repeated the assertion more than once besides speaking of him often. But, in any case, at the beginning it seemed so far in the future that I could not believe it would not have been proved correct.

'He is very busy,' I begin and, sounding unconvincing to my own ears, elaborate. 'He is trying to stop there being any more wars.' By forming a third brigade for Sindhia, I think and try a different argument. 'Sometimes people cannot do as they choose,' I say. 'And Papa is in the employ of a great king. That he does not come to see us does not mean he does not wish to come. So many other people need him, no one else can do what he is doing.' She does not ask what it is that he does that is so important that he has not seen his children for almost a year. 'He is very brave,' I assure her. 'And I know we will see him just as soon as he is able.'

I doubt that she understands 'alf' of what I have said but she is satisfied, gives me a hug and runs off to find Ali, almost bumping into Gulzar who is coming in. I explain the welcome change in her behaviour.

'You did well,' says Gulzar. 'If only someone could explain to me the ways of men who are never satisfied with what they have and always look to take what is another's.'

I think at first she makes a criticism of my husband, which, despite her great sympathy for me, is entirely unlikely. She sees my moment of uncertainty and softly adds: 'I speak of his master, Sindhia. Your husband does his duty.'

***

He writes at last as the hot season begins, making excuse for his long silence of his ill health and lack of reliable messengers and the fact that he has been constantly on the move between the cantonment at Koil and Delhi. He has appointed an Englishman to help form a third battalion, mentions as did Faiz the discord within the alliance, and the possibility that Holkar might even make traitorous accord with their old enemy Ismail Beg,

'In short, my dear, I know not what the coming months may bring. I beg you to remember me to our children and know that I do not entirely forget you. De Boigne'

I fold the page and am about to slip it into my bodice for, though his tone is impersonal, I know I shall derive some comfort from holding close to me something that he has touched. But then I notice an addition, written on the reverse and clearly in great haste.

'I have left it too long to tell you what I know you have already heard. The girl, Mihr-un-Nissa, was given to me by her mother, she said in gratitude for sparing their lives in battle. It was not the noble gesture she would have it appear for the girl is of most unagreeable disposition and the adopted rather than true daughter of this royal lady. I must acknowledge that neither was it noble of me to accept the girl, for I only intended her to live with me in an inferior situation. I would have you assured that never did I envisage the matter impinging greatly on our relations and, in the event, I soon ceased sharing her company. De B.'

33

1853 Lower Beeding May

Caroline is back. Her raised voice wakens me and her heavy tread upon the stairs warns me of her approach. She frowns when she espies the pipe and sniffs at what must be the close and unhealthy atmosphere of my chamber, but I am not ready to rise.

'Do please open a window. I should like to take luncheon in bed. Which Mary can bring me to save you the trouble.' Another placatory offensive, which, however, does not entirely please, so then I hasten to reassure her that she is not displaced. 'She has done very well, thanks to your instruction and good example.'

Still she appears unhappy and I see at last it may be on her own account.

'How was your visit? Do your preparations proceed?' I wait for her to order her story.

'They will go well enough, thank you, ma'am,' she says, smoothing her apron most forcefully over her stomach. 'But they did hit a hitch owing to my intended's parsimony.'

I did not expect to be made party to such confidence and, reflecting that perhaps I am the only one to whom she can express her frustration, encourage her to go further.

'How so?'

'Well, I told him I want new bed linen and tablecloths and all as wuz only natural, and what every bride would want and does have. And he says to me ...'

I grasp the whole situation sometime before she has finished describing it, not least because I am more party to the state of James' finances than she appears to be herself. If she did have such valuable information she might better appreciate his attempts to economise. I feel

173

a good deal of sympathy for her. *You are not the first woman to be misled by her man.* And then I wonder: *What would you say if I confided in you?*

'So I told him, I said, "I shall buy as I see fit and the bills shall be to your account. And when we are wed I shall keep the books myself or there will be no wedding."'

'And?' I might fear for her disappointed hopes did she not now look triumphant.

She looks at me a moment as if I am a puzzle she cannot make out then shrugs dismissively. 'Well, he agreed of course, didn't he.'

Well done, Caroline. I silently congratulate her and think it a good moment to make my intentions plain. 'Caroline,' I say. 'I wish to make you a wedding gift of ten pounds. Might that meet your linen bills?'

She is quite taken aback, her hands fly to her mouth, which had become an 'O' before they covered it. 'Oh ma'am, that is most generous, most generous indeed, I thank you. Thank you.' She clasps her hands and looks pensive for a moment almost as in prayer, but her more worldly thoughts soon become apparent. 'But ma'am, in that case, since James has already agreed to the linen purchases, then I'm thinking I might look again at equipment for the kitchen, for last time the tinker was around he had some fine implements and utensils that I craved.'

Her eyes feast awhile on this inner vision, her young face flushed and glowing with anticipation, before she recollects her present place. 'Oh ma'am, here's me quite forgetting. Luncheon'll be served in no time, no time at all.'

And it is not long either, before I am installed in the warm and sheltered nook where I had thought to sit the evening before and, as I had then desired, can allow the hazy sun to warm my body and, before I die, relive the joys that once were mine when I was young, so very long ago. Perhaps they will at last triumph over the sorrow that besets my soul.

1793 Lucknow

All summer we have depended upon the letters from my brother-in-law for news of Benoit's welfare and whereabouts. He has faced down the expected uprising from General Holkar together with Ismail Beg and prevailed upon Sindhia to show lenience upon the latter when captured. He then marched to engage with Holkar which, being in a narrow pass, became a hard and bloody battle but which turned into a complete victory. Sindhia is now master of Hindustan and my husband is '*surely at the zenith of greatness. Sindhia trusts him entirely, never has a European gained from a native prince such esteem. He told me that though he owed his being and his heritage to his father, yet it was de Boigne who taught him how to enjoy the one and make use of the other.*'

I do rejoice at knowing Benoit safe and at his great success and acclaim, but cannot help but wonder what Sindhia means when he accredits him with teaching him how to 'enjoy his being'. I shall not be truly happy until, and unless, he writes to me himself.

My long wait ends in November when I receive his summons to join him in Delhi. It is Ali's second birthday, and we light our own fireworks to mark our joy. Benoit sends a troop of cavalry to escort us, the countryside being in a most disorderly condition, where travellers are in constant danger of attack. My father chooses to accompany us, which greatly pleases the children, who by turn ride on horseback with him each day. The Nawab loans us several *raths,* his womenfolk have many such at their disposal, so that we may have space for the children to sleep and play on the journey and we pass through Lucknow in fine fashion, passers-by pausing to see who might be travelling in such style, and the sounds of the horses' hooves resounding from the buildings on either side.

It is a long journey of near two weeks but a fine time of year to travel, neither too hot nor yet too cold. Much of the countryside is green for at last we have had rains. There are wide fields of grain, interspersed with many large ponds where we see buffalo wallowing or grazing knee deep in the surrounding luxuriant grassland, pass whole trains of bullock carts and camels. At one point we are accompanied by a very large herd of buffalo one of which, that has clearly just enjoyed a mudbath, lurches against the side of our transport, causing the children squeal in delight.

My husband rides out to meet us at our last halt, a few cos from Delhi when some of our party has gone ahead as usual to make camp and prepare food. As it happens, I have been travelling alone for the past hour and, when my carriage stops, I part the curtains and see him, mounted on a fine black steed, surveying the cavalcade. He notices me, swings from his horse and hastens to greet me, hand outstretched to help me alight. His face appears stern or, perhaps, unsure of our relations after so long apart and I am sad to see how thin it is become, drawn from sickness and the hardships of the last months.

'My dear,' he begins and bows to me a little, then steps back hurriedly for I have bent to touch his feet. He raises me quickly with both hands and stands looking down at me, seeming very large and powerful.

'We hear how great you are become.' I feel as shy as when first we met. 'As mighty as a king, on whom the Emperor himself depends.'

He flushes a little, looks away and shrugs off the compliment. 'For a while,' he says. 'The game of power is never ending, and many a player has lost all by overplaying his hand. Look from your carriage tomorrow when we pass through the ruins of all those forgotten empires and kingdoms. Delhi is no place to encourage delusions of permanent glory.'

And then he shivers, and I see the sweat on his brow.

'I am cold,' I lie. 'Perhaps winter is come early. Think you our accommodation ready? I would order us a *samovar.*'

Do I imagine a softening in those dark and brooding eyes that have looked upon so much bloodshed and death? Is it perhaps evidence of a relief in one who has had to make so many difficult and instant decisions on which many lives depended, that someone else is taking charge of him? Is he glad I have come? I like to think so and it gives me encouragement for the resumption of our conjugal life.

'Take this,' he sweeps off his heavy cloak and wraps it round me, then takes my hand in his arm to lead me to the principal tent, as the rest of our company, with many shouts and whinnies, amidst the clip clop of hooves and jangling of harness and trundling of wheels, rides into camp.

PART IV

Love and Glory

34

1794 Delhi January

We enter Delhi like returning heroes. Just outside the city, we come to a halt and Benoit rides back to the carriage where Gulzar and I sit with Banu and Ali.

'Pray descend,' he says, dismounts, extends his hand to us and lifts down the children. 'We must change our transport for the last approach.' And I know from the smile that flickers around his mouth that it is to be a pleasant change even before I spy the elephants that await us. He strides ahead with a child on each arm and I hear their excited squeals as they too guess what is to happen.

My father heads our procession with half the cavalry, my husband is mounted on the first elephant with Ali and Banu, Gulzar and I on the second, the bullock carts behind followed by the rest of the cavalry. Our mounts are richly caparisoned, their *howdahs* of gold and azure with canopies of silk, our *mahouts* clad in white suits girdled in gold, with blue plumed turbans on their heads.

As we process down Chandni Chowk, the people and traffic part to allow us through. We have a fine vantage point of the shops and stalls along the way and into the crowded alleys of the bazaar beyond, unlike the last time we were here and staying at my uncle's, when we had to push through the crowd and our view was very restricted. We can also see past the gateway of the great caravanserai and understand why people rate it the most magnificent building outside the fort, with its gardens and lakes to make welcome visiting merchants. I wonder if the rest of our party will be accommodated there or within the fort, which looms larger than ever I remembered, the great red walls stretching far on either side of the towering entrance porch. As we approach, the gates open to allow us passage and from my lofty seat I can appreciate the carved lotus flowers around the arch.

It becomes darker as we pass through, for we traverse a long covered area, which is perhaps the thickness of the outer walls, and where there are guards quartered at several levels. We emerge into daylight once more and, as Benoit's mount draws level with another building, Gulzar and I are startled by a sudden and very loud fanfare of drums, trumpets and cymbals, which is repeated as we pass and we can then see the musicians seated within. It is a splendid noise, though quite overwhelming, and I hope that the children were not alarmed and cause displeasure to their father.

We next enter a vast courtyard enclosed by two storey buildings, with a large square tank at the centre and wide roadways leading off at each side. In the far left corner, a large and grand building set on a high plinth, accessed by steps on all sides. I see the horses and bullock carts turning away to the right while our elephants cross to the far side and kneel, with much rolling and pitching of the howdahs. Benoit climbs down from his elephant and lifts out the children, who run to greet me as we too descend.

'Papa says the music plays every time he passes,' says Banu. 'And that building is called a *Naqqar Khana,*' she adds helpfully, pointing back whence we have come.

'And Ali not scared,' Ali stoutly assures me and looks at Banu, daring her to contradict.

I have been told of such ceremonial welcomes but have never heard one and certainly never been the recipient. The true object of such honour joins us.

'Papa, can we have a Drum House at our home?' Banu asks.

He looks down, so far down, at his daughter who gazes up at him, her adoration plain, while Ali takes his hand and jumps up and down in his continuing excitement.

'Banu, this is to be your home, while we are in Delhi,' he says gravely and does not smile as her face, while she looks in every direction, displays her incredulity.

'All of it?'

'No, all of it belongs to the Emperor but he has given us one house, which is at some distance from here. In fact it is across three more courtyards. We shall take a palanquin for it is a very long way to walk and we shall stop along the way to greet the Emperor.' He turns to me. 'It is almost noon, the hour when the Emperor daily gives audience to his nobles. The *Diwan-i-Khas* is beyond that gateway.' He indicates a fine arched entrance. 'The large building you see in this courtyard is the Diwan-i-Am for other audiences.'

My father appears behind us, having evidently given his horse to a *syce,* and picks up Ali, while Gulzar takes Banu by the hand and we make our way to a number of palanquins.

We are deposited at the base of a marble terrace that supports a large building also of marble. The Emperor sits at the far side of a great pillared hall on an immense high gold throne canopied in gold, with a further canopy over that. There are steps leading up to the throne, on three sides on which are seated members of the Imperial family, I guess, and perhaps Ministers. A small crowd of petitioners await their turn to ascend and greet the Emperor but attendant servants lead us straight to the foot of the steps.

'General de Boigne and family!' one announces and the Emperor indicates that we should ascend.

'Your Majesty.' Benoit bows low as he takes the proffered hand and introduces us.

Shah Alam is of dark complexion with a small white beard. He has a fine, sensitive face despite his cruel disfigurement, and is clearly listening attentively to compensate for his lack of sight. He speaks in a low, cultured voice.

'Come, children, let me see you.' He indicates that they should come closer and reaches out until he can place a hand on either head.

They are entirely awed and barely able to give their names, and I too am quite overwhelmed at the thought that I am here at the centre of the Empire, as the wife of an honoured man. At a nod from his master, an attendant steps forward bearing a red silk cushion on which rest a child-size *talwar* and *katar* for which Shah Alam carefully reaches. He holds them out to Ali.

'Take these, my son,' he says. 'And may you be as valiant as your esteemed father.'

Benoit steps forward to help Ali take the child-sized sword and dagger, which I can see he has not at all anticipated. 'Your Excellence is gracious to so honour my son,' he says, making a deep bow.

And still the Emperor's courtesy is not exhausted. He turns in my direction. 'You must come to one of our *mehfils*,' he says. 'I hear you are musical and I am a great lover of *ghazals*.'

'Your Highness is most kind,' I whisper, and only then realise that he has addressed me in pure Persian, and that I have responded in similar fashion. To my husband and the children he spoke in the more common hybrid tongue. 'Although my talent is small when compared to the great musicians who play for you.'

'Nevertheless,' he nods his head and smiles. 'And my ladies also will be most glad of a visit from you and your cousin. And how is your sister, the Lady Faiz?'

'She is well, I thank you.'

He greets my father and enquires after my mother and I am astonished that he pays us such attentions, whilst to my husband he speaks almost as a supplicant. 'Pray, General, when you are rested and if I may engage your most valuable attention, do come to my apartments. I would speak with you of some household matters.' And he makes a dismissive gesture as if he will entirely understand if this should not be convenient.

It is only as we descend and back away from the dazzling presence that I see how faded is the carpet on which we walk, and how many of the fine stones of the inlay on the marble pillars are missing, and how threadbare the dress of the retainers. As we leave the hall I read an inscription above the doorway:

'If there is a paradise here on earth,
It is here, it is here, it is here.'

Benoit meets my eye and nods gravely for it is clearly no longer true.

Our palanquins take us the remaining distance, which is, indeed, considerable. We pass through two more gateways, across two very large courtyards, until we reach an area of elegant pavilions set amongst trees and gardens which stretch to the far encircling wall of the Fort. We stop by one pavilion that sits a little aside in its own well-tended garden.

'The Emperor's private apartments are there.' Benoit indicates a complex of pavilions to one side. 'And those of the *zenana* beyond. Come. I hope it meets with your approval.'

He leads me up a short flight of steps to a spacious verandah or terrace, open on three sides, the roof of which is supported by elegant pillars and sculpted arches, along the top of each of which are large rings where in the hot weather we may hang awnings. It will be a fine place to receive visitors. Beyond this, I find a suite of inter-connecting rooms around a small private courtyard where a fountain plays in a large basin. The children race ahead of me and I hear their squeals of approval before I can make my own assessment, but there is nowhere to find fault. The carpets and wall hangings and all other furnishings are richly coloured and new or newly cleaned, the plasterwork without cracks and freshly painted.

I rejoin Benoit, who is waiting on the terrace. 'It is all very fine.'

'Did you find the staircase?' He leads me back to the main bedchamber where, in a corner behind a curtain, there is a spiral flight of stairs. I climb them and find myself on the roof, where there are twin *chattris,* each topped with shining gilt cupolas, giving a splendid view of the Yamuna. A pair of large turquoise butterflies, such as I have never seen elsewhere, flutter so close I feel the breath of their passage.

'I like it very much,' I say, turning, for Benoit has followed me. 'I can see nothing lacking for our comfort. Indeed,' I continue to look around and am becoming puzzled. 'It appears that we are especially favoured.'

For, as I look more closely, I begin to notice that neighbouring buildings are not in such good state, their walls being discoloured and darkened by damp, and growths of weed sprout from cracks in their masonry and obscure windows and doorways.

Benoit sighs. 'I have written to Sindhia on the subject of the conditions in which the Emperor and his household live, for I find them sorry indeed. As you will doubtless see when you visit the ladies.'

***

An ageing eunuch escorts Gulzar and I into the centre of the *zenana* complex which houses the Emperor's wives and female relatives. He points out the most magnificent pavilion, the Mumtaz Mahal, once the home of Shah Jehan's favourite daughter, Jahanara, where he caused one of her many secret lovers to be boiled alive in a cauldron, having received word that he had hidden there.

'Some say it was from jealousy,' the old man informs us, opening his eyes wide to ensure we understand his meaning.

Today's inhabitants huddle miserably in faded clothing, thin shawls wrapped round their shoulders, or lie shivering on dirty mattresses under equally unclean covers. But they welcome us with great courtesy and make a place for us to sit, where we are instantly surrounded by a large number of the ladies in the chamber, all attempting to speak and gain our attention. Finally, one older lady, a senior wife perhaps, is pushed forward.

'We are hungry,' she says. 'All of us, all of the time. The Emperor's close household receives a fixed portion of meat and rice daily and two loaves of bread, but there are five persons and servants also to share this. Everyone besides, whether Queens like myself, Princes or Princesses, eunuchs or female slaves, every day we have only two seers of barley to every three people to bake into bread.'

'So every day,' a slightly younger woman takes up the story, 'The Emperor invites one of his Queens to join him so that she may occasionally eat meat.'

'Very occasionally,' corrects a woman whose hair is still free of grey but whose cheeks are sunken like those of a much older person. 'For there are two hundred of us.' She laughs, revealing gums entirely bare of teeth

'When I was a girl this was still a beautiful place.' One very old lady leans forward and touches my arm to gain my attention. 'We could eat the most luscious apricots and mangoes fresh plucked from the trees, which, if they have not been felled for firewood, are now blighted from years of neglect. We had running water for every chamber, and pools and water chutes and fountains all fed by the bubbling *Nahr-I-Bishisht*, the River of Paradise.' She pauses, her face lit by her joyful memories and I can see how very beautiful she once was. 'Now look at it!' She gestures sadly at a dried up reservoir by the entrance that is so piled with rubbish that we had not recognised its true nature. She grasps my hands as we leave. 'Prevail on your husband to help us,' she pleads. 'He has the power.'

'I will try,' I promise, thinking how easily I could have been in her situation.

As we walk back to our apartments, we see unswept detritus drifting between all the buildings and find that we are walking on grown-over channels that once kept the air cool and fresh in the hottest season.

'He is trying to help them,' I tell Gulzar, who knows this already.

'Perhaps the evidence of your own eyes will strengthen his argument,' she suggests.

'My life might have been similar.'

'I know.' She takes my hand briefly. 'But for the grace of Allah.'

And very soon, it as if the long months of separation are a dream, so completely are our good relations re-established. Benoit is busy attending to his duties, but often able to return to us during the day and in the evening and he appears to relish family life more than ever before.

***

'I have received a letter from a Company officer in high position in Calcutta,' he tells me some weeks later when we are taking our ease after dinner. In fact, I am massaging his temples and forehead with aromatic oil so that he may later sleep more easily.

'Colonel John Murray asks me to use my influence to prevent the irrevocable decay of the Taj Mahal and I am of a mind to view it myself to ascertain its condition. Since I know that you regret not having visited it when at Agra, it occurs to me that you might care to join me? We should leave the children here rather than subject them to another lengthy journey.'

'I should very much like to see the mausoleum,' I respond. 'I had not known that it was in any serious disrepair.'

'I have already spoken to Sindhia on this matter also,' he says. 'But found him unsympathetic, appearing to value only the richness of the material. There is a small allowance intended for the maintenance of the building, but, whether from the avarice and parsimony of the Hindoo caste in general, or the Mahrattas in particular, as also their abhorrence of all that is Mahomedan, I fear that it will not be applied to its intended purpose.' He sighs, his forehead again creases with fatigue and anxiety and I renew my massage.

35

1794 Agra February

Dawn is just breaking when we visit Mumtaz' mausoleum and, despite having gazed at it so often from my perch in Agra Fort, I am quite unprepared for its beauty. We enter by the southernmost and main gateway and emerge into formal gardens, quartered by watercourses with the marble basins of fountains at each corner. But I am barely aware of these features since my eyes are drawn straightway to the Taj Mahal itself. It stands on a raised platform at the far side of the gardens, its great central dome and four smaller surrounding domes silhouetted against the lightening early morning sky. The vision, slowly tinted by the pink of dawn, is framed by minarets at each corner of the platform that together create an image of perfect symmetry.

We make our way first to an ornamental plinth at the centre of the garden and, taking care on the steps, I can see that the marble underfoot is dirty and the water green and stagnant giving only a dim reflection of the magnificent building. The extent of decay becomes more apparent the closer our approach.

Just as in the Red Fort, where there were dense inlays of semi-precious stones, in many patterns of wondrous invention, each requiring uncountable separate pieces laid together, now there are cracks and gaps where the green and yellow jasper and precious red cornelian have fallen or been prised from their settings. Once delicate and intricate carvings around the high arches are chipped and discoloured, if not fallen away entirely, and the porphyry-inlays depicting sacred words from the Quran are in many places illegible. I look at Benoit in dismay and see that he too is most concerned.

We go inside where the floor and walls are also damaged and the exquisitely perforated marble screens surrounding Mumtaz' cenotaph, each miraculously carved from single pieces of marble, are in places broken away. Here again, much of the precious inlay, the lapis lazuli, purple onyx and green malachite, is missing.

'Her actual tomb is below the ground, beside that of her husband,' Benoit says, which news almost brings tears to my eyes.

'Oh, I am glad! I did not know he was ever brought here.'

'You care so much for one who killed his own kin to ascend the throne?' he asks, when we are back outside in the dazzling light of sunrise. 'And whose son killed his brother for the same reason and whose daughters were bitter rivals and led lives of dissolution and worse?'

'And who spent so extravagantly on this construction, money which could surely have benefited his people.' I am standing on the wide terrace gazing back at the now brightly illuminated building from a distance which once again obscures most of its blemishes. 'And yet, he was capable of such great love, it was done for love.'

Benoit is silent and I wonder if he disagrees, will perhaps assert some other motivation, perhaps of a more political nature. Instead, he indicates that we should walk further to the edge of the terrace, where he leans on the parapet and looks away across the Jamuna towards the distant fort at Agra.

'There are contradictions in many characters,' he murmurs in a voice so low that I almost do not hear and hold my breath as I see he wishes to say more. 'A man can love and yet betray that love.'

Still I remain silent, my eyes cast down, for I know now that he speaks of himself.

'You may hear a story of a girl, Zinatt. Have you heard this tale?'

I shake my head dumbly, suddenly very afraid, for he has never yet spoken to me of the other girl, Mihr-un-Nissa. I feel faint and perhaps I gasp or sway for he reaches out to support me, but I step back, not wanting him to touch me.

'She is the daughter of a Nawab, now living with her mother in Delhi, who tricked me into promising to take her daughter into my house. Twice only she permitted me to see the girl and only at a distance and much painted in red, white and black. This I only discovered when she was mine, when her true colour and form turned out to be very inferior to the beauty as seen and said to be. I made her presents of jewels and clothes and gave her a monthly allowance. But I never touched her. I swear *je ne l'ai jamais touché.*'

His tone is become so insistent that I lift my head and meet his troubled eyes. 'It is good that I hear this from you. I thank you for this courtesy.' I say and, perhaps from relief that I am not to be abandoned, suddenly find I am able to smile. 'Why, I do believe even Mumtaz had to share her husband with more than one other. Many more in fact.'

'You are too kind,' he shakes his head. 'Don Queiros was right.'

'Oh?'

'He wrote to tell me that you are a treasure. When he was finding you accommodation in Lucknow, he wrote to inform me that you were insistent that he not waste my money, and told me that I was lucky to have you, that you are a treasure.' He reaches a hand into a pocket of his tunic and withdraws a small box of black velvet. 'So please accept from me and wear this very small treasure.'

The box contains the most beautiful ring I have yet seen of heavy gold filigree inlaid with diamonds, sapphires and emeralds and holding a single great ruby at its heart. I put it on one finger and hold it up and become fascinated as I watch how it glows and sparkles and dances in the sunlight. He takes my hand at last, kisses my fingertips and draws me close.

'And we will take what steps we can to save this monument to love,' he adds.

1853 Lower Beeding May

The sun has crept round the corner of the house to find me in my nook and announces its arrival with a triumphant flash and glitter of reflections from my most beautiful ring. Not for the first time I gaze into the very centre of the ruby and try to guess its secret. Where diamonds dazzle and emeralds distract and sapphires have a somewhat superficial and inscrutable allure, it has always seemed to me that a ruby swallows the light in depths as unfathomable as the very sun.

'He surely loved you very much.' Mary is staring at the ring, having placed a tea tray on the bench beside me.

I was close to snatching my hand away from scrutiny but am tempted to hear more of such sweet opinion. 'It is certainly worth a great deal,' I concede, tentatively, so that she is encouraged to continue.

''Tis more'n that.' She is quite certain. 'My Gran says -' she breaks off. 'Sorry, mum, I mustn't – intrude. Ms Goldine said.'

'Oh but I should like to hear what your Gran says,' I assure her, thinking that it is more the company of her own sympathetic soul which I desire to detain awhile.

'Well,' she glances quickly at the ring and then her gaze drifts somewhere into the distance so that she tells me without making claim on my attention.

'Jewels've a meaning, my Gran says, not that she's got any. And maybe they have powers. Like gold cures inflammations, leastways on the eye, you know when you get a stye?' She points to one of her eyes. 'My Gran can cure them, with a rub of her wedding ring. I've seen it myself and folks come back again and again, 'n say it's like a miracle, they're so -' She breaks off and looks down at her boots in sudden confusion. 'Sorry, mum, there I go again, runnin' on. I like talkin' to you.'

'I like listening to you,' I assure her. 'I would like you to tell me what jewels mean.' I pat the seat beside me and hold out my hand in invitation.

It is the one with the ring and she sits and takes it in both of hers, and looks at the ring and then at me, her head on one side, considering, I fancy, how much truth I wish to hear. 'T'were a gift from your husband?'

I nod and inwardly smile at her tact which she has surely also learned from her grandmother. She concentrates on the ring and, pointing at each stone in turn, delivers her verdict.

'Diamonds are for innocence, the giver's or the recipient's, t'would depend on the intentions of the giver.'

I become more interested. 'Go on.'

'Sapphires are for love and emeralds success in love.'

'Oh,' I say, unaccountably excited in despite of my better judgement. 'So that is why I find the one a little untrustworthy and the other evasive, though both are beautiful.'

She regards me gravely and I wonder if she truly has the sooth-sayer's gift, for her expression seems that of a much older person and the tone of her voice offers consolation for suffering of which at her tender age she can have no experience. 'But the ruby, this wonderful great ruby, stands for a contented mind.'

'Mary!' we both start at the sound of Caroline's distant voice and Mary jumps to her feet.

'Shall I pour the tea, mum? Or - '

I wave her away. 'I can do it,' I say. 'Best attend to your other chores.'

And she leaves me alone to ponder, not Benoit's meaning in selecting this ring, for I doubt he ever heard of, let alone would have credited such associations between minerals and humankind, but whether he would have remained contented with me as he was then, but for unexpected events.

1794 Delhi February

We are a day's journey from Delhi and Benoit travels with me in the *rath,* having given over his mount to be led by one of the escort party. He is sleeping peacefully with his head in my lap, his health much improved, I think, by this time away from his responsibilities. I am near sleep myself when I hear the jangling of harness and a horse's whinny as it halts beside us. There is a cough and a soft call.

'General?'

I peer through a chink in the canopy and an unseen uniformed rider hands me a letter bearing the Royal seal of Gwalior. Benoit sits up to break the seal and open it.

'Sindhia is dead!' He blinks and scans the page again, as if unsure if he is still dreaming. 'Of a fever, near Pune. His nephew Daulat Rao is the new ruler. He is fifteen.' He sighs deeply, closes his eyes for a moment, then sits up straighter and begins to button his tunic.

'I shall have to go on ahead to Delhi,' he says. 'I wish you had the company of your cousin though these men are amongst those I most trust, even without your father's presence.'

I know this. 'I will see you tomorrow.' But I am very sad to have our intimacy thus curtailed and, for the rest of the journey, wonder what new trials await him and ponder the ways of the Almighty who, without warning, cuts us down with no regard for wealth or power or position. Sindhia was at his most mighty, his kingdom the most powerful in India, his once great rivals, the Rajputs, now his vassals. He might have founded a dynasty that changed the course of the whole nation, but with his death surely there will again be conflict and change as different rulers wrestle for power.

When I arrive home, Benoit tells me: 'Some are saying I could myself become ruler.' He is watching my face for my reply.

'But you will not.'

He nods and I can see he is glad I understand. 'Sindhia made me, I shall remain loyal.'

It is not long before he receives other offers. 'Shah Alam has offered me the position of *wazir*, thinking I can restore the power of the Empire.' He shakes his head in disbelief. And again: 'The King of Afghanistan, Zaman Shah, has sent his ambassadors to offer me half his kingdom if I will establish his dominion in India.' He laughs. 'It is flattering indeed.'

'And yet you are not tempted.'

Instead, he sets himself to restore law and order over a vast territory, where the old Imperial system that was established by the great Akbar, has entirely broken down and once cultivated fields have been overtaken by the jungle where tigers roam. He wants to provide protection for villagers, a reliable supply of water and fair assessment and collection of rents and taxes. Despite opposition from young Sindhia's ministers, he manages to improve the situation of the Emperor and his household with an increase in their allowance and other income and he also obtains a small grant towards the upkeep of the Taj Mahal.

But it is all a great burden and he becomes increasingly dependent on his pipe to give him relaxation and temporary escape. There is less and less time when we are truly together.

One hot night when we are sitting on the rooftop and, as usual, I have prepared his pipe, I beg him to let me share it. 'Your duties keep you from me by day, let me accompany you in your dreams.'

But he waves this away. 'You cannot,' he inhales deeply, his eyes closed. 'I must face my demons alone.'

But I sit beside him and gaze across the Jumuna as the lengthening shadows cast by the great fortress wall slowly disappear into the deeper gloom of night.

1853 May Lower Beeding

My corner of the garden is now in shade and my own demons remain unassuaged. I need a pipe to pursue my own dreams, I decide, for it is strange indeed how entire decades of time leave but the slightest trace in one's consciousness. What governs the choice of such moments I wonder, and, were it possible, would I wish to recall the whole? I make my way into the house to ask for one to be brought to me in my bed. Caroline is about to go home, but obliges me nonetheless with only a token display of disapproval. She does not yet know Mary has almost mastered the task.

36

1794 Delhi Summer

'Banu! Ali!'

They are playing as usual in the grounds of the Fort with the many children of the Royal household. Gulzar has been sitting on our steps keeping careful watch, for some of the little princes and princesses are run quite wild and not at all as one might expect of the offspring of such cultured parents and grandparents. They have discovered how to turn the Persian water wheel, that used to feed the River of Paradise, by lowering buckets into the Jumuna and filling those remaining on the wheel. It is most certainly not without danger and so far I have prevented my two children from any involvement, though it is good to see how once the gardens might have looked when all its hundreds of long-stolen silver fountains were in operation.

Banu emerges from behind some shrubbery, with Ali in close pursuit, both with faces flushed with exercise and excitement, leaves in their hair and mud on their hands and clothes. It will surely be necessary to bath them both before we can go out.

'Come children, it is time to get ready.'

Banu adopts her particularly ingratiating stance, hands clasped as in prayer, head tilted, eyes wide and fixed upon me.

'Can't we play a *little* longer, mama, please?'

'Little longer,' echoes Ali.

'We are going out with Auntie and Uncle, you will have a lovely time there too. I will count to one hundred.'

'Two hundred.'

'One, and I am starting now...'

They disappear again into the undergrowth and I see them emerge a little further away chasing a skinny child of about seven, whose skin is darkened by the sun and whose clothes are torn and dirty. He climbs a tree to avoid being caught and begins to throw things down at my children beneath. I guess it is last year's dried up fruit or nuts but it could be stones he carries with him. I run after them and take their hands before they can escape me.

'One hundred!' I announce and drag them, protesting, indoors. 'We are going outside the city,' I tell them and, before they can protest again, add. 'And so we have to go by bullock cart.'

They are of an instant amenable at the prospect of this adventure and the princeling turns his attention to the persecution of a piteously crouching kite that drags a broken wing along the ground as it attempts to escape and calls uselessly to its luckier brethren wheeling far above in the high blue sky.

***

In September, the weather begins to improve at last. Benoit has suffered more than one bout of fever during the rains and is very pale and quite reduced in girth. At my urging, he has remained sitting in bed to conduct some of his business on the day that we receive a letter from the Nawab. In truth it is more like a parcel, being of such thick paper and so tasselled and gilded that it bears heavily on the outstretched hand of the servant, who enters with it resting on a silver salver. When I have succeeded in untying the several silken cords that bind it and broken the large wax seal I find an invitation to his son Wazir Ali Khan's wedding in the spring.

A handwritten note from Asaf-ud-Daula himself informs us that besides hoping most sincerely that we will be able to forsake duty for pleasure and grace this most auspicious occasion, he trusts that the knowledge that he is also inviting my parents and Major Palmer and his esteemed wife may sway us in favour of acceptance. I hand it to Benoit affecting indifference but he is not fooled. He looks at me, his head on one side, a slight smile playing about his lips.

'You would like to go.'

I shrug, but know my eyes betray me.

'I cannot spare so long from my work. In fact, I must soon go to Koil for I fear that, without employ, my army may become undisciplined. You may go, take the children, it is sometime since they saw their grandparents.' But then his shoulders slump and he lies back on his pillows with his eyes closed.

'You are exhausted.' I go to his side and place my hand on his forehead. 'And the fever has returned.' I will not leave him. 'Oh,' I say lightly, 'There will be another opportunity I am sure. And I shall request the fullest report from my mother.'

1795 Koil December

The town of Koil is quite a different place compared to my last visit, much repaired with its streets are full of carts transporting all manner of foods, fodder and materials for construction. There are many more shops and stalls and workshops busy with the sound of hammer and anvil. There are also hundreds of military men making purchases, supervising their loading for transport, or at their ease in and outside teashops. The cantonment has indeed benefitted the area as Benoit predicted.

He has left the greater comfort of the *rath* to ride on horseback the remaining few *kos*, the better, I guess, to announce his returning authority. I see its effect as sauntering soldiers straighten and salute and call the attention of others to do the same, so that their General is treated to an impromptu guard of honour all along the way. It is entirely deserved in fact and, yet again, I think how fortunate I am to be his wife.

Our new home is a fine flat-roofed house, almost a small palace, set in walled grounds slightly to the east of the town, on the way to the cantonment and fort. We approach through high gates along a wide gravel path across lawns shaded with large trees, all of which recalls to my mind the Residency and is, I think, rather in the English style. We are greeted at the porticoed entrance by a small crowd of servants dressed in fine white costume, led by Mahmud who has clearly been busy arranging this new establishment.

'There are important messages, Sahib.' He beckons forward a boy who holds several sealed documents on a silver plate.

Gulzar takes the children off to bathe and change, but I linger in my dusty travelling clothes, watching Benoit pace the verandah, breaking each seal in great haste, his expression becoming more tense and concerned as he reads, until finally he sighs and sets his shoulders with resignation and comes to face me.

'It seems the Nizam of Hyderabad is about to make war on Pune,'

'Must you go?'

'No, our army in Pune outnumbers theirs and, like theirs, is equally divided between cavalry and infantry.' A note of amusement enters his voice. 'Although they do have the advantage of a troop of female infantry, dressed in British redcoats.'

'What?'

He looks up and acknowledges my surprise with a smile. 'Their duty being to protect the harem which accompanies the army in a long caravan of elephants bearing covered howdahs.'

'Which will surely not facilitate progress!'

'But,' his expression has become again grim, 'He, the Nizam, is attempting to bribe Sindhia to defect from the Maratha alliance and join him.'

'Which would render your own position most uncertain?'

'Indeed. Although here,' he indicates a third letter. 'Your brother-in-law tells me that that they have also made similar overtures to the Company, particularly concerning the two British regiments stationed there. Kirkpatrick, the Resident, is firmly asserting Company neutrality, but he and a small party are accompanying the Nizam's army. Meanwhile, envoys of the Marathas, of the Peshwa not Sindhia, seek to divide the Nizam's supporters...'

'And so?' My heart is sinking at the prospect of such continuing confusion and unrest.

'I can only wait on events and continue to order matters here as I had intended. But I cannot pretend that it will make my work any easier.' He extends his hand. 'Come, let us survey our new abode.'

A large dining room opens directly from the garden and adjoining that, a great hall designed for the reception of official guests, a few small rooms opening from this for their accommodation. Our family apartments are in the back of the house set around a courtyard with a tank all in our Indian style. As in the public area, the furnishing is plain and unimposing, which I prefer, although Gulzar and I will soon set to making our rooms more comfortable for everyday life. There are many servants to help us, many more than we have employed in the past. I send word to Preethi asking if she wishes to join us but discover that she is soon to be married, while Sita is already wed and with child. So I send a gift to each and occupy my time with the children's education and amusement.

Benoit is occupied from early morning until late at night. Almost daily he holds a *durbar,* when the road outside our gate is quite impassable due to the waiting palanquins and horses belonging to local dignitaries or their emissaries. He has European visitors also, whether passing through or living on properties in the area, for he seeks with them to develop trade in indigo and salt petre in which the region is rich and, besides, he often departs to inspect his troops or regulate the affairs of his extensive domain.

The Nizam's army suffers a complete rout at the hands of Sindhia's troops, due largely to its unwieldy organisation and the revolt of his womenfolk who had threatened to unveil if he did not retreat to a safer haven for the night. It would be amusing, comments Benoit, were not they not now besieged in the same fortress and dying of the combined effects of starvation, thirst and cholera. I am as much concerned about the effects of so much work and worry on his health.

My mother writes in April with much more diverting news, of the wedding of the Nawab's son. '*Lucknow has never seen such marvels, nor I think will it ever do so again. Can you imagine a procession of 1200 elephants, some with howdahs of silver, with our dear Nawab on an uncommonly large elephant covered with cloth of gold, accompanied by four hundred dancing girls on platforms held aloft by bearers? And either side of the road artificial sceneries of bamboo work very high, representing bastions, arches, minarets and towers, which were but part of an artificial fort five miles in circumference....*'

The wedding feast was held in the Nawab's gardens in two immense tents made of exquisite cloth costing ten lakhs rupees, the ground between the tents was covered with fireworks and, at every step the elephants took, it was as if the ground burst and threw up stars into the heavens, the garden itself was illuminated by hundreds of transparent paper lanterns and the bridegroom's robe was stitched with jewels costing twenty lakhs rupees. All of this met with great approval, according to my mother, with one exception.

'*Of course Mirza Abu Taleb Khan had to be the only one to spoil the entertainment with his usual criticisms of the Nawab's extravagance. Personally, I think that the people, however poor, would rather have a spectacle such as this on which to feast their memories for all the years to come than rice and lentils today. My especial embraces to my two dear grandchildren. Your loving mother.*'

37

1853 Lower Beeding May

My beloved mother's presence seems as vivid as if she were sitting beside me. Was she with me in my dreaming? Is that where we go in dreams, to meet with the souls of our dear departed? How I should like that to be true. Meanwhile, her phantom is fast retreating into the obscurity whence it came, and I am powerless to retain it as I am recalled to the present day.

'Ma'am? Ma'am? Are you well?'

She is peering closely at me, lines of worry etching her young forehead. I shake my head to clear my thoughts and, with the greatest of difficulty, smile and sit up.

'Oh Mary, I have been dreaming. When you are as old as I, dreams become as real as the everyday.'

She nods gravely as if she understands. 'I were afraid you would never wake.'

'I was dreaming of my mother, who is of course long since passed from this world, but whom I still much regret.'

'My ma died when she were giving birth to me,' Mary confides. 'T'were my Gran as raised me.'

'That is very sad.' I would like to say more but Mary is yawning. 'My dear, is it not time you were in bed?'

'I was on m'way, Ma'am, when the thought occurred, Miz Goldine being out, as you'd like a morsel to eat.'

She goes out to the landing and returns with a tray that gives off a most appetising aroma as she sets it on my lap. There is cheese toasted onto bread with some apple chutney beside and a cup of milk.

'Thank you, Mary. I think you know my needs better than I.'

'Will I stay with you?'

'No no.' I begin to eat with a show of enthusiasm that becomes wonderfully unfeigned. 'This is tasty, Mary, I thank you. And will see you in the morning.'

And here is another wonder. I wish to see another morning, now that there is Mary's bright face to greet me.

'You're welcome, ma'am.' She yawns again. ''Tis only summat to take you through the night.' She bobs a curtsey and is gone to her room, and as I lie waiting for the return of sleep, I recall how often I sat by Benoit's bedside that year, when he was wracked by fever, to take him safely through the night.

1795 Koil July

I have perhaps been dozing and I open my eyes to find him staring past me, into some imaginary distance.

'Still they come, wave after wave, laughing, blind to their own destruction. Why do they not see and cease?'

I lean towards him. 'Who? What phantoms assail you?'

'Look!' he sits up, seizes my arm in vice-like grip, and points. 'Rathors, the proudest bravest warriors that ever lived. Ten thousand horsemen, Rajput nobles all, flashing silver in their mail and helmets, so sure of victory against our lowly infantry, assured that under their daring charge, the musket men will turn and be cut down by their scything swords as they flee. But, do you see, it is Rathor blood that is spilled, again and again are they torn apart, flung to the ground and trampled by their terrified horses that are entirely unused to meet these unyielding lines of blazing fire and cracking volleys of shot.'

His voice dies into a whisper. 'Ah, the pity of it and the waste. How many did we kill, any one of whom I should have been proud to call my ally? Upon whose side I might have fought had fate not otherwise decreed. And why? For what?' He shakes his head and falls back on the bed.

I do not know of which particular battle he speaks, only of the eventual outcome. 'You brought peace,' I assure him and cool his head with a cool damp cloth. 'And you are restoring order.'

'For how long?' He sighs deeply as I begin to stroke his forehead. 'Who is friend, who enemy? Who should rule?'

While he sleeps I compose a new *ghazal* and sing it softly, hoping to comfort him in his dreams.

'Kings would not be supplicants if my love ruled the land.
Queens and princesses not starve if my love ruled the land.
My love is wise and just and good and all would praise his name.
For there would be lasting peace if my love ruled the land.

The jungle would be cleared again if my love ruled the land.
Wild animals would leave the towns if my love ruled the land.
Disorder and injustice rule, the poor take all the blame.
They know their lives would be restored if my love ruled the land.

Palaces would not crumble if my love ruled the land.
But nor would more be built if my love ruled the land.
Princes would respect the law, their murderous rivalry tame.
Government would be fair for all if my love ruled the land.'

***

He is again working from his bed, receiving emissaries, dispatching orders. But it is afternoon and they have all gone and the children and I have joined him for a quiet hour or so. Also with us is Marcel Aumont, a young French sergeant, who has been with him on many campaigns and is used to serving his personal needs. The sergeant has come to live with us and at this moment, through conversation with him, Benoit is attempting to teach the children some French. Banu is making some progress.

'La!' she exclaims suddenly pointing in the direction of the front entrance. 'Un cheval!'

The approach of a horse is not very unusual in itself, of course, there being hundreds in the cantonment besides those of visiting civilians; rather it is the hour that is unusual. Marcel goes to investigate and returns with news of a visitor, a young English traveller who desires very much to make the famous General's acquaintance and has come a long way to do so. Benoit gets up and goes to meet him, returning a half hour or so later in high spirits.

'Splendid young fellow. Only eighteen but a good head upon his shoulders. I've left him having a bath and will meet him at four for dinner and then show him around. He showed a great interest in seeing the troops.'

'Perhaps he is a spy,' says Marcel softly and then shrugs and grins when he sees my husband's frown. 'But perhaps I am not so much a friend of the English as you, *mon general*.'

I think to change the conversation. 'He has had some refreshment?'

'Indeed, indeed, we sat in the hall together. Well, this is an unexpected diversion indeed!'

He is very pleased, flattered, but also amused and entertained by this young man's company and we see little of him for the next two days. Ali is upset when he sees the two of them take a ride out into the plain on an elephant to see the horses of the bodyguard where they are at present freely grazing, for he has been promised just such an excursion. He is however summoned next morning and the one after to join them for breakfast, which upsets Banu.

'Why am I not invited too?' she sulks. 'I want to meet this Englishman whom Papa likes so much.'

'Because you are a girl and Ali is a boy,' snaps Gulzar and both Banu and I stare at her, surprised at her unaccustomed anger. Banu in fact is on the point of weeping for she is not accustomed to unkindness from her aunt who, however, immediately softens and takes her in her arms. 'Girls and women do not go out in the world as do boys and men,' she says. 'It is the way we live.'

But later, when we two are alone, Gulzar returns to the topic. 'I too thought it surprising your husband did not call for Banu or even let us all meet together. Since we are well accustomed to European company and, besides, this visitor being so young.'

I make some excuse, and she does not argue for her words were spoken in haste. But she is right, I think, and feel accordingly slighted, whilst knowing I will never mention the matter to my husband.

***

'Do you know what I am thinking?'

It is a few days later in the quiet of evening before the time when the fever often returns and we are sitting together, Benoit and I, looking at a pale sunset. Now that it is September, it is not so hot and I am optimistic that he may remain well, for each bout leaves him weaker.

'I am thinking I should return to Europe.'

My heart begins to beat very quickly. I have long feared that this moment might come, but that makes it no less of a shock. I watch the sun slide below the horizon and the atmosphere turn briefly golden while I try to compose a calm response. 'You wish to see your home and family?'

He shakes his head. 'It is not my wish but rather a choice based on circumstance.'

'Your health.' I almost make it a question and hold my breath for fear there is another reason, but he nods.

'I think I could not survive another such season. I have been in India - ' he stops to calculate. 'Seventeen years! Without furlough.'

'We could go to the coast,' I suggest, still unsure as to his whole intent. 'Many do.'

'It is a possibility,' he agrees. 'Kirkpatrick himself has requested leave to do so, I hear, in order to recover from the effects of the war.' He pauses. 'Do you not desire to leave your country?'

I sit up straight, my heart pounding so hard I think he must hear, and open my mouth to give my customary response, '*I will go where you wish.*'

But then he adds, 'Will you not come with me?'

In an instant my future is changed and, at last, it seems, secure. Relief and joy flood through me in converging waves, recalling that moment long ago when I was set free from a future of concubinage upon the death of the Nawab of Pundri. I turn to him, the man who rescued me from my widowhood and give him my heartfelt response.

'I should not wish to stay without you.'

***

Banu snuggles up to me in the howdah whence we are watching the great parade. It is December and quite cold, even though it is the middle of the day.

'Papa looks sad.'

He sits alone on a large, magnificently caparaisoned elephant, saluting as battalion after battalion ride and march past him for the last time, near ten thousand in all, an entire brigade, the foot soldiers resplendent in their uniforms of scarlet English cloth, or the blue quilted material of this country, the cavalry in green and scarlet on horses as well-fed and groomed as themselves. They are splendid men, strong and ruddy-faced from an active life spent largely outdoors and they hold themselves erect with pride at their competence and accomplishments. We are too far to see if their faces show other feelings, of regret perhaps at their general's departure, uncertainty as to the future, a little fear even that it will never again be as glorious.

Benoit's face is gaunt, the features sharpened by the loss of flesh, and I know how thin his body has become, though it is not betrayed by his uniform and he holds himself as straight as ever. And Banu is right, his expression is of great sadness.

***

We leave Koil on 25th December and make our splendid progress to Lucknow. We are in a procession of four elephants, one hundred and fifty camels, innumerable bullock wagons, all with their attendants and drivers, and an escort of six hundred and ten cavalry, each man armed with a pair of pistols, a gun and a sword.

I am lying in our tent, whence I can see him sitting outside, smoking as he gazes at the star-studded sky. From time to time his broad shoulders rise and fall in what must be a sigh. He is so clearly regretting all that he has had to relinquish and takes little comfort in knowing it is wholly his decision, nor how much his young master regrets his loss. I helped Benoit write his letter of resignation and I read young Sindhia's reply.

'*You are the pillar of my state, the right arm of my victory. Your presence is required in my Councils and my Brigades. Come with all speed. Without fail. It is my order and my petition to you.*'

But Benoit could promise only that if his health is re-established he will return, and I do not think he believes this very likely, for he added a strong warning to Sindhia to avoid all contest with the English and to disband his battalions rather than excite their jealousy or risk a war.

Lucknow 1796 January

'You must not go to France, nor even Savoie.'

Colonel Martin, our old friend and host, is showing us the plans for his new house. He has decided he will remain in India. They are grand indeed, if a little over-adorned for my taste, for a very large site outside the city by the Gomti, with colonnaded walks on either side of the main entrance that will afford shady places to stroll.

'I have said it is to be my mausoleum,' the Colonel informs us. 'For the Nawab has already expressed interest in the building.' He smiles, a trifle sly.

'Aha! And could never live there if that is its purpose so will see no point in acquiring it?' Benoit laughs aloud. 'You are cunning, *mon vieux.*' He laughs again then points to the lines of cannon along the river bank and the two enormous East India Company lions guarding the entrance 'And yet there are such strong fortifications.',

'Ah, those,' muses the Colonel. 'They will hold flaming torches in their mouths and prove, I trust, a fearsome deterrent should any enemy choose to attack. We live in uncertain times, *mon ami*, I do not believe the French have ended their attempts to oust the British from India. As to what is still happening in France … you must have heard what has happened to our dear friend Antoine Polier? In February last? He was killed, together with his French wife, lynched by a Revolutionary mob.'

'Mon Dieu! I should have known!' Benoit is clearly shocked.

'I thought such news would reach you or should have written myself.' The Colonel is most apologetic.

'You have been greatly occupied, *mon cher*,' Benoit assures him, 'and, I hear, done the Company great service.'

'Oh, I have long been a friend of the English,' the Colonel replies. 'As have you. I hear you lately lent them a regiment to put down some rebellion? I think you will receive a fine welcome in London. Whence, by the bye, I have learnt other news, good news.'

'Warren Hastings' acquittal,' my husband nods. 'It will be very good to find him there, his honour restored.'

'Perhaps you may be able to enlighten some of those London-based Company men as to the true conditions of service here.'

'Perhaps. And I trust they will soon reward you for your valiant leadership in appropriate manner.'

The Colonel sighs. 'I have said it is the rank I crave, the salary I can do without. I daresay we shall reach agreement. But I intend to make opportunity to press my case if it is not already forthcoming.' He nods to emphasise the point. 'I plan to put on an entertainment for Sir John Shore when he visits next year. Including a grand firework display.' He looks at me.'I do hope you will not depart before that. Though it will be poor recompense for missing our last spectacular. The Nawab's son's wedding. I cannot compete with the Nawab.'

'We cannot remain another hot season,' I say, as much to convince myself. 'Health is more important than entertainment, however splendid, as I know you know well.'

'And I guess there will be fireworks in Europe,' Benoit affirms. 'Since a large number of the firework makers here are French.'

He speaks lightly and I do not think he will change his mind. But I can see the uncertainty in his eyes, he knows no more than I of England and what lies ahead, and enlists the children's enthusiasm for our journey, though his stories, perforce, are of Savoy.

'The first hot air balloon was launched in the town where I was born,' he tells them. 'I used to play in the very park, Buisson Rond, whence it took flight. In winter there is always snow which covers the whole ground for many months of the year. It is white and looks very beautiful, but it is very cold and you must wear coats of fur in order to keep warm. Also when there was snow, we used to race each other downhill on chariots without wheels.'

I am sure the children can imagine little of this, no more can I, but they are enchanted nonetheless and, for the moment, forgetful of all we shall leave behind, their loving grandparents before all things.

'Why do these chariots not have wheels?' Ali wants to know and I guess is not satisfied with his father's response for he repeats the question, more than once. 'How can they run without wheels? Papa? Papa?'

38

1853 Lower Beeding May

Ali's childish voice resonates so clearly in my ears that it is sometime before I can reconcile myself to my surroundings. I then remember that the day of my long grown son's arrival must be near and summon Mary, but it is Caroline who appears and this suits my purpose better. First, however, I must enquire about her more pressing concerns, the wedding being but a week hence.

'I trust your arrangements proceed? All is in hand?'

'As near as can be, marm, I thank you, though I keep thinking of summat else and to be sure He is no help whatsoever. But then you knows what men are like, never wanting to spend no money on what they sees as fripperies and suchlike ...' she breaks off abruptly having been taken by a habit of speech into uncharted territory.

But, far from being upset, I am in sympathetic mood. 'Oh indeed, I believe they have very little idea of household management whatsoever. Caroline, *if* your intended is not too busy with matrimonial matters,' we exchange a look of knowing conspiracy, 'I wonder, would you ask him to descend the trunks from the loft? I think he must ask Albert for assistance, for they will be unwieldy.'

Caroline frowns, despite our mutual goodwill. She does not like the sound of this at all. 'And where should'ee be putting them, ma'am?' she enquires, her voice full of doubt.

'The library,' I reply with confidence. 'For I shall sit there to sort them out.'

It is as she feared. She begins to wring her hands, quite unconscious, I am sure. 'But the books, ma'am, should you not be doing them first? With Mr Charles coming an'all?'

'It is *because* Mr Charles is coming that I wish to open the trunks.' I smile reassuringly. 'For there are items I may wish to give him to take home for his family.'

She is not happy, foreseeing continuing disorder, which she fears will displease my son and cast aspersions on her housekeeping abilities. We agree a pact. I promise to make all haste clearing both books and trunks, and she to complete her self-assigned tasks as regards the beating of curtains and carpets within the next two days. She rolls up my bedside mats forthwith and, as she leaves me with her dusty burden, Mary enters with my breakfast and a letter, newly arrived.

'Lovely writing, ma'am,' she observes and is clearly reluctant to depart without discovering the identity of my correspondent.

Of course I recognise Charles' script, of which I have always been proud, but hasten to satisfy her curiosity with ceremony. I take a brass letter knife from the bedside table, slit open the seal and scan the contents.

'*Charles.*' I read the last word aloud. 'It is from my son, Mary, he is arriving from London, where he has business to conduct, on Thursday, a few days earlier than expected. Please tell Caroline and see what you may do to assist her. I am afraid it will harry her still further so we must both do what we can to reduce her burden.'

I mean to make short work of my breakfast and be up and dressed and downstairs within the shortest of time. But still I linger and begin to daydream, remembering how long it took Benoit to complete his business before we could leave Lucknow.

1796 Lucknow May

'I have appointed Joseph Queiros to be my attorney,' Benoit tells me one hot morning.

He is sitting at a writing desk, pen and ink before him, and holds a roll of closely written parchment with both hands. 'Together with two others whom he has recommended. Listen,' he holds up the parchment and adopts dramatic pose. 'The above-named *do hereby agree to do, act and perform all other matters and things in and towards the premises requisite and necessary as fully as I myself might or could do, were I personally present and I do hereby ratify and confirm all and singular whatsoever my said Attorneys or their substitute shall legally do or procure to be done in and touching the premises."* The "premises" having been set out at the beginning of the document. Perhaps I should have been a lawyer!

'This will secure your interests? Of course I know that you trust Mr Queiros but, if one were to consider the wording alone, there would seem to be fair room for negotiation. Or dispute.'

'Which will make work for another lawyer!' He laughs, briefly. 'But stay, I must tell you of one specific matter to which they will attend on my behalf.' He frowns and looks away. 'It is about the two girls about whom I told you. With whom I was briefly – associated. I am making provision for them to be paid some allowance and you should know since your brother-in-law has engaged to pay a proportion and you may hear of this and wonder why.'

'I know he must have good reason.' I busy my hands in folding the end of my veil. 'Though confess I am confused as to his involvement, if glad these women will have some means to live.' I *am* glad that my husband should honour the responsibilities incurred by his past conduct, but I shall be more pleased when the matter is complete and never again a topic of discussion.

'He owes me some money. A considerable amount,' Benoit explains. 'And he has now engaged to repay his debt through a monthly payment to Joseph for the benefit of the girls, who, through Claude, will also each receive 40 rupees monthly from the produce of my *jagir*. I have also sent a purse of money as a gift to the mother of one, this through the good offices of your sister who knows this lady. Now you know it all.' He takes up the pen, dips it in the ink and, with great speed, signs the document.

***

Over the weeks remaining, the children and I spend most of our time with my parents, who dread our imminent departure and in fact seem to me of a sudden shrunken and aged.

'I shall never see you again,' my mother weeps, not for the first time, clasping one or both of the children to her for as long as they allow.

I think it a fair assessment, and could myself weep at the thought, but combine with my father to scoff and assure her to the contrary. I am very glad that they will have Gulzar's company.

'It is by no means certain that we shall not return when my husband recovers his health and can resume his duties,' I say. 'And also very likely he will have to come on personal business one day and the children and I may accompany him.'

'How goes his business?' My father seeks to change the topic.

'Oh, he is continually engaged in purchasing, packing and arranging shipping for a variety of goods which he plans to trade in Europe,' I say. 'Varieties of textiles mostly, for clothing or furnishing purposes. He has already had some successes in such ventures, including some crimson taffeta, of which I did see a sample, which apparently sold well in the city of Edinburgh, which is in the far north of England.'

'It is in Scotland,' Mirza Abu Taleb Khan corrects me, when this fact is later repeated to him by my mother. He too visits when he can and confesses himself a little envious that I am to see the world.

'Even thirty years ago England was a very dream world,' he says. 'I have read descriptions of its lush pastures and healthy livestock, why even the peasants are fat. And the scientific inventions! Windmills, watermills, watches – I daresay there are now three such wonders for every letter of their alphabet. The English carry their passion for mechanics even into their kitchens where the writer says he saw a 'very complete engine' used to roast a chicken!'

'Oh brother, what rubbish are you talking!' my mother rolls her eyes. 'You would risk such a journey just to see a machine which can do no more than a servant boy on his first day of employ? You would leave your family, even Hussein?'

Abu Taleb has a small son, Hussein, not yet two years old, who was born quite long after his various siblings and is become the greatest joy in his father's life, accompanying him to most places. Even now I can hear him shrieking commands at Banu who, I guess, is sitting with him on the swing seat or pushing him on Ali's outgrown wooden horse.

'I shall go nowhere while Hussein is young but one day perhaps – I should like to frequent the coffee shops where gentlemen sit and read the daily newspapers and discuss the affairs of the world. One can always thus find company, even if a stranger newly arrived in a city. And then in the evening sit on velvet seats to see an entertainment in one of London's many theatres and after supper visit -'

'Stop!' my mother covers her ears. 'You may keep your fantasies for the company of the General, and my husband, if he so inclines.'

'Dear lady, I meant to say: and visit the shops that open until late at night and the paved streets lit by so many lamps that a stranger would think them there to celebrate the wedding of the King's son. I mean to go one day, to France also when it is safe.'

'I hope you will,' I say 'And visit us. It will be good to see your familiar face.'

For the closer the event becomes, the more apprehensive I feel and part of that fear, which I confess to no-one, has been sown in my heart by Boulone.

'The further he travels from India, the further from you your lover may drift,' she declares and I can see how possible this may be, however stoutly I assert that the only alternative would be worse.

'Then would you have me stay here alone? For surely he will wish the children to have an English education even if they were to return here afterwards.'

'Half breed children will be no more welcome there than they are here,' she retorts. 'However well educated.'

But this I will not believe. 'William and Mary Palmer are well accepted in London as soon I shall see for myself.' Which thought cheers me greatly.

***

I leave my beloved Lucknow in August with a mix of the most powerful emotions. My mother has pronounced herself incapable of this final farewell, Gulzar remains with her to give her comfort. I gave her a golden locket of European design containing a curl of each of the children's hair. No words could express my gratitude. And I promised my mother that, once established in London, I should ask my husband to let us sit for a family portrait or at least a miniature and send it to her.

211

Now only my father is here standing shoulder to shoulder with Colonel Martin. I close my eyes as my father embraces me, wishing to imprint the sensation in the very marrow of my bones,

'I will visit you,' Colonel Martin salutes me. 'In England or perhaps in France. Once my house is constructed and there is peace.'

But when he embraces Benoit there are tears in his eyes. '*Bonne chance, mon cher ami*,' he says. 'Goodbye.'

As their figures dwindle into silhouettes and finally disappear around a bend in the river, I fancy that the city itself now mounts a last conspiracy to remind me of what I am losing as we pass the places of so much that has been precious to me. There is Captain Ganj and a view of the Residency complex on the higher ground above. There Mr Wombwell's bungalow, where I was so happy to set up my first home, not knowing for how brief a time this would be. Here Colonel Martin's town house, where perhaps even now Boulone gazes from a window, unsure whether she should envy or pity me.

We pass the Nawab's palace, the Daulat Khana, below which are moored a number of his pleasure boats, shaped like peacocks, gilded and painted and upholstered in rich brocade and cloth of gold.

'When I grow up I am going to be a nawab and have peacock boats,' says Ali.

'You can't *decide* to be a nawab,' Banu informs him. 'The Emperor has to ask you and first you have to be very brave and clever. Like Papa.'

'As well as good luck,' adds Benoit and then I remember my earlier intention.

I search quickly in a bag and find the bundle of moong beans from Ali's *chhathi* still tied in their green cloth. Several times over the last four years I have thought to cast them but not found a good place or, if in a suitable place, not had them in my possession. Mid-river is surely ideal and it pleases me to think they will start their mingling with the waters of the world from my dear river Gomti.

'Look children,' I show them the beans and tell them as simply as I can whence they came. 'Perhaps we may give Ali the good luck to become a nawab. You can throw them into the water.' Which they do with great enthusiasm.

'And now can we throw some for me?' asks Banu, then seeing me hesitate, droops her lower lip. 'Or is it only for boys?'

'No it is not,' I reply carefully, 'But your grandmother and Chachi were not there when you were born so I do not have any for you, but - ' I am thinking quickly how best to comfort her when, to my surprise, her father speaks instead.

'I did not have any beans either, Banu. So you and I shall have to make shift together without.'

At this she is quite satisfied and takes his hand, the better, perhaps, to make shift.

Further down river, I recognise scenes from paintings in Colonel Martin's house that recorded Mr Zoffany's journey up river on his visit to Lucknow. I see rocky outcrops with precarious temples perched on top, villagers watering their buffalo in the shallows and *ghats* where others wash themselves or spread their clothing to dry or burn their dead. Benoit seems happier to have at last set out on our long journey and points out other places: the Company opium and silk factories, the rocks where Mrs Hastings's boat was near wrecked in 1782, the year that he himself first visited Lucknow.

'Our own craft,' he says, 'is a pinnace, a rather superior vessel. And this is a good time to travel,' he adds. 'For we do not have to quit the boat and travel any part of the way by land, the water being neither too shallow, nor too deep and fast flowing which the Ganges certainly can be, as you may see when we reach it.'

Near a fortnight is passed before one morning we wake to a complete transformation of scenery. The land is flat, of brilliant green, with lines of swaying palm trees and grids of watery fields where peasants wade thigh-deep tending their crop, which I know must be rice, though I do not remember ever having seen it grow. The air itself is heavy with moisture and my husband is sick and remains in his cabin in Marcel Aumont's care, while the children are tired of the few toys suited to such confined conditions and their favourite amusement is to tease each other. I am sitting between them trying to keep the peace as our boat leaves the Ganges for the smaller Hoogly and we at last near Calcutta. I should like to pay more attention but they are a distraction, reaching across me, trying to reach each other, pulling on my clothes...

39

1853 Lower Beeding May

'Tis tight Ma'am.' Mary is attempting to insert me into a dress of bottle green bombazine which I do not like and scarcely wear, for it is indeed constricting. It is evident she has been tugging awhile for her voice has become urgent and I have paid no notice.

'There is an additional opening, Mary, down one side, I do believe, Caroline had the seamstress add a placket. There, t'will fit.' I shrug my shoulders to ease the final passage of the bodice and Mary rehooks the buttons at the side and laces the front.

'The trunks're brung down, Ms Goldine says to say.' She stands back at last, a little breathless. 'And heavy they was t'be sure.'

'Oh you didn't yourself lift them?' I am vexed that James and Caroline should have so tried a young girl's strength.

'Albert was a'gone t'market,' she says. 'And Miz Goldine says since Mister Charles is acomin' 'tis a matter of urgency and we all must lend a hand.'

'Then I must certainly lend mine,' I determine and, leaning on her arm, make my way to the library, meaning to make short work of sorting the contents.

There are four trunks, all constructed of fine hard wood and newly dusted. Only their leather bindings betray their age for these are cracked and frayed from use and lack of lubrication. Someone, most likely Caroline, has thought to open one and place a chair conveniently close by and I sit me down and prepare to inspect the contents. The writing on the side is still clearly legible: *General De Boigne M/S Kronborg Calcutta/London.*

'That was my husband,' I point. 'This the name of the boat on which we travelled from Calcutta to London. Have you heard of

Calcutta?' I see she has not. 'It is a fine city in India, or so it was then, with clean, paved streets of fine villas, whitewashed and painted like marble. It was mostly inhabited by Europeans of whom I had never seen so many.'

Only they were almost all men and boys. I remember Benoit telling me there were well over sixty thousand in the city, but perhaps only a couple of hundred ladies and some children. He recalled his previous visit in '82 when he was thirty-one, with no position and more or less penniless having only the benefit of a letter of introduction to the Senior Member of the Company Council. And, even this might have served him little but for the fact that this man was on close personal terms with, and recommended him to Governor Hastings, which entirely changed his fortune.

'Did you stay in a fine - villa?' Mary pronounces the new word with care.

'Very fine. It was near a river just north of a great open space, called the Maidan, where the soldiers from the Fort used to exercise and my children could play.'

'Your children, Ma'am?' She is surprised for, I realise, she knows of only one, but I shall not enlighten her just now. And I have just remembered something else. We were scarce arrived when a servant announced a visitor, someone with whom my fate was to be closely intertwined though none of us yet knew it.

1796 Calcutta September

Our visitor enters without further ceremony in evident expectation of a welcome. He is a man of dark complexion, tall enough, though shorter than Benoit and more portly, with the beginning of a double chin, and long dark, rather greasy hair tied back in a pigtail. There is a sheen of perspiration on his forehead, I guess he is hot in the long black coat and breeches that seem almost the uniform here. He is, perhaps, a few years my husband's junior. Benoit bounds to greet him, clasps him to his chest and kisses him on both cheeks.

'Anthony!' he exclaims, stepping back and still clapping him on one shoulder in his enthusiasm. 'I was not sure if you were in town.'

'As you see.' His friend spreads his hands with a smile. 'But perhaps not for much longer. I plan to go to London.'

Again Benoit shows his delight. 'As do I!'

Still his friend smiles as he inclines his head. 'So I have heard already from the very reliable newsmongers of Calcutta.'

'Allow me to introduce my wife, sister-in-law of Colonel William Palmer, whom you may have met when they were in Calcutta.' My husband turns to me. 'This is Mr Anthony Angelo Tremamondo of a famous family of fencing and riding-instructors to the Royal family of England, and friend of Hastings on whose recommendation he established a riding school here, which entirely revolutionised the training of cavalry in Bengal. It is true,' he insists when Mr Tremamondo begins to wave a dismissive hand. 'Even Hastings' enemies welcomed your appointment. My wife's father is a cavalryman,' he adds, 'previously in my service, but now returned to that of the Nawab in Lucknow.'

Mr Tremamondo bows and would perhaps kiss my hand if I offered it. I have a strong impression that he is already apprised of all this information and yet does not admit it, which rouses my mistrust.

'We can discover the London business world together!' My husband continues enthusiastic as he conducts Mr Tremamondo to a couch and sits beside him.

'Gladly, my dear friend, if I had half your powers of investment!' Mr Tremamondo is again self-deprecatory, or obsequious. 'You are now by far my superior in wealth and reputation.'

1853 Lower Beeding May

My step-nephew John Palmer, by then a banker of considerable standing in the city, was a much more welcome visitor, I think. It was he who found Amrita Bose to help me in Calcutta and then through the journey to England. Her plan was to find similar employment for her return passage and thereby save enough money for her dowry, being from a very poor family in which there were too many girls. I remember finding Amrita's manners a little rough at first, but she had a cheerful disposition, the children liked her and, most usefully, she knew the locality and where best to buy produce. It was through her introduction that we ate our first potato, a starchy vegetable which I discovered absorbed well the spices in which it was prepared...

'Of what are you thinking, Ma'am? Shall I leave you? Shall you rest?'

Mary is gazing at me, surely a little fazed by my long silence and immobility.

'Oh, of when I first ate potato!' I laugh. 'No do stay, we must make progress in our unpacking. Pray pass me some of that clothing which I fancy was also purchased in Calcutta.'

I pick up the garment on top of the pile in my lap, a day dress made of the finest white muslin embroidered with a pattern of small blue flowers. I remember the tailor saying it was a popular material in England also. I found the long skirt quite an encumbrance at first.

He made a shorter dress for Banu in the same material. I can see her still, taking care to display her long matching drawers that were frilled with *broderie anglaise*. And we both wore bonnets trimmed with ribbons, while Ali's first outfit was of white cambric knee breeches and a short jacket of blue brocaded stuff. I thought we made a handsome family group, though we took few outings together.

Benoit suffered frequent feverish attacks, which left him very weak. Amrita told me more than once and with undue relish, that Calcutta was an unhealthy place for Europeans, and suggested a visit to the cemeteries of St John's Church and St Paul's Cathedral to see how young many were when they died and, often, how soon after their arrival. But I took the children only to healthy places such as the Botanical Gardens across the river, where we saw many exotic plants for the first time, including China peaches and several varieties of tea, also from China.

It was on one such outing, I recall, some weeks into our residence, when my husband had accompanied us, that, returning by carriage taking a different route, we passed a long and impressive building of beautiful proportions...

1796 Calcutta September

'It is the Writers' Building,' says Benoit. 'Where many Company recruits start out, whence issue the future Residents and Assistant Residents and others of the British administration. I should like to see this phenomenon for myself from the inside, if you would not mind waiting a while. I am quite sure it is not a place for ladies or children.'

I see him in conversation with a doorman, who soon returns with some European official who clearly welcomes my husband and takes him inside.

I quite expect a wait of some half an hour and the children are already tired and hungry. 'Let us count the windows of this building,' I say and plan to require Banu to then multiply this number by the number of sides of the building or perhaps first divide it by the number of floors. Ali will require simpler diversion. But within a very short time Benoit rejoins us.

'It is like a large school,' he says. 'Very noisy, quite ill-disciplined and containing boys as young as thirteen, who appear to receive very little in the way of education and perform the most routine tasks. What parent would send a child so young so far from home to such a life?'

'And how long will they live? Amrita told me many die soon after their arrival.'

***

He is even more shocked another day when, his health having shown some improvement, he accompanies Mr Angelo (this is how we are to address Mr Tremamondo) to a popular eating place in the city. Again he returns after a short time and this time he is angry.

'Look!' he shows me a greasy patch on his tunic. 'And here!' he points to a red mark on his cheek. 'Can you imagine that these are but the accidental result of a total lack of courtesy and decorum amongst my dining companions? All of them English! Animals I should call them, if animals did not show more sense.'

'What can you mean?' I help him out of his tunic. 'Had they drunk too much alcohol?'

'Undoubtedly some had, even most, but still I have never seen such behaviour. In so many years amongst men, amongst soldiers far from home and in frequent danger. Never.'

'What behaviour? Is it too disgusting to tell?'

'No.' Suddenly his anger is spent and he sighs and throws himself flat on the bed next to me. 'They were slinging their food at each other across the table, across the room. Half chickens, pellets of bread flicked hard enough to injure as you can see. And finding such amusement in others' discomfort. Why, my assailant only laughed and shrugged when I did protest.'

'Did no other object?'

'No. But Anthony said that on occasion such food fights do become serious and end in a duel.' He turns to me. 'Do you not think it shameful? Do you not wonder to what society we are bound?'

'I do, most certainly I do.' I reach to touch his cheek. 'But I do not think London can be quite like Calcutta for will there not be more equal numbers of females? Will there not be mothers and sisters to care for and civilise these boys?'

He turns his face and kisses my hand then pulls me close. 'And wives and lovers in whom to lose the dark side of their souls,' he whispers fiercely in my ear, as he pulls up my gown and moves on top of me.

40

1853 Lower Beeding May

'Tis a pretty gown, ma'am.' Mary cocks her head to one side, her unspoken question plain. *Why do I thus sit motionless, pondering so long this one item of clothing?* I see that she has emptied the trunk and its contents are in neat piles on the floor while I am clutching this gown to me as if to admire the effect in an invisible mirror. I drop it hastily to my lap and turn to her.

'The material is very delicate, it is long since I felt such.'

She fingers it tentatively. 'I never saw as fine. 'Tis furrin', ma'am?'

'Indeed, and unavailable here these many years since England began to produce her own such cloth. It was the first dress I possessed, Mary, just before I came to this country.'

She inspects it more closely. 'Such fine embroidery. Forget-me-nots. English flowers.'

'So they are. I did not know that then, only that it was popular with the European ladies at the time.'

'Reminding them of home, most like.'

'Most like,' I echo, impressed anew by her instinct and then, on impulse, add: 'Please take it, it is more a young girl's style. And if it does not fit, you may make of it some underwear or bed linen or what you will. A nightcap for your grandmother perhaps.'

She holds back, doubtful.

'And then perhaps you will forget-me-not. When I am gone. For there are some years wear left in it, longer than in this old body of mine, I do daresay.'

I speak lightly but she regards me gravely and does not rush to deny this truth. Still she hesitates. 'M'z Goldine'll be thinkin' I'wuz askin'. Or takin', which is worse.'

'Miss Goldine need not know,' I assure her and then, more kindly, add: 'And there are surely other items I can give to her. And more to you also. So help me now and let us make some haste. I think one pile there for my son,' I indicate, 'another there to offer others, for I would give also to my friends in Horsham. Here beside me things that I might keep and somewhere throw what might at least make rags. This for a start.' I hold up a faded shawl made of the finest Cashmere wool that has clearly long since given sustenance to moths of some description. It is riddled with small holes. Mary takes it to the far side of the room.

We do make rapid progress, the pile for Charles accommodating several of his childish outfits that, already too small for any of his many sons, may yet fit my great grandchildren present and future, or even prove a plaything and clothe some doll. I add the better of some table linen, one or two silk neckcloths, several ornate waistcoats - which I fear will be found too old-fashioned but may be of interest - and, entirely as curiosities, two heavily embroidered *topis* of the style the British called 'Mogul', each with matching *jootis*.

In my selection there is as yet only one ivory back-scratcher, one small embroidered cake box for which I may find another purpose, and a plan of the Taj Mahal that I shall study at leisure. All that appears to remain is some nondescript cloth that was perhaps included for the purposes of wrapping, but I have reckoned without Mary's sharp eyes.

'Look, ma'am,' she extracts a yellowing scroll of thick paper and hands it to me with some excitement. 'Is it a secret map, d'ye think? A treasure map? Like pirates draw?'

I unfurl it and recognise Benoit's sober script, which yet has the power to cause a moment's pain. 'It is but a shopping list, Mary.' I peruse it more closely. 'Or more precisely, a list of goods my husband shipped from India.' I begin to read aloud. '£5250 in gold and £30,000 worth of personal effects.' Mary gasps. 'Including,' I skim the long list, '577 table napkins, various quantities of Ninsooks, plain and flowered, carpets, gold and silver pettecoat pieces...' Mary's eyes are drifting to the other as yet unopened trunks.

221

'Chintzes, Cashmere shawls, sheets, a small black trunk of pistols, which clearly we do not have, eighteen waistcoats, two bundles of Indoostanne prints...: in all, forty –three bales weighing near nine tons – he gives the exact weight – and costing £143 15 shillings and 3 pence in freight.'

Oh, my careful husband, whom some thought mean but I believed of the noblest disposition.

'It is not all here.'

'No, indeed, for he took the majority. And of course some was lost in the wreck.'

'You was shipwrecked, ma'am?' Mary's eyes are round with wonder.

'Our ship was wrecked,' I correct her. 'But fortunately after we had disembarked.'

'Such stories you must have to tell, ma'am, that I should like to hear. One time,' she adds hastily and drops her gaze, already regretting the boldness that is the fruit of her extreme curiosity. She busies herself making neat the piles, using some of the old cloth to tie them loosely until we should add to them.

'Oh, but I should like to very much,' I say, suddenly eager to have an audience for my memories, if in a somewhat edited version. 'It is, I guess, the stuff of storybooks and we have made adequate progress for the day. Come let us both take a more comfortable seat and I shall begin.'

When we are both sitting by the fireplace, I in an easy chair, Mary on the hearth rug beside me, I begin my tale which, long ago and more than once, I used to tell my children.

'We left Calcutta in late November 1796. A *budgeroo*, a small and shallow craft that is known here as a barge, took us three days down river to join our ship that lay in deeper water in the Bay of Bengal. The crew were mostly Bengalee *lascars*, not very experienced, nor yet, I suspect, well treated or well paid. Our Captain was an American and, though of a bad-tempered disposition, mercifully knew his trade and steered us safely past banks where the water was of an alarming shallowness.'

Mary closes her eyes and leans against my knees and I am encouraged to continue.

'The other danger we faced was from prowling French ships, for this was a time of frequent war and one French frigate had but recently captured several vessels. We passed one English ship that had been set ablaze and for this reason dropped anchor in a place of shelter and were glad to be sailing under a Danish flag, Thus delayed, we had soon finished our supplies of fresh food and were reduced to eating biscuits and salt butter. Our discomfort was increased by the flies that were so numerous that we had to hold our hands to our mouths when we spoke lest they go down our throats. After a week or so, we learnt that an English Man of War from Madras in the south had captured the frigate and we could again set sail.'

Mary is very quiet and I wonder if she has fallen asleep, but when I remain silent she speaks.

'And then?'

'We very soon put in to some island, one of the Nicobar archipelago, for it was necessary to replenish our supplies of water and to trade cloth and tobacco and some cutlery for supplies of fresh foods, pineapples, plantains, limes and other fruits. I remember we obtained ten coconuts for one cheroot, a very small cigar costing less than a farthing in Bengal, while a coconut, you may not know, is a rich food and drink beside for inside it has the sweetest milk.'

Mary shifts a little. 'And so?'

'We took on also live ducks and chickens. The people there were most obliging, in appearance of a Chinese cast. The men wore only a cloth tied around their waist, we scarce saw any women, for I think they stayed hidden from strangers. They lived in houses of wood and bamboo with thatched roofs like a stack of corn, though some were of three stories. I think they were good boat-builders also, and all in all it seemed a pleasant place to live. Indeed, one of our lascars may have found it so, for he absconded and we should have lost him had not the natives returned him, perhaps to preserve our good relations. Then was I saddened and ashamed for our Captain, on putting forth, told us, laughing, how he had tricked these charming people of half the cloth which he had promised.'

Mary clicks her tongue. 'Then next time they will not be so obliging.'

'Indeed. Many people do not look to the future consequences when they act.' I take a breath and continue. 'For some time then we made slow progress, for there is a region of calm in the vicinity of the equatorial line and one is obliged to make wide diversions to take advantage of the little winds there may be. I know this because my husband was in frequent conversation with the Captain and other passengers who had made the journey before and he explained it to me. He also showed me how the positions of the stars were changing as we continued south, some quite disappearing until we again headed north.' I close my eyes the better to imagine...

I see his shape against the starlit sky, an eager child on either side, for they are not much used to his attentions, especially when he is sick.

'See there,' he lets go Banu's hand to point. 'We call that star the Pole star, most important for accurate navigation, but soon it will be below the level of the land. Already it is much lower than before.'

'Then shall we be lost?' asks Banu, again taking his hand.

'I think not,' her father replies. 'I think our Captain will find the way and do you know how?'

She thinks a moment. 'Perhaps new stars will appear when these are gone?'

'Yes indeed,' he praises her. 'To him the heavens are as a map that he can read and chart our course.'

'And yet we do not voyage amongst the stars,' she wonders. 'So can the sky be mirror to the earth?'

He looks down at her while he considers a response. 'In some measure,' he agrees. 'If one can but see the correspondences.'

And then she turns and calls me to them...

'Are you well, Ma'am?' Mary has taken hold of my hand and her face is near to mine.

There are tears sliding down my cheeks which I dash rapidly aside with my other hand. 'A little tired, perhaps.'

'Then must you rest,' she scrambles to her feet. 'And tomorrow we may continue?'

'Indeed we should. Both my unfinished tale and our task.'

41

1853 Lower Beeding May

We have resumed our places as before, only today Mary has lit a small fire, the month proving itself unreliable as predicted, and, no doubt due to this warmth, we have been favoured with the additional company of the cats. The contents of another trunk lie dispersed, including various unfaded lengths of damask that I remember I once intended for summer curtains. Perhaps I still may have them made, unless my son would take them for his castle.

'Where were we in our story?'

'Star-gazin', ma'am, and'n th'doldrums.'

'Doldrums?' It is a word I did not use.

'My Gran told me.' She is pleased to explain. 'Her brother was a sailor.'

So my history has another listener. The thought pleases me. 'Then may she also be apprised of this next phenomenon. For some distance south of the equatorial line, we encountered a strong yet steady wind, that blew from the south east and could enable a speedy and complete circumnavigation of the globe, I learnt, but for the intervention of the land, of the continents of Africa and South America. Even so, such winds are favourable to commerce, and for this reason named by merchants "the trade winds", for there are many hundreds of miles of open ocean.'

'With ne'er a sight of land, ma'am? Were you not afraid?'

'Certainly. For a storm blew up, the winds grown more erratic, great gusts that whipped the water into waves that washed the decks and pitched us high and low, up and down, as if we were on a giant horse. Have you seen the sea?'

'From a distance, ma'am, from the Downs, once, when I was young, I went to Lewes town, t'see a relative, with m'Gran. And we climbed high above the town and could see so far I never would ha'credited it.' She inclines a little more against my knee, she has said enough.

'So, the ship was tossed as if it were a child's boat made of paper and we kept in our cabins, small and dark as they were, for one could scarcely walk, not without holding fast and stumbling. And the noise of the wind in the timbers! I think I hear it still, such a groaning and a creaking that we could scarcely sleep, together with the cranking of the pumps working day and night. Oh yes, I was alarmed!'

But remained calm, I think. Amrita was often sick, being much upset by the motion of the waves and of course I did not want the children to be afraid, though hard it was to keep them distracted and amused...'

'I cannot set my soldiers straight,' Ali complains. 'They slide this way and that and lose themselves under our beds.'

'And I cannot see to read or sew,' says Banu. 'Shall we sing, Mama?'

She touches my hand and I hold her close.

'Something to cheer Papa,' she says.

For he is ill again, though mostly lost in opium dreams and in Marcel's care in the cabin adjacent. I begin to improvise.

The world is like the ocean, never still, always in motion,
We breast the waves of life, endure sorrows and face strife,
Lost but for our Guide, who ne'er leaves us and provides
Starlight and heavenly charts that map our inmost hearts...'

My voice is faltering, my inspiration wavering when I hear Banu take a breath and I let her suggest the next refrain, which is quite a different mode and tempo.

'Oh God our help in ages past
Our hope for years to come
Be Thou our guard while troubles last
And our eternal home.

I join her in another verse.

Time like an ever-rolling stream
Bears all its sons away.

They fly, forgotten as a dream,
Dies at the opening day.'

We are about to sing the next verse when we are startled by a timber cracking, the noise of something falling and we clutch each other in great fright.

'Beg pardon, ma'am.'

We turn, Mary and I, startled to find we have eavesdroppers, two, Caroline and James, in outdoor wear and arm in arm standing in the doorway. I understand how I must have sung aloud and my dream of Banu become the reality of Mary and realise also that I am not as sad as I might have been until a very short time ago. Silver runs in past Caroline and James, salutes me with a muddy paw on my arm and licks my face when I bend my head to his. Meanwhile, Mary has jumped to her feet and is looking about her for some employment. But Caroline is calm, scarce pays her heed and addresses me directly.

'Sorry to surprise you ma'am, only we was passing, and thought to look in to see if all was well,' says Caroline. 'It having turned chill and all. And then I hears your voice, ma'am, and couldna' help but be intrigued, it not being of its usual tone. And then we finds the pair of you singing like you was in church so we thought best t'keep quiet a while, only he,' she jerks her head at her fiancé but with a humorous glint, 'He has to lean too heavy on his stick and breaks it and near falls over.'

'Sorry, ma'am.' James is busy righting a small occasional table which stands to one side of the door with his now useless stick dangling from one arm.

I wave all this aside. 'I was telling Mary how I came to this country many years ago.'

'M's Bennett was tellin' me the true story of her adventures,' chimes in Mary. 'Her voyage here around the world, 'cross oceans wide and deep.'

Caroline lifts her brows, no doubt even more surprised than I at Mary's eloquence, but, I hope, not put out at my favouring her protégé with more intimacy than I have ever shown her.

'I could continue if you were of a mind to listen,' I offer. 'Pray draw up some chairs and warm yourselves before you continue on your business. And what say we all take a warming sip of Madeira wine. In the sideboard, Mary, where you will find glasses too.'

227

'So.' I pat my hair and take a breath, unused to being the focus of such attention. 'For four long days the storm raged on, the hatches battened fast, so that we sat in darkness except when we burned a candle. We were like prisoners confined in cells, or, but for the constant noise and jarring of the structure of the ship, might have thought ourselves already the inhabitants of the nether world. It called to my mind the words of our poet, Hafiz:

Dark is the night and dreadful the noise of the waves and whirlpools; Little do they know of our situation who are travelling merrily on the shore.'

'There's more troubles at sea,' Mary whispers.

'But the storm did slowly die,' I continue. 'And we climbed on deck at last to take some air and were in time to see a miracle. For there, on either flank, flew birds with wings extending near four yards, facing down the gale with seeming tireless determination.'

'Are they our guardian angels?' asked my son and I thought that he was right, the more so for, as they veered away north to find another ship in distress, the sun broke through, and lit up all the underbelly of the clouds and reflected off the sea beneath. And the wind settled into one direction, and the fast scudding clouds became our outriders and our escort until around noon when we heard a joyful shout from up aloft where a crewman kept watch, while he clung to the crows' nest at the mast head.

"Land ahoy!"

'Oh! how we all scrambled to the side where he was pointing, you might think the boat would tip, but it did not, sturdy as it had already proved to be. We could but see the dimmest mounds at first, that broke the skyline and might have been dark cloud deceiving us, but becoming more distinct until it was clear that it was for sure the shape of solid land. Then did we cheer and thank the Lord and praise the Captain and his crew, all of us in joyful tumult knowing death defied and danger passed.'

There is a moment's silence before James speaks.

'What land was it, ma'am?'

'Africa, the continent of Africa,' I reply. 'Some two hundred miles north of the Cape of Good Hope where next we sailed, keeping always the coast in sight, until we could drop anchor in a sheltered bay and go ashore.'

'Was there no danger then?' Caroline wants to know.

'From the French, you mean? Oh there were several other ships and two men of war to protect us.'

'Oh,' she is surprised but continues with her original thought. 'I was meaning from local people, the Africans, the savages. Was they friendly?'

'Well, we landed at a town called Capetown, which even then was a well-established port, accustomed to receiving ships for the purposes of replenishing their stores. Indeed, I imagine it is to this service that it owes its origin. And it is inhabited by English and Dutchmen, the natives being their servants, or, more accurately I guess, their slaves, for I know not why else they would remain in their employ, so little did they seem to benefit from it.'

'My! Such a distant place to choose to live!' Caroline shakes her head. Her pity seems all for the benighted Europeans unwise enough to leave their homelands, and she looks at James with a small smile of satisfaction, I suppose at her superior situation.

'I am a little ahead of my narrative,' I continue. 'For I should like to describe our landing place as it is surely unique in the whole world. There is a mountain like a great table that so looms above the town that one feels it may at any moment fall upon one's head. But we heard that the local people sometimes for pleasure contrive to have themselves pulled up the precipice by means of ropes and pulleys to enjoy the land at the top, for it is a verdant place clothed in flowers and sweet-smelling herbs which affords magnificent views of the sea and countryside beneath. We did not ourselves stay long enough to avail ourselves of this diversion.

'However, once accustomed to the feel of firm land under our feet, (which, though most welcome, is a very strange sensation after the weeks of allowing for a floor that is constantly in motion,) we did explore a large garden in the town that was also full of flowers and delicious fruits. We ate there the sweetest grapes imaginable. Meanwhile, my husband accepted an invitation to inspect an English garrison on an adjoining bay whence we heard a fine cannonade salute as he approached.

'And then we met and walked the wide paved streets of the town, which seemed a paradise after our recent experience, and were invited to dine, together with our Captain, at the house of one lady, I forget her name, only that she was known as the Princess of the Cape. She was in the habit of entertaining weekly and we were fortunate to benefit from this hospitality. We met there another resident, a young married Irish woman, beautiful and courteous, who helped me arrange for our clothes to be freshly laundered, not before time. As you may imagine, the atmosphere below deck was quite foetid on account of the inadequacy of washing facilities and what things were washed did not dry in the salty air.'

Caroline is nodding sagely. I have in fact included such homely detail for her sake.

'However, I paid quite dearly for this service which gave me some surprise.'

Again she nods, as if it is as she would have expected of a foreign place and then we are all surprised by a loud 'Halloo!'

'Why, it is Charles!' I recognise his voice and moments later hear his approaching strides. He stops short in the doorway, astonished to find us so assembled and, perhaps, to see us all rise to our feet as if caught in some impropriety. My companions back respectfully away as he hastens forward to embrace me.

'What celebration is this? Are you wed already, Caroline? I thought t'was next week and I may be invited.'

'It is, sir, and you would be most welcome.' Caroline colours quite prettily and curtseys, which is unusual.

Charles bows in response, for he is kind and courteous, this son of mine. Yet how old he looks! Never tall, despite his size at birth, he appears shorter than I remember, having, I see this plainly, grown stouter. And his hair is surely thinner than last year and too carefully spread across his near- bald head. All this serves also to prove how old am I, but that is not what makes me sad. Does not every mother wish their children ever young? I remember that he has not met Mary and introduce them. Tongue-tied, she forgets to curtsey so, in part to cover her embarrassment, I tell him of our recent activities and that I was recalling our journey to England. He casts a cursory look at his allotted pile of his father's possessions, and says he will examine it the morrow. He is more interested in my story of our voyage.

'How old was I? Five? I wonder what I would remember. Perhaps you should tell me.'

'Do you not remember the angels, sir?' Mary's tone is urgent. 'The birds, sir, that you knew really was angels.'

Charles is bemused and I hasten to explain. Sadly he does not. He shakes his head.

'I do remember some things, Mary,' he says. 'The fish that flew! Do you remember, mother? Three or four yards high? And many fell in the boat and were eaten, but I would not eat them for I thought them magical but you said they tasted not unlike bird?'

Our listeners are doubtful until I nod my head.

'And waves like mountains? Though there perhaps it is a child's exaggeration. But the whales! Like great fish, four times as long as the biggest elephant in my father's estimation and throwing up huge plumes of water, fifteen yards high. They have to come to the surface to breathe, Mary, for they are not fish but animals like us. Captured by us for their fat and their bones.'

She knows this. 'I will never wear a corset for that reason,' she avows.

'You will when your waist is not so slender,' says Caroline and James eyes his future bride and laughs.

'And did you mention the ceremony when we passed the equator, Mother? I remember that. There were three sailors, daubed in red and yellow paint, one holding a book,' he proceeds to act the part. 'One a trumpet and one most extravagantly dressed as Neptune – god of the sea. And all the males on board were obliged to be cleansed of their sins in a tub of sea water.'

Now I remember. 'Your father refused, he thought it a ridiculous farce.'

'He gave them a gift instead.'

'Several bottles of brandy, so they were not displeased!'

'I also remember the black cliffs of St Helena, where Napoleon later ended his days. We moored extremely close to shore and I wondered why. The sea must have been very deep. And we visited some other islands where the sailors caught turtles and we ate their eggs. And once we thought we saw a French ship and the deck was cleared for action and I was disappointed it was a false alarm. Such excitement for a five year old boy!'

James is twisting his hat and looking at Caroline who nods. It is time for them to leave.

'Your room is ready, sir,' she tells Charles before turning to me. 'And we had a good clean all through and young Mary is well able to cook for two and I have laid in stores and Albert will do what heavy work is needed, so I hope that everything is adequate for I can spare no more time, 'tis unfortunate timing, and these books and all...' she is becoming breathless with her anxieties.

'Do not worry,' Charles waves away her apologies. 'We shall make shift together, I have no doubt. Off with you both and think only of the coming happy day.'

PART V

Betrayal

42

1853 Lower Beeding May

'This side of lamb is very tender,' Charles demonstrates how cleanly cuts the carving knife. 'Being quite out of practice I thought I would *mammock* it. Isn't that what they say in these parts?''

'I am surprised you remember.' I laugh as I take a mouthful, and then smile at Mary, who is standing behind his chair. 'I think it to be very well cooked.' She bobs her appreciation but remains in place, her hands clasping and unclasping, her smooth young forehead twisted in a small frown.

Charles turns and speaks over his shoulder. 'We have all we need, I thank you.' Still she does not shift.

'What is it, Mary? Did you need to tell me something?'

'Oh ma'am,' she bursts out. 'The shipwreck, ma'am. You was going to say.'

'So I was.'

'What shipwreck?' Charles' fork is arrested in midair.

'After we landed in England, when your father lost his goods.' Mary has edged closer, her eyes fixed on me. 'Come, sit,' I pat the chair next to me. 'Eat something. There is not much to tell.'

Charles lifts his eyebrows but cuts a slice of meat onto a small plate and places it in front of Mary. She nibbles at it while I speak.

'We reached the channel between France and England in late April and had the intention of putting first into the wide and safe harbour of Portsmouth, but received warning of a mutinous situation at Spithead. For the same reason we could not sail up the River Thames into London and so put into Deal, which is at the mouth of the river and almost on the North Sea.' I break off some of my bread and give it to Mary. 'We were, as you may imagine, mighty glad to disembark at last and eager to complete our journey. Somehow, I know not through what communication, we were met by a fine carriage sent by my husband's banker and transported at once in comfort to our destination. And I have always been glad of such an introduction, for it was May and the countryside was lush and fragrant, the county of Kent being similar to Sussex. Sweet drifts of blackthorn blossom along every hedgerow, carpets of bluebells under the unfurling beech trees… it was not as I had expected. And I never forgot, indeed it was my consolation when later in I was cold and wet and suffering from the smoke of a thousand London chimneys. So, all in all, we arrived at our lodgings in Great Portland Street in fine humour, and good health, my husband's having improved steadily as we sailed north.' I pause to eat some more.

'But then…?' Mary prompts me softly.

'Indeed.' I swallow quickly. 'Then we were safe but our ship was not. Somewhere between the port of Deal and the Danish coast it was capsized and sank with all aboard, I believe, making good their escape but with the loss of all its cargo, including my husband's possessions, which were not insured since we were travelling with them. I have never understood why our goods were not disembarked with us, whether by error or intent, but, as you may imagine, the event cast a very great shadow over our first weeks in England.'

'All those costly things,' Mary muses. 'For I found a list,' she informs Charles. 'Gone to the bottom of the sea. Maybe the captain thought to steal them for himself.'

Charles is becoming tired of the conversation. 'More likely he needed it as ballast to complete the journey and planned to ship it back in another vessel,' he asserts. 'In any case, Father got much of it back by employing divers and received compensation besides. I have seen the documentation, which he kept in full.' He pushes aside his plate and Mary understands and hastens to clear the table and bring dessert.

When she has at last withdrawn, Charles' face acquires a look of concern which I know well and which annoys me.

'And how is dear Cesarine?' I ask to forestall him. 'And Ernest, newly married and no doubt soon to continue the family line!'

'Well, all well, I am glad to say, and beg me to give their compliments as ever.'

235

As ever, I wonder what image Charles' large family can harbour of me, the foreign recluse they have never seen. Charles used to issue half-meant invitations to visit but I never accepted. He has received rightful recognition of his status and is happy, that is enough for me. I do not want to complicate his situation. And he should not interfere in my affairs as he seems set to do.

'Mother,' he begins, 'I am pleased to see you in such good health and having established so democratic a household regime which should serve your interests well.'

'However?'

'However, there are proprieties one should observe. Mary–

'Mary?' My tone is sharp, but he persists.

'Mary is young and untrained. You should not spoil her.'

'Mary is very young and motherless. She needs some care.'

'She will not learn her place.'

'Stop!'

'She may exploit you.'

'I will not listen. I do not care. She reminds me of your sister. She is the same age.'

'Ah.' He looks down, defeated as I knew he would be, though in truth this is the first time I have formulated my feelings so clearly, thinking only that I am grown fond of Mary. He holds up his hands in submission. 'I do not wish you to be hurt.'

'I know.' I reach to touch his hand. 'I shall retire and see you in the morning. Ask Mary to stoke up the fire in the library if you wish to sit and smoke a while. Sleep well, my dear.' I stand and bend to kiss his cheek. 'I am glad to have you under my roof again.' But he is wrong about the effect on his father of the sinking of the *Cronborg*.

1797 London May

'Another day spent waiting for some office boy to deign to do his duty.' My husband is again in ill humour. He is used to giving orders, not waiting on another's pleasure.

'Do you make no progress?' I hasten to help him from his outdoor garb to sit in greater comfort. The children have gone with Amrita to a park nearby.

'A little,' he sighs. 'I have hope of some trade off t'wixt shipping brokers and salvage company. But I expected London to be less convoluted.'

'There is corruption? Bribery?'

'Perhaps.' He shrugs. 'But enshrined to such a high degree they call it rules and regulation. Through which the newcomer must find a way. I daresay I shall yet require the services of lawyers and accountants and others of the parasitical professions to show me how. And I had not realised,' he sits up straight and regards me. 'How very large the Company, how great a part it plays in this nation's wealth. Come to the City with me tomorrow and you shall see.'

***

'This 'ere's the City,' our driver shouts. 'Where is it yer wan'?'

'Fenchurch Street,' my husband calls back. 'The new public house, the East India Arms.'

I have some time to inspect this City within a city for our way is congested with horse-drawn vehicles of many sizes and description, and persons rushing hither and thither across the street and in and out of the buildings on all sides. I watch in fascination, finding them exotic, as of another breed. Their clothes are mostly dark, their expressions intent and their eyes fixed ahead, though the day is fine and the sun shines even in these narrow chasms. There are important-looking men, coattails flying in their passage, most with retinues of boys to carry their papers and hurrying to keep pace. Young men, smartly clad and eager with ambition, dodge the traffic with practised ease, taking the stairs to office entrances two at a time, passing older men, some thinner and more threadbare, tired perhaps, yet quite as purposeful and at home, for this is their habitat too. It is a noisy place, the rumble of carriage wheels and the clopping of horses' hooves in concert with a constant shouting, shot through with frequent louder exclamations in protest at the way obstructed, and all accompanied by much thrusting and jostling.

We are passing a large stone edifice, quite plain though flanked by two equestrian figures, when our driver points with his whip and shouts over his shoulder.

'That there's bin East India House long as I c'n remember,' he says, with an air of fond proprietorship. 'But 'twas thought not grand enough for the Comp'ny's present status.' His voice seems to convey both disdain at the vanities of man and admiration at what he can accomplish. Pride also, perhaps, since he is an Englishman. 'Won't be long afore they've all shifted to the new which ain't far now... See,' he calls when we shortly turn a corner, 'That there's to be the new.'

The atmosphere becomes dustier, passers-by cover their faces with their kerchiefs and I wish I had my veil, for an entire side of the street is under construction.

'It is huge.' I am obliged to crane my neck to take in its full extent.

It is very long indeed and several stories high, of imposing grey stone with a portico supported by six great columns, above which some large sculpture is in final preparation. Our carriage is halted by a wagon loaded down with marble that, having halted at the entrance, is pounced upon by a swarm of workmen holding hods and shovels, who swiftly unload and transport the cargo to the interior of the building, where soon perhaps it will become the floor of some grand office at the very centre of the Company's great dominion.

'See that there sculpture,' the driver indicates aloft. ''Tis the King, see, George the Third, and his three accompanying ladies are Britannia on her lion, Europe on an 'orse, and the one that follows is Asia, on a camel.' He gives a brief laugh and seems about to say more when, perhaps noting my complexion, he stops and turns back to face the way ahead.

'There are few other ladies in this City,' I remark to Benoit as we alight at the East India Arms, which marks the end of the Company building. I spy only one in fact, an aged woman sitting on its step, a basket of flower posies in her lap. She catches my eye.

'Come and buy!' she shows a toothless mouth. 'Lilies-of the valley! Blood red carnations!' She sees that I am tempted.

Benoit takes my arm and hurries me on. 'You may see one or two, on business like ourselves. There are ladies rich enough on their own account to have investments.'

We pass a narrow opening between two buildings that is packed with men waving their arms and calling out, as traders do their wares. There is a strong and pleasant smell of coffee.

'They call that Change Alley,' he says. 'It is where much of the business of the City is transacted, in and out of the coffee shops, the selling of stocks and shares, the fixing of prices, the making and the losing of whole fortunes.'

'Yet where are the goods on which this wealth is based?'

I would ask more but know he is still bitter at the possible loss of his own, and feel also that he is near as perplexed as I at the whole proceedings.

'That is where we are going. Come.' We take a wider turning that leads into a courtyard, off which are alleys lined with shops and stalls selling all manner of daily requirements. 'This is the Leadenhall Market,' he says. 'Watch where you walk and hold close your purse.'

There is refuse and dirt aplenty and eyes whose business it is to watch for careless strangers as well as gullible custom. Yet on the whole, I like the place for it reminds me of the bazaars at home. There are other women here, both selling and buying, and there are items that I should like. I turn aside but my husband scarcely slows his pace.

'This is a short cut.' He urges me on until we reach the far side of the market and turn a corner. 'There,' he stops and points. 'That is where the Company stores its goods.'

It is astonishing. A complex of towering buildings six stories high, that occupy an entire block of land, thus forming the sides of several streets. Viewing it from what appears to be the front, I lean so far back that I am forced to clutch my bonnet to my head, yet still cannot quite see to the roof.

'It is vast.'

'This particular building is the original, known as the Bengal Warehouse, constructed about twenty five years ago,' my husband tells me. 'The rest has been added in the last few years. The whole being constantly packed full of cloths of every kind, ivory tusks, a myriad different spices and chests of Chinese tea.'

There is indeed an endless stream of labourers pushing trolleys, loading and unloading wagons that are laden with bales and boxes and chests, entering and exiting the building in so constant and regular a fashion that one might almost be watching a mechanical device.

239

'Do you smell the spices?' I close my eyes and inhale deeply. 'Cinnamon, nutmeg, cloves and something else...'

He sniffs several times then takes a deeper breath. 'It is myrrh, I believe. A welcome antidote, is it not, to the other smells of dust and sweat and animal excrement and rotting vegetable matter. London is not so clean as Calcutta.'

There is scorn in his tone which I do not understand. 'This building is surprisingly elegant for one with so simple a purpose.' I point to the rows of windows that are generous in size and in pleasing proportion to the whole. 'It certainly seems built to endure.'

'Then perhaps its purpose is not quite so simple.' Benoit's face is grim. 'Do you not think all would be as impressed as we are and think how rich and powerful the Company must be? And will remain? How much confidence that must inspire in its investors present and future? And, with its sister building, can you now see how the Company bestrides the City and be the less surprised if its stocks are the belweather for the rest of the market, its fortunes determining those of the whole country. For so I have been told.'

I remain silent, still wondering at his black mood, he who has always been the Company's friend, but he continues.

'How little space would all my goods have occupied in that place.' He sighs. 'How paltry is my wealth.'

Now I understand and hasten to cheer him. 'But you are one individual, this the common repository of the possessions of many, where you may yourself choose to invest when you have retrieved your fortune, as you will.' And he has moneys previously sent to London, I know, though do not now remind him.

'I may,' he corrects me, but pats my gloved hand nevertheless. 'Perhaps you are right,' he adds. 'Though I begin to think that the climate of Europe may suit my health more than my temper.'

'Oh, I daresay in very few months you will feel quite at home here.'

As shall I, I determine, unless, that is, he decides we should return to India. I have made my home in many places and shall do so again in London.

43

1853 Lower Beeding May

'Is London much changed, Charles?'

We are breakfasting together, our table set by the window, the morning-room awash with sunlight. He sets down his coffee cup to consider.

'Since my visit last year? London is ever changing and growing fast. Taking in more villages in its surrounds - not that I ventured from the centre.'

'I rather meant – I was thinking of when - '

'When you last lived there? Oh Mother, that was near fifty years since. Of course it has changed. There are many more theatres with facades like Italian *palazzos,* covered shopping arcades and great museums, the National Gallery and splendid housing developments west of Regent Street. Elegant terraces around and over-looking Regent's Park. Horse busses, trains, the docks so greatly enlarged to enable a vast increase in trading.' He breaks off. 'How many times have I offered to take you to see for yourself? Especially when there was the Great Exhibition in Hyde Park. One may still visit the Crystal Palace in fact. Perhaps I will bring some of my family and you can meet at last.'

'I am much too old to travel so far.'

'We will see.' He does not pursue the matter. 'I do remember some things from those days,' he says instead, I know to please me. 'We used to walk from our first house to a park, which I know is now Regent's Park. Do you remember?' It is not the first time we have revisited this scene, perhaps he thinks I have forgotten.

'Marylebone Park. To feed the ducks and swans upon the lake.'

'And I did not believe you when you said I should beware, that swans though beautiful, can be fierce and break a man's arm with a sweep of their wings. And one day there were baby swans and I would go too close and Ann...' He breaks off, unsure now how I shall respond.

I close my eyes tightly. 'Go on.'

1797 London May

I hear birdsong, ducks quacking, the whoosh of swans landing on the water and children's voices laughing. They have run on ahead of me.

'Beware the swans, Ali,' I call. 'They have big beaks.'

'Like peacocks,' he calls back laughing, though the swan hisses and, rearing on its legs, flaps its wings.

'They're not a bit like peacocks, silly,' says Banu, pulling him back.

'Their wings could break your arm.'

'I'm not frightened.' He shrugs her off.

I have almost reached them. 'Ali! Stop!'

Banu catches hold of his coat though he continues to protest. 'Papa said so,' she tells him firmly.

'Papa's right, Ali.' I reach them, quite out of breath and behind me hear a horse approaching at a canter. 'They wouldn't dare break Abba's arm,' he asserts, arms akimbo. The horse stops close by and he turns. 'Papa!'

'You have found some fine amusement! The countryside in the city!' He does not dismount and addresses us from on high. 'Do you think they wear sufficient clothing, Helena? And you, you are shivering I think. You must buy some good thick English clothes. Ask Mrs Blane to assist, she will know what is best.'

'I did think you would bring a carriage,' I explain.

The horse paws the ground and tosses its head.

'Mama said we could drive and see the street lights when it is dark,' adds Banu.

'Another day, *ma petite.*' He has forgotten that he promised. 'Be a good girl and help your mother with your little brother.' And he clicks his tongue at the horse, which begins to sidestep away from us. 'I have business to attend to. My application for naturalisation, to see some schools your Uncle William recommended, for you must go to school. And arrangements for your baptism.' The horse mouths its bit. 'Charles and Ann. Will you like your new names, children?'

'Why must I have a new name, Abba?' Ali asks, but his father has turned away.

'When may I expect you?' I call out.

'Late, my dear Helena, I am going to the theatre, with some new acquaintances. Do not wait supper for me.' He cracks his whip and the horse breaks into a trot.

'Why must I have a new name, Amma?' Ali looks up at me, his eyes dark and troubled.

'Because Papa says so.' Banu is upset too. 'Don't be a goose.'

'I'm not a goose.' Ali's face turns red as he tries not to cry. 'I'm not, Amma, am I?'

'And Maman has a new name.' Banu is relentless. 'Helena, after our French grandmother, Helene. And Bennett, after how the Irish said Benoit. Helena Bennett.'

'Grandma isn't French.'

'Our *other* grandmother. Honk, honk!'

Ali screams and tries to hit her. 'Stop it! Stop it!'

'Yes, do stop, Banu. And please remember that your French grandmother is no longer alive. Look, children, see how fast your father rides.' I crouch between them and point across the park where the horse now gallops away from us at full speed, then put my arms round them both and hold them close.

'Where's Papa going?' Ali sobs.

'Hush, Ali.' Banu is again his kind sister. 'Look at the heron. Do you remember the herons in India?'

I shiver and stand up. 'Come children, it is getting a little cold.'

Ali protests at once. 'I don't want to go.'

'We are going to see Mrs Blane.'

'Auntie Begum!' His mood is transformed.

'You may just call her Auntie.'

243

'And then are we going to the shops?' Banu takes hold of my hand and pulls. 'And shall we see the street lights?'

'Auntie Begum told me she will get a puppy. Can we have a puppy?'

This is Ali, who has taken my other hand and is pulling in the opposite direction.

'Oh children. Yes, no, I don't know.' How I want to please them both.

1853 Lower Beeding May

Charles has taken hold of my hand. 'And then, or maybe it was another day, our father came a'riding by in great haste upon a black horse and said we must change our clothes and go to church and change our names.'

'That was certainly another day when you were baptised.' And I was not there. 'I am sure we should have had more warning to prepare for such a ceremony. But you are right that he announced it in great haste.'

'Did you mind, Mother? Being given such a fabricated name? I have often wondered. So has Cesarine.'

Has she, indeed. Somehow I did not expect ever to have occupied her thoughts. Perhaps we should have met. I think back.

'I believe I found it preferable to '*Mrs Begum*' which had been my title until that point. Mrs Madam. It is inelegant, do you not think? And besides, I was eager to accommodate my new country where I was already finding enough to make me feel welcome. Acquaintances from India who included me in their invitations to visit. Your cousins, William and Mary, to whom I had been so close when they were small. I was so very happy to see them again. Do you remember the first time we went to visit them? We took a boat from Westminster Pier down the Thames to Greenwich, such a lovely place with the Palace so elegant on the banks of the river and the parkland rising up behind with the King's Observatory at the top. I could quite understand why their step-mother did not wish to leave London.'

1797 London June

'So I told him, if you wish to go to India, go, but leave me here with the girls.' Sarah Palmer sets down her cup on its saucer and reaches to pat my hand. 'I am sure India has its attractions but I have found London an altogether pleasant place to live.'

'Greenwich is certainly splendid.' I respond. 'It rather recalls to my mind the city where I used to live. Lucknow.'

She raises her eyebrows but the name appears to mean nothing to her.

'Where William and Mary also lived.'

She inclines her head and looks across her elegant sitting room to where William stands in earnest conversation with my husband and Mary sits on a couch, with Banu on her one hand and Ali on the other. I follow Mrs Palmer's gaze and admire anew my dear nephew and niece. William is seventeen, strong and good-looking and in other company but my husband's, would look tall. Mary, who seems to have already overcome my children's shyness, for they are competing eagerly for her attention, is very pretty, her dark hair gathered high but for several artful curls that frame her face. I guess this to be the fashion for her stepmother affects a similar style, if with less pleasing result.

'Well I trust that they too have been most happy living with me here in their school holidays.' She smoothes her gown, which is of a muslin that is surely of Indian origin. Indeed, most of the European ladies I have seen appear to wear our fabrics. 'Have you not?' She raises her voice to address her stepchildren.

I do not greatly take to my brother-in-law's first wife, finding her manner artificial and this is not, I believe due to loyalty to my sister. But I daresay she puts a brave face on past difficulties and is discountenanced by our meeting. In any case, it would seem she has acted beyond her duty in providing hospitality to her stepchildren and they seem to like her. Mary calls across to her in friendly assent to the question, while William crosses the room, kisses her hand and bows.

'You have given us a second home, dear second mother, and a most tender refuge it seems to me after the rigours of military academy.' He steps back to include us all in his subsequent speech. 'And Mary and I are filled with joy to be able to welcome you to London.'

How proud my sister will be of her son and daughter when she again sees them, I think, but how cruelly deprived of their company has she been all these long years while they were growing. Whatever difficulties I may face in living here, I shall not suffer that.

'I have been discussing my future with my uncle,' he tells us. He has two more years at the Royal Woolwich Academy and then intends to return to India. 'Since I cannot follow in my father's steps, my uncle has offered me his most valuable advice and assistance.'

He refers to the laws passed most recently by the Governor General, which prevent the sons of mixed racial parentage from entering the Company service. Benoit has already helped many such young men by recommending them as recruits to one or other of his officers. He now claps William on the shoulder. 'Your parentage will yet stand you in good stead with any Indian prince.'

'And he speaks Persian as well as he does English,' Mary tells us. 'I only wish the same were true of me.'

'I shall be extraordinarily obliged of any introduction that you may make on my behalf, Uncle,' William bows again. 'And endeavour to acquit myself in a way that does you honour. However,' his eyes take on a determination quite at odds with his deferential demeanour. 'Since I am entirely certain that I could never emulate your great achievements, I think I shall not remain a soldier for long. I shall try my hand at business, perhaps with my dear cousin's assistance.' At this point he smiles at his stepmother and I understand that he refers to her son, and my step-nephew, John in Calcutta. 'And uncle does not think me ill-advised.'

Benoit shrugs. 'In a situation of such constant flux it is hard indeed to know in whose service one might best prosper. And my own career, of which you are kind to speak so highly, turned on as many incidents of good luck as judgement. And business is most certainly a surer path to fortune than soldiering.'

'If I shall make a fortune it will be honestly, Uncle. I know Father and you were great friends of Mr Hastings but on this point Mr Burke is surely right. Our Indian society is every bit as civilised as that of Europe, and in their pursuit of wealth Europeans have no right to destroy it. I wish to live there and make my contribution.'

246

'I too,' Mary speaks up. 'Although I suppose I shall have to marry someone first.'

'Bravo, both of you,' says Benoit. 'Although,' he addresses William in particular. 'Hastings too loved India as does your father. And I. But it is difficult to serve two masters.'

'Papa, if William and Mary are going back to India shall we also go?' Banu wants to know.

He smiles and turns to her. 'I think it very likely,' he says, and her little face alights with happiness. 'But meanwhile you and Charles must begin school. You have stayed at home long enough. I have made arrangements.' Both children look apprehensive. 'Ann shall go to Miss Eliza Barker's in Hammersmith.'

'Which is my school also,' says Mary.

Banu's expression is instantly transformed. 'Oh, if Mary is there then I shall be perfectly happy to go too,' she says and I feel the first loosening of the ties that bind a mother to her children.

44

1853 Lower Beeding May

'Did I not go to the school that cousin William had attended?'

Charles pushes aside his plate at last. I have long finished my breakfast but been happy to see my son enjoy a hearty meal. I stand and move towards a pair of armchairs by the window that looks onto the garden.

'Let us sit in greater comfort.' I sit in one chair and Charles takes the other, stretching out his legs in perfect relaxation as we resume our conversation.

'Yes, it was Mr Clarke's School for Boys,' I agree. 'Your uncle, William Palmer, recommended it. Which was a reason for me to begin to feel more settled in this country since I wished to remain close to both of you. In fact, I think at this time I felt much more settled than your father.' I speak lightly but Charles begins to argue.

'Now it is you who misremember.'

'I do not think so. Several times he said that he wanted, even intended, to return to India.'

''Tis wishful thinking, mother.'

'I remember clearly.' I am becoming a little impatient. 'And besides, there was less for me to return to than him. So much was changing already in Lucknow. My mother wrote to me that Asaf-ud-Daula, the Nawab, had died at an early age and his son, being of a less cooperative cast of mind, was then deposed within months and his elderly uncle put in his place. By the British, who, as a condition, received half his kingdom. It was a sign of greater changes to come. It was ceasing to be the city I had known and loved. Marriages like ours became less acceptable, their offspring also.'

None of this means very much to my son. 'Father obtained British naturalisation, Mother, in January '98. I have seen the document. He intended to stay.'

'But he did not find the way of life in London suited to him,' I insist. 'He told me of his visits to London clubs where he saw English 'Nabobs' returned from India drinking and gambling away small fortunes in a night. It was entirely hostile to his temperament, as you must know. Especially since some of them had gained their wealth through private deals whilst in the Company employ, despite Mr Hastings' attempts to stamp it out.'

I should not have said this last, for it means even less to Charles, is ancient history and unnecessary to my argument.

He remains adamant. 'My father never spoke to me of such things.'

'Well, I was there and you were not, not at an age to understand, that is.'

There is vitriol in my voice and I know I must stop. I love my son, he is all that I have left. I lower my voice and try to explain.

'Your father was a soldier, a great commander of men, he had been at the very centre of events, wielded great power and influence. How could he be content with polite conversations in coffee shops and drawing rooms? Surely I have told you how in India he held durbahs like a king, where other kings and princes were glad to pay him court? And how he sometimes called you to sit beside him and you were dressed in silks and gold and wore an embroidered turban like a little prince. And how the first time you were afraid and did not want to go...'

1794 Koil December

'Amma, I don't want to go.' Ali wriggles and twists in my arms as I try to fasten the diamond pin which holds the shawl in place over his shoulders.

'Hush now, be still, Ali, you must look your finest for your abba.' I hold him more firmly between my knees and adjust his little turban-styled cap, which is a small copy of that which his father is wearing today. 'There now, does not your suit feel soft and smooth? Do you not like the colour?' He turns his face away from me and frowns as I continue. 'What colour is it, hmm? Red? Purple?'

'Blue.' He mutters, still sulky, staring at his feet, presently sheathed in the finest leather worked with gold thread.

'Blue like...mmm, the sky? Or...'

'Uncle William's eyes?' We have played this game before. 'Or - a peacock?'

'Yes, yes! Clever boy.' I kiss his cheek and hug him. 'And you are beautiful as a peacock. Come now!' I lift him in my arms and hasten out of the chamber towards the great hall where my husband gives audience.

Ali clasps me tightly round my neck. 'You are coming with me?'

'Only to the entrance, *beta,* I cannot go further.'

He begins to cry. 'I won't go alone.'

'Hush, hush, I will be watching, with Banu and Gulzar chachi. To see what a big grown up boy you have become, helping your father with his important business. Look, he is coming to meet us, so dry your tears quickly before he sees.'

'Come, Ali.' Benoit takes him from me and they walk hand in hand up the red carpet to take their seats side by side upon cushions on a raised dais at the far end of the hall. And then I climb to the gallery and, together with Banu and Gulzar, watch from behind the jali as a great many local nobles, or their ambassadors, arrive and salaam first to Benoit and then to his sahibzada, his first-born son and presumed heir, before taking their seats on mats spread for them around the room, where they make a splendid impression in their finest apparel of every rich fabric and many colours.

They present nuzzurs of gold or silver to my husband, who takes it off the cloth on which it is laid and places it on a low table before him. Some give smaller offerings to Ali, who, I see with pride, quickly learns to touch them with his right hand as a sign of acceptance before his father places them also on the table in a growing heap. I am proud also of my husband's bearing, for it is as courteous and dignified as that of the Emperor himself.

1853 Lower Beeding May

'You told me many stories,' Charles is obstinate, and I find myself cajoling as of old.

'And the prince for whom your father had fought was fast falling foul of the British, for he was young and poorly advised, and he begged your father to return. And would not at first appoint a successor. So naturally your father was most tempted to return to a position of such importance in a country long his home. Which he did love and whose history might in fact have been different had he returned. Yes!' I see I must insist. 'Others have said it. It is not my prejudice.'

'But he didn't return.' Charles speaks as if he holds the trump.

'Because he met Her,' I scream. 'There, now you have made me mad again as you have long thought me.' I heave myself to my feet and stumble from the room, calling to Mary as I reach the stairs.

'My pipe, Mary, quickly my pipe.'

1798 London Spring

'I have met with an old friend whom I have not seen these thirty years, not even knowing if he still lived.' Benoit's joy is infectious.

I laugh. 'Thirty years? Before even you went to India?'

'We served together in France, in the Regiment of Clare before I went to the Russian Army and our ways diverged.'

'An Irishman?' I have some memory of my husband's history.

He nods. 'Daniel O'Connell. *Comte* Daniel O'Connell,' he corrects himself.

'How so?'

'It is a long story, longer perhaps even than he has to me imparted, but, having received from the French King the '*honneurs du Louvre*', which includes playing cards with the Queen and the Dauphin and riding in the King's carriages, it seems, perforce, he required a title.' Benoit laughs loudly. 'And he has married a Frenchwoman, a widow and a Comtesse in her own right, and knows

251

many of those here who have fled the Revolution. And tonight he has invited me to dine.'

'I am glad.'

I speak sincerely and remain glad for him, even when these evenings alone become more frequent and spill into the days, and the occasions when I accompany him become infrequent. But visits to Mr Angelo and his large family do include me. They live not far from us in Howland Street, Soho. I also attend the christening of one of his sons, Warren Hastings Bennett, named after both my husband and Mr Hastings who are the child's godfathers. Mr Hastings remembers me.

'How is my dear friend William Palmer? Soon to receive his proper recognition at last with his appointment as Resident in Pune. And his lovely wife, your sister?'

Mr Angelo watches with disapproval writ large upon his florid face. He does not like me being accorded such favour and we do not like each other any the more for our increasing familiarity.

Some days I go visiting alone, having been very happy to find Dr and Mrs Blane returned from Lucknow, and through them have formed one or two new acquaintances, with John and Mary Walker in particular. Mary is of my age and has a son Michael who is six years old like Ali, or Charles as I must now call him. We are watching them play together with a large set of tin soldiers together with Mrs Blane's two slightly older boys, while Banu-Ann reads in a window-seat, story books being her new passion. At some point today I have misaddressed both my children.

'Do not take too much mind.' Mrs Blane sees my difficulty and perhaps senses some unhappiness. She pats my hand. 'Your children will fare better here with English names. And no doubt begin to correct you.' She hesitates. 'You know we have formed the intention of moving from London? Well, we have found a place, Wickfield Park, it is to the west of England, near both Bristol and Bath I believe. You must all come and visit us there and perhaps, Nur my dear, I shall not call you Helena unless in company, you may find a property nearby for I know your husband has expressed some interest in having a home in the countryside.'

'I think he would prefer the space and freedom that it would afford,' I agree. 'He could certainly keep more horses. I think I

252

would like it also, London being a great deal dirtier and noisier than I imagined.'

But one Sunday morning I hear him singing in the hallway below, surely for the first time in many years, and, still unbathed and in my dressing gown, descend to find him tying an unusually colourful neckerchief round his collar, whilst considering the reflected effect in a looking glass. His face is flushed, his eyes glitter.

'Are you well? You don't have a fever?'

He turns, startled, and frowns. 'I never felt better. I have been invited to a music party with the O'Connells.'

'How I miss hearing music.' I speak without thinking.

'This is not your sort of music,' he retorts, much more sharply than he need. 'It is French music, you would not enjoy it.'

'Oh, I did not expect to be invited,' I quickly respond. But I am wounded nonetheless as I see how distant he has become and how little he cares for my feelings.

At this moment the front door bell is rung and he opens it himself to admit his friend. Daniel O'Connell is tall and slim and dressed in style. As he steps over the threshold he spies me and sweeps off his tasselled three-cornered hat in a low bow, revealing long fair hair tied behind his head in a ribbon. He walks forward to kiss my hand, appraising me with startling green eyes slightly narrowed. I think he finds me plain.

'*It is early morning,*' I want to say. '*I am not yet properly dressed.*' I say: 'I am very happy to meet so good and old a friend of my husband, Comte O'Connell.'

He bows again and smiles. 'I hope you are finding London agreeable, *madame*.' He is handsome, perhaps a few years older than my husband, has a kind face, and, according to Mary Walker, a good reputation. He seems about to say more but my husband has become impatient.

'We should leave,' he says and, without meeting my eye, takes his hat and walking cane from the stand beside him, turns his back and is gone from the house, leaving his friend to make a hasty and apologetic retreat.

'Au revoir, madame, enchante.' He replaces his hat and wheels away, in a small flurry of swinging tassels.

253

Watching the two of them hasten down Great Portland Street, arms round each other's shoulders and chattering like schoolboys, I wonder if perhaps I should acquire some French to facilitate my own participation in London society. But Daniel O'Connell does not again come to the house and, it seems to me, that for the next few weeks my husband contrives to avoid me almost entirely, until I think I must confront him and ask for an explanation. Yet am I utterly confounded when he tells me of his own accord.

'I am shortly to be married,' he announces. 'To a French girl, Adele d'Osmond. I shall make a financial settlement for you and the children. Mr Angelo and Mr Richard Johnson will be my agents in all such matters and help you find alternative accommodation.'

1853 Lower Beeding May

'Oh Mother, I am sorry.' Charles has come to find me in my bed. 'You were in such good spirits that I was only trying to stop you once again dwelling in the past.'

It is insufficient excuse but I am willing to negotiate our appeasement. 'It is just that I think you misunderstand how greatly was I injured by your father's rejection,' I say. 'It was so sudden, his decision already complete. And so soon after we had come here. Why did he bring us, if only to abandon us? Can you not imagine?' Perhaps not, I think, since your own marriage appears to have been so entirely contented and fulfilling.

'It was better that we came, was it not?'

'For you, yes, and for this I have always been thankful.'

'And Adele is not all bad. She has always been most charming to me and Cesarine. And trusted me with her financial affairs.'

'I do not wish to hear of it.' I hold up my hand, thinking he might show more sympathy. But I am determined to let nothing further spoil our time together. 'Enough of the past indeed!' I sit up from my pillows. 'Let us dine together and tomorrow I shall accompany you to Caroline's wedding.'

45

1853 Lower Beeding June

'We should purchase a more comfortable conveyance, perhaps a cabriolet, as you appear inclined to remain in the countryside,' remarks Charles as he drives us to the church next day.

Since we have not yet discussed the matter of my moving this time, despite my fears, he must base his opinion on his own judgement of my condition and find it satisfactory.

'I must say,' he continues. 'That I have always felt most content on returning to this corner of the world. I have such pleasant memories of holidays spent here.'

'You were indeed happy to have a proper home at last. And we have the Walkers to thank for that, it was they who said that land hereabouts being at that time cheap, the turnpike not having reached it, your father should purchase a small estate and settle us more comfortably.' I do not miss this opportunity to remind him of his father's earlier unkindness.

'I took a walk early around the grounds in Silver's company and found it all in good repair,' he says.

So he has been spying on me, in order to assess my competence, I think, but say only: 'I have good tenants, on the whole. And I consult John or Michael if in need. Or Pitfold Medwin, in Horsham.'

'I saw John and Michael in London, they send their greetings.'

'And Mary?'

'She was unwell and confined to bed, but she too sent her love to you.'

'I shall write to her. The Walkers have always been good friends to me.' *Especially in my hours of greatest need. It was to Mary*

Walker I wrote as soon as my husband had left the house after telling me of his forthcoming marriage.

1798 London May

'You must stay with us,' Mary states. 'From this day.'

She has come immediately on receipt of my note and finds me still sitting at the window whence, only one hour since, I watched him walk down the street and away from me for ever.

'Oh Mary, I did not expect – I only sought your sympathy and advice. What am I to do? Why did he give me no warning?' My voice breaks and I am again helplessly weeping. 'How can I deserve such cruel treatment?'

'Hmmph.' Mary stands and pulls the bell cord to summon Amrita. 'We shall not stand by and see you so dishonoured. And meanwhile you shall let us care for you and give you a home as long as you require it.'

Amrita comes running. She too is in a state of confusion, her comfortable situation thrown into doubt.

'Please pack your mistress's bags,' says Mary. 'I will send round for them later. The remainder of your possessions,' she turns to me, 'and those of the children, can be collected at another time.' And she sweeps me off in her carriage to her fine house in Russell Square.

1853 Lower Beeding May

The trap stops with a jolt as we arrive at the church. Charles ties the pony to the fence and helps me dismount and we walk up the path and into the church together, arm in arm. Caroline's family and friends turn and acknowledge us with respect and, for once, I feel I have a rightful place in this world which for so very long I have had to face alone.

I am glad I have come to see Caroline in all her glory. She is radiant as a bride should be and fairly glides up the aisle on her father's arm, her gaze locked to that of her future husband who awaits her at the altar steps. She wears a deep blue gown that lends grace to her sturdy figure, and will be serviceable on many occasions after this day, and her hair is dressed higher than normal in a most becoming fashion with a coronet of lilies-of-the-valley. She carries a simple posy of the same and leaves a trail of their sweet scent behind her.

1798 11th June London

The heady perfume of the bouquet of pink roses carried by Charlotte-Eleonore-Louise-Adelaide d'Osmond, known as Adele, reaches me in my place in the small curious crowd that has gathered outside the Church of Saints Anselm and Cecilia in Lincoln's Inn Fields. We have watched her alight from her carriage and take the arm of her father, the Marquis d'Osmond. Her slender figure is swathed in creamy silk that is elaborately ruched and ruffled round her shoulders and bosom, leaves bare her slim white arms, cinches her tiny waist in a sash and falls in frilled flounces to the ground. Her abundant yellow hair is half piled in curls on top of her head, the remainder cascades down her back. By chance she catches my eye for a moment as she passes. She does not know who I am, nor even perhaps of my existence.

I would think her pretty as an angel but for her expression, which is of extreme pride and disdain and especially unpleasing in one so young. She is seventeen, my age when he married me. Which was less than a decade since, though none would guess from my present appearance, wrapped in the dowdiest dress, in an old woman's bonnet that covers my own lustrous hair and shadows my still unlined face.

I have stood here and watched as the guests arrived in their finery, learning their identity from a well-informed bystander. A bishop to perform the ceremony, an archbishop to whom the bride is related, dukes and duchesses, marquises and marchionesses, counts and countesses and Louis XVI's Controller of Finances, all of whom have fled France following the fall of that regime. I myself recognised our ex- Governor General Sir John Shore and his wife, now Lord and Lady Teignmouth, who are surely guests of my husband. And I saw Him enter also, in some kind of military garb, with a fine cocked hat and accompanied by Daniel O'Connell. The architect of my misfortune, for it was he, I have heard, who negotiated the marriage settlement. The fatal invitation, however, to the music party was procured by Richard Johnson, one of those appointed by my husband to look after my interests on his behalf.

Dear Mary Walker has found out all. Mademoiselle Adele is to receive a dowry of £2,500, an income of £500 per annum for her parents and he has given her a diamond ring worth £110 and other jewellery besides. Also a grand piano from Broadwood's, for it seems she is musical too, my successor; she was amongst the singers on that fateful Sunday morning only six weeks past, singing with the one-time music master to the Queen of France no less. Once again he fell in love with a voice - if he ever loved me. He has been heard to say that he is in love for the very first time. This I overheard Mary tell John. They think he has lost his senses. Should this make me feel less despised and cast aside?

Monsieur and Madame de Boigne are to live in Portland Place in a large house on which he is expending much in refurbishment. I am to receive £200 a year plus expenses for the children, who are each to receive a generous sum that invested, will later afford them a reasonable income. Mercifully, I am entrusted with their care. Or, more likely, he sees no place for them in his new life. Filled with such bitter thoughts, I wait with my fellow onlookers, who are mostly old women, for the end of the ceremony to see the newly-wed couple emerge. I imagine I can hear each pledge their troth.

'*If any man can shew any just cause why these two may not lawfully be joined together let him now speak or else hereafter for ever hold his peace.*' No doubt there is silence. No-one considers me a just cause, though there are those there who know me. The Blanes, God bless them, declined their invitation and have now left town, though not before Dr Blane declared the bride's nationality proof of his long-harboured distrust of 'the Franks'. The Walkers tried to persuade me to let a famous lawyer argue my case, but I refused. If my husband wishes to leave me, then why would I wish to prevent him?

'I require and charge you both, as ye will answer at the dreadful day of judgement, when the secrets of all hearts shall be disclosed, that if either of you know any impediment, why ye may not be lawfully joined together in matrimony ye do now confess it.' He is silent. I am no impediment. Let God be his judge.

'Do you, Benoit, take this woman to be your lawfully wedded wife, to have and to hold, from this day forward, for better for worse, for richer for poorer, in sickness and in health til death do you part?'

'I do.'

I see him turn to her, hold out the ring that seals their union and place it on her left hand as I clutch my breast thinking my heart must break at last.

1853 Lower Beeding June

Perspiration beads my forehead and moistens the palms of my hands. I am breathless, near fainting, I need to be outdoors. As I rise to my feet, Charles raises his eyebrows and begins to stand, but I wave him back, hasten from the church and collapse on the surrounding stone wall of some family tomb.

'Ma'am? Are you ill?'

I hear Mary Piper's voice but the face I see, though very similar, with its calm dark eyes and red-brown skin is that of an old woman. I close my eyes in confusion and open them again to see both Mary and, from their close resemblance, surely her grandmother, gazing deep into my face. I had not noticed them in the congregation.

'No. Or perhaps yes. I was remembering –'

Mary's grandmother nods as if she knows exactly what ails me. 'Funerals is similar,' she says. 'They brings back other such.' She reaches into a pocket, extracts a phial and holds it to my nose while Mary gathers leaves nearby and presses them to my temples.

'Is she recovered?' My son appears, his expression a mixture of concern and annoyance.

'Twas the closeness of the air, sir, in the church,' says Mary as her grandmother fans me with the end of her shawl.

It is a convincing show and Charles' displeasure subsides as the church doors burst open and the congregation spills forth and lines the path.

'Come then,' he takes my arm, 'We should salute the happy couple.'

They emerge, Caroline and James, he blinking in the sunlight, a little dazed, she the very picture of happiness as they parade before us. Someone hands round a basket of flower petals of which I take a handful and cast it over their heads in blessing. When They passed by I threw dead blossom that I had scraped from the ground and cursed him for his desertion.

'Well, Mother, we have paid our respects. What say we find an inn at which to dine so that Mary may remain for the wedding breakfast? I have a fancy for some English roast beef and those batter puddings in gravy that can only be found in this country. And tomorrow I propose we seek the benefits of sea air and take the train to Brighton. It is some time since I went there. And you too, I daresay.'

46

1853 Brighton June

The sun is warm on our faces as we drive the few miles to Balcombe station, the breeze a caress on our cheeks. The trees are in full leaf, even the oaks, clad in a light bright green that almost dazzles. Swathes of white marguerite daisies cloak the banks on either side of the lanes, and intermingle with dense clouds of cow parsley pierced by pink and white campion and, more rarely, patches of purple orchid. Yellow iris sprout in ditches and, on every pond, water lilies begin to unfurl. If I should step down and inspect more closely I know I should find any number of smaller flowers, scarlet pimpernel, blue periwinkle, trefoil and clover, vetch and ragwort....

'It is a beautiful day.'

Charles smiles. 'It is how I remember every day when I was young and used to roam here.'

'And I feared for you, for it was wilder then in these parts. We were quite cut off from the world, with the Aldridges being one of very few families of standing.'

'I feared for you when later came so many temporary labourers to work on the reclamation and the parish was said to be a place of open fornication and incest.'

'I recall. But it was exaggeration. None troubled me.'

***

The gleaming engine pulls into the station, announcing its arrival with a great sigh of suppressed steam. How General Martin would have enjoyed these new marvels of the age, machines that can pull carriages in their train sufficient to carry a hundred persons and more. I was less impressed on my last trip, for then the evidence of construction was recent, the cuttings raw, the embankments ugly intrusions on the landscape. In so few seasons has nature made these features her own. Whole trees have taken root or been planted, and, beneath them, low growing shrubs and wild flowers and grass entirely green the chalk and mud scars that had so grieved me; whilst travelling high above the landscape gives almost the illusion of flight, without the dangers of false wings or inflammable balloons.

I gaze across treetops, with a bird's view of woodlands, see fields of half-grown wheat, oats, barley - it is hard to tell at such a distance - buttercup pastures where cows and horses graze, deep meadows surely almost ready to be mown for hay. Summer in the countryside is a busy time of year and everywhere there are folk in carts heading to market, others walking along rutted tracks and hedge-lined paths between farms and cottages, carrying implements, sacks and baskets. Yet others bend and crouch in fields of fruit or vegetable, picking, weeding, digging, every one of them intent upon their task, unconcerned, or so I hope, by the spying eyes of strangers.

Sometimes we pass on viaducts over entire villages and are afforded a moment's glimpse of scenes which, for the inhabitants, are entirely familiar and may indeed encompass their whole lives. So superior and detached a viewpoint I find a little discomfiting after a while, but my spirits rise again as we approach the northern face of the glorious sweeping rise and fall of the South Downs. When travelling by road, I used to anticipate that moment when we reached their crest and the sea filled our forward gaze to the very horizon and the heart lifted to meet the over-arching heavens. Our train heads heedless into the dark entrails of the earth to arrive, by a number of cuttings and smaller tunnels, at our destination.

The road down from Brighton station is steep; not so long ago it was a place of open grassland like the surrounding Downs where sheep graze in their hundreds, rabbits burrow and chalk-loving plants like sea thrift, scabious and harebells thrive. Now our way is lined with elegant tall buildings housing shops and apartments and rooming houses and we walk on paved pathways raised above the road.

'Do you remember how we used to be obliged to descend from our carriage lest it should run upon the horse in front?'

Charles nods. 'And again on ascending if the gradient was too extreme. But sometimes the driver let me take the reins and himself would walk.'

'Oh see now,' I point ahead. 'How improbably high does the sea appear to rise between the buildings, as if it must flood down upon the land. Though one knows 'tis but a trick of perspective, the illusion is hard to shift. What?' I catch Charles looking at me, a small smile curling one corner of his mouth, which broadens as he speaks.

'Only that your remark recalls to my mind my younger children. They enjoy a novelty of perception that dulls with age.'

'It is a while since I saw the sea.' I am pleased that I amuse him. It is a very long while since our relations were so easy.

'Perhaps you should enjoy a change of scene more frequently.'

His tone is thoughtful, but changes the subject as we reach the seafront.

'East or west?' It is always a point of consultation and usually a matter of little preference. Today however, Charles has a mission.

'I should rather like to visit the Baths and discover if they are still in operation since Din Mahomed's sad demise,' he says. 'I had intended to visit his London establishment and enquire but found no opportunity.'

We turn to our left, the east, whence it is an easy stroll towards the pier where once we came to see the Queen disembark. The tide is at low ebb, revealing wide expanses of flat sand where herring gulls patrol and search for worms. It is a little cooler than inland but very pleasant nevertheless. After some hundred yards we stop at an edifice several storeys high, built at an angle to the seafront and newly painted in large letters.

MAHOMED'S WARM COLD AND VAPOUR BATHS

A sedan is drawn up outside, windows are open and several ladies and gentlemen stand on balconies gazing out to sea.

'Perhaps one of his sons continues to manage it as well as the establishment in London,' I say.

'Arthur,' Charles replies. 'Perhaps. I should like to discover. Will we enter and enquire?'

'You go,' I urge. 'Let me sit here someplace in the shade. If perchance the widow is there, then I shall come and pay my respects.'

I find a bench against a cobbled wall and gaze down over the banked up pebbles of the beach to the sunlight glinting from the gentle ripples of the sea. To my right, a number of fishing vessels are drawn up on the stones, and behind them is a row of black wooden huts in front of which a few fisherfolk mend nets and gut the day's catch. To my left there is loud shouting and splashing from a group of hardy boys, who leap continually into the water from a harbour wall, only to race back up the beach and repeat the exercise. Directly ahead, I know, lies France but the horizon appears limitless and I can believe it stretches straight to India. In fact, of course, one would sail west, down the channel separating this island from the European continent and retrace the course that brought me here.

It is a very long time since I considered whether I might return, but here, with only water dividing me from my homeland, I feel anew the attraction and I wonder if Din Mahomed ever felt as I, looking out across these waters every day. Perhaps not, for he was so well settled with his Irish wife and so very successful. Shampooing Surgeon to the King! Who would have predicted such achievements when first he came here? Surely not even Mirza Abu Taleb Khan, who met him in Ireland on his way to London and visited me soon after, as he had promised he would, it seemed a lifetime since, though it was but three or four years. It was when I was living in rented rooms above a shop on the corner of Wardour Street and Oxford Street, the unfashionable end of Oxford Street.

1800 London

'Din Mahomed is a very fine man and well set up already in a town known as Cork, with a most respectable Irish wife and several children,' Abu Taleb opines. 'And Dublin is an even finer city, with such brilliantly lighted streets and chemists' shops with glass vases filled with differently coloured liquids that quite put me in mind of the windows of our Imambara, and parks for recreation, particularly Phoenix Park, that made me sensible of the just sentiment of the English gentleman in India, who considers that country as merely a place of temporary sojourn and have their thoughts always bent upon retiring to their native land. And though I found that I could only keep warm by walking several miles a day, I am convinced of the beneficiality of the climate to the temperament. It inspires valour over hardships, encourages the pursuit of immortal fame. One cannot be idle, the mind does not wander.'

'Is everything here to be preferred in your opinion?' I interrupt at last.

Abu Taleb looks around my shabby sitting room as if it is this upon which I have requested his opinion, frowns briefly, shakes his head as if to clear it and then considers, forefinger to his lips. He does indeed look stronger, more substantial, perhaps because his clothing, while of our style, is of warmer stuff, some thick embroidered brocade and he wears a fine woollen shawl draped elegantly around his shoulders. But, his beard being clipped to a narrower frame, his face too appears fleshier while his moustaches have been allowed a little growth so that they take an imposing upward turn. Abu Taleb is enjoying his travels.

'I neither understand nor approve of this predilection for erecting statues in every square, of generals and politicians. It seems to me to be approaching idolatry,' he says at last. 'Do you know, one statue sold recently in London for forty thousand Rupees and it had lost its head and all its limbs! But this is a trifle. London is as full of delights as I expected and I have to say that I am exceedingly well-treated, being much invited and sought after in the highest circles, including those of Royalty.'

I make appropriate expressions of surprise and admiration.

'Some think me a Prince,' he laughs. 'Which as you know is indeed one meaning of 'Mirza'. And I do not go too far to disabuse them of this notion, while the few Indian ladies like yourself, who have accompanied their husbands and children on their return to England, are doubtless too kind to unmask me. Do you know Mrs Ducarrol? Why, she is so fair and so accomplished in all the English manners and language that I was for some time in her company before I could be convinced that she was a native of India. This lady introduced me to two or three of her children from sixteen to nineteen years of age, who had every appearance of Europeans.'

I do not know this lady and had had few meetings with any such before my husband's desertion rendered me indisposed, if invited, to social gatherings. But Abu Taleb does not wait for a reply.

'I have decided to write a full account of my travels upon my eventual return to India,' he says with a smile of satisfaction. 'Din Mahomed has already written a book containing some account of himself and some about the history of India. Just now I am composing an ode to London...'

I cannot begrudge Abu Taleb his success, for his journey was prompted by grief and desperation. I know from one of my mother's letters that, not only has he lost his much beloved son, but also, upon the death of Asaf-ud-Daulah, his position and all means of income which had the further unhappy result that his family and retainers all but abandoned him. I do not quiz him on this and he says only that he was most grateful to accept the invitation of a friend, a Scotchman, one Captain David Richardson, to accompany him to Europe.

And yet I cannot help but see the contrast to my own sorry situation. I have long removed from the home of my kind friends the Walkers, though I still visit, and been forced to dispense with the services of Amrita (an acquaintance of the Walkers has taken her on until she should find a return passage). My rooms are small and draughty, the air entering being full of London soot and the endless noise of passing traffic. I am ashamed to receive visits from any but my closest friends and family. And my impressions of London are principally gathered not from glittering social occasions, but from long and lonely walks through the streets and squares of the city. Perhaps these do enable me to withstand hardship, for I contrive to put a brave face on my undeniable misfortune.

'Please tell my dear mother, when you see her, that you found me well,' I tell Abu Taleb. 'My children are often with me and make excellent progress in their schooling. I have good friends who make me welcome in their society.' And, for more general consumption, in case he should converse with others about our meeting, I add: 'My situation is quite sustainable due to the General's provision.'

After he has left, I take a walk which seems to prove my argument for, in almost every doorway, after the shops have closed, poor wretches make their temporary home and sleep, and many of these are my countrymen, *lascars* often enough, too old or ill to find employment. There are men and women, servants and *ayahs*, who, like Amrita, found a one way passage but no return, or were promised a ticket home but then, on arrival, denied the necessary funding, and yet others whose employers, sometimes of many years standing, have died. I stop sometimes to hear their stories, give a few coppers if I have them, share tidings of 'home'.

One dark and rainy afternoon I am walking home from some small errand when a woman's voice calls my name and there in an alleyway see Amrita, huddled in a filthy blanket, her once rounded features drawn and dirty.

'Come home with me.' I help her stand. 'And stay some nights.'

'They threw me out,' she relates her story, between mouthfuls of potatoes in gravy. 'Your friends' friends. Saying I did not work hard enough.' She becomes indignant in the telling. 'They only had three servants and expected me to do all the heavy work, the fireplaces, even the chamber pots.' She shudders at the memory. 'I said '*I was a lady's maid*' but they said t'was immaterial and bade me leave.'

Her story is common enough. 'Servants here cost more to employ,' I tell her. 'Which is why I have none that live in. Could you find no other situation?'

She looks away and is silent for a moment. 'I met a man,' she says at last. 'A Bengali, a *lascar*, who like me, planned to better his situation before marriage. He said why did we not put our assets together for two can live more cheaply than one, until we should find a return passage.'

'You were to marry?'

She sighs. 'I thought so. For many weeks he went daily to the docks to make enquiry until at last he found a place, on a ship that was leaving the next day for Barbados. Of course, on such a voyage there was no place for me. But he said not to fret for he would make enough profit to buy our passage home and off he sailed, never to return. But that wasn't the worst of it,' she speaks before I can console her. 'For I was expecting his child, though he did not know it.'

267

'Where is the baby?'

'Oh it died,' says Amrita. 'Soon after birth, it was a sickly thing and I was ill also, for many months. Better I had died with it.'

'I will help you as I can,' I say and find her a place in a respectable hostel where she may do some sewing to earn her food. I can scarce afford the cost but soon it is unnecessary, for one day when I visit she is gone. One of the other inhabitants says she left on the arm of a man and I pray that it is her *lascar* and that her story will have a happy end.

Oh I am certainly more fortunate than many.

1853 Brighton June

'Mother?' Charles has returned. 'Forgive my long delay. When he heard that I am having some pains,' he points to the top of his left arm. 'Arthur, whom I know – it is his brother Horatio who now manages the London baths and I have promised to visit him when next I am there – Arthur insisted I try some new herbal massage.' He rotates his shoulder with caution. 'I think it is better.'

'I have been comfortable,' I assure him. 'But now I am hungry. It must be the sea air.' Indeed, a wind has picked up and the sea is running in and the sand has almost disappeared.

'There used to be an oyster bar not far from here.' Charles takes my hand and leads me down a passage so dark and narrow that one might easily pass it by. The walls on either side are so close that we must go singly.

'This reminds me of bazaars in India,' I say. 'I should not like to come after dark alone.'

'Indeed,' laughs my son. 'For likely as not t'would be smugglers you would meet, carrying in their moonshine and other illicit goods.'

I am accustomed to rest after the midday meal, but when we have eaten Charles has a fancy to see the Royal Pavilion once more and it is but a short walk.

'Surely this also reminds you of India?' says Charles, as we survey the white plastered domes and minarets and elegantly sculpted entrance porch. 'I think there can be no other such in England.'

'It does, but less so since I have learnt the resemblance to be superficial' I say. 'It is what Caroline would call a "mock beggars' hall".'

Charles laughs. 'I have no doubt she captures her meaning precisely but am quite unable to guess what it might be.'

'A building that is grand on the outside but inside quite mean and inconvenient.'

Charles laughs again. 'Ah! Well, that rather fits Cesarine's opinion of Buisson Rond, which is grand in its outward aspect but has remarkably few rooms in which one can actually live. But I hardly think that can be true in this case.'

'The Queen found as much, by all accounts.'

'She too has a large family,' he acknowledges. 'And, one imagines, has more need of bedrooms than luxurious banqueting halls and music rooms. For there are such - ' He breaks off in embarrassment. 'I saw them when I came here, soon after it was built.'

'Which was soon after your marriage, I recall, and when you were on one of your first business missions for your father? Which, by chance, was when She was here, the invited guest of the Prince Regent. I recall you telling me in some detail when you visited me soon after.' I am unkind but, after so many years, jealousy and hurt can still provoke my anger.

He flushes and attempts some defence. 'She was here only as the companion of her father, who was then French ambassador at the Court of St James.'

'And is also your Godfather, though I was not invited to that ceremony. But come,' I take his arm and propose a diversion to change our mood. 'Let us take a carriage ride along the shore. I should like to gaze some more at the ocean before we must return. This has been the happiest day. Thank you, my dear.'

And yet, when our train emerges from the tunnel and the long line of the Downs is behind us I find myself glad enough to be going home and say as much to Charles.

'I know that you have long since preferred the countryside to the town,' he says with caution and I guess what is upon his mind and interrupt.

'Oh indeed! When living in London I used to visit the British Museum only in order to look out from its windows, for it gave a glorious vista of rich meadows and verdant fields all the way to the villages of Highgate and Hampstead, which were just visible upon the hills. No doubt it is now all built upon.'

He nods, pauses and resumes his intended speech. 'There may yet however come a day when you will need to ...'

'Hush, I know, but pray that I may die before that day.' I hold up a hand to stay his protest. 'It must be said. I am past eighty years old. But thanks to your company, today feel very well indeed, despite our exertions.'

I settle more comfortably into my seat and look from the window as the train leaves a cutting with a hiss and a whistle to travel along a long viaduct that affords a wide view over farms and fields and woodland, all suffused with the clear golden light of a midsummer evening. A distant deer turns its gilded antlers to watch us pass.

'Look!' I turn to Charles to share this sight but find he is asleep, his head dropped to his chest, his mouth slack, and so, left alone, my thoughts return again to the past. How tired I grew of London's soot and grime. And of living under such close scrutiny by my banker.

47

1800 London

'What is this, Nur Auntie?'

Mary Palmer, my dear niece, is visiting. She leans over my shoulder where, seated at my bureau, I am attempting to reconcile my accounts before visiting Mr Angelo. As I must every month, more if I have a special request, as when I wished to visit the Blanes last summer and had not money enough for the coach. Which I did obtain, though not before I had endured a sermon on prudent living, a subject on which Mr Angelo prides himself an expert, though I am sure it is from necessity, not choice, and on account of his ever-expanding family

Ann is sitting in the window seat nearby, learning some French grammar. She has her eyes closed and only her lips move as she silently rehearses her lesson. At ten, her face has lost its childish curves and one can imagine her as the young woman she will all too soon become. Mary takes the notebook from under my nose and proceeds to walk about the room reading aloud and growing more indignant by the minute.

'18 requests for pocket money 3 shillings; a penknife 1 shilling; a pair of gloves 3 shillings; prayer books and Christian doctrine for Miss A.B. one and sixpence; a great coat for G.P. 1pound 1 shilling; 25 times coach to take Miss A.B. to school 10 shillings and sixpence; bisquits for Miss A.B. 1 shilling; 25 oranges for G.P. 1 shilling....what? Must you count every orange?'

'Well, there is an additional allowance for George Polier when he is with me. Currently he has entered a House at his school and comes to me only for the holidays.'

'And if you or Ann or Charles eat one of George's oranges? It must be hard to keep such close account.' She tosses the book back in front of me. 'How much is He spending on that fine house in Portland Place? And is he not planning to buy Clive's palace at Esher? And what about all their travelling? For a beginning, there was £169 for a chaise and a further £82 a short while afterwards to paint it.'

'How do you know all this?' Ann asks sharply.

'Which adds up to much more than your annual income, Auntie, I do believe.' She turns to Ann. 'People gossip, Ann. And many of them think that your mother has been harshly treated. And, Aunt,' she turns back to me. 'My father wrote of his great surprise that this Mr Johnson is one of your accountants, for it is the very same person who was recalled from his position as Assistant Resident at Lucknow for business mis-dealings, on account of which, and a short time after, he was also recalled from his next position at Hyderabad. And my father knows this well because he was sent to Lucknow by Mr Hastings to investigate suspicions of corruption amongst Company officers. But I do not think he will tell General de Boigne, whom he has always held in such high esteem.'

'My father has made a most generous settlement on Charles and me,' Ann protests. 'For when we are of age.'

'I am glad,' says Mary. 'But meanwhile, your poor mother has to live in inferior accommodation and count her pennies. Surely you can see that. It is not the life to which she has been accustomed. It is wrong.'

She stamps her foot in emphasis at which Ann throws her book to the floor and confronts her with tears in her eyes.

'Perhaps my papa requires Mr Angelo to keep close account so that he may not be cheated and can see that his money is being spent as he intends,' she asserts and runs from the room.

Dear Mary, she has always taken my part and even refused to go to her cousins' christenings though her own father requested it; while William, bless him, on hearing of my deserted state, wrote that if he were only in England he would challenge the General to a duel.

'Oh Mary, I shall miss you.' She is about to leave for India, this will be one of our last meetings. 'But I think you should go after your cousin for there is reason in what she says also.'

272

'You do not receive enough, Auntie. That is the principal fact of the matter. But I will go.'

I watch her tall slim figure leave the room. How could she not be handsome with both her parents so good-looking? She has her mother's delicacy, together with her father's bearing and a determination all her own. Her parents will be filled with joy to see her once more, but I wonder how easily she will fit in to their life there again and whom she will marry. My sister has written with pride of her son's return.

'William, Captain William Palmer, has taken the place in the Hyderabad Finglas battalion vacated when one William Linnaeus Gardner, friend of my husband, and also having an Indian wife, left to join Holkar's forces. These are now ranged against those of the young and, despite my husband's best efforts, impetuous and ill-advised Peshwa in Pune, whilst the young Sindhia is apparently so lacking in principle and understanding that he will surely not long retain his position. These two young men between them cause my husband endless trouble and mortification.'

She wrote also that the entire Mahratta alliance is in danger of falling apart, which will certainly affect the position of the British. Indeed, she said it is what Wellesley in Calcutta hopes for and, very likely, actively encourages. I daresay my brother-in-law conveys a similar analysis to Benoit, who has apparently quite recently again indicated his intention of returning to India. *'Perhaps he intends to bring you with him?'*

She expressed her continuing dismay at my husband's defection, but her principal concern for the moment appears to be the liaison between James Kirkpatrick, the Resident at Hyderabad, who is my brother-in-law's great friend and ally, and a young girl whom Faiz has befriended. This girl is closely connected to Ministers of the Nizam, broke off her engagement to another and has already given birth to James' daughter. It is becoming quite a scandal, but one that seems very remote from my situation, almost to take place in another world.

I am much more affected by her other news: General Martin has died, before even he could move into his splendid new house. I write immediately to Boulone with my condolences. Joseph Queiros is to buy the old house, which pleases me since he was ever my friend.

Mary returns after some time, arm in arm with Ann, who runs to me and kisses me on the cheek.

'Oh Mama, I am sorry for my ill humour, only I have had to listen to so many slanders against dear Papa at school.'

'Oh?' Both Mary and I are surprised.

'That he is a secret supporter of Napoleon. That he behaves like an Oriental despot and mistreats his wife ...' She breaks off in confusion. 'Not that I care for her, only...'

'No, you are quite right to take issue,' I soothe her. 'Firstly, he was and always will be a friend to the British and does not consider himself a Frenchman, of that you can be quite sure. As to the other-', I must suppress my secret joy, 'I guess he is not accustomed to the niceties of European manners, having been so long in the East. And perhaps Madame de Boigne is ignorant, if not careless, of this circumstance and acts in ways that make him jealous.' I know very well, from my great ally, Mary Walker, that Benoit has stormed out of at least one of Adele's singing performances for just this reason.

'I have heard that she is far too closely attached to her parents, to her father in particular, on several occasions has returned to live with them, and that this is the cause of much discord,' says Mary. 'One would think,' she raises her eyebrows disdainfully, 'That a girl of her age should understand that her first duty is to her husband.'

'Poor Papa,' Ann sighs. 'He is not happy.' She sits down suddenly beside me and leans her head on my shoulder.

1853 June Sussex

The train comes to a sharp halt at Balcombe Station. Charles still sleeps, his head now resting on my shoulder. I shake him awake and we clamber from the carriage just before the guard blows his whistle and waves his green flag. When we have retrieved our pony and cart from the inn and are on our way home, Charles apologises for his lack of company on the train.

'I don't know why I am so fatigued,' he says. 'Perhaps it is due to the sea air.'

'Or perhaps the massage?' I suggest. 'No matter. I have been enjoying some memories.'

He looks at me askance, with some suspicion.

'Of your cousins, William and Mary. And my sister. The letters she used to write.'

'I have found some letters,' says Charles. 'Amongst my father's papers which I thought I should put into some order for Ernest, who has said he should take on some of the management of the estate.'

'What letters?'

'A great deal that will be of little interest to you, his business contacts, his Le Borgne relations, issues relating to his many philanthropic activities in Chambery... '

'And?'

'I have brought some. I will show you. Letters from myself, one or two from you.' He pauses. 'And one from Ann.' He switches the pony on its flanks. 'Gee up, Beauty. We want to be home before it is dark.'

'Let us read them tomorrow. It has been a long day. And I will find any still in my possession to show you.'

***

There is only one and, though it is some years since I have read it, I know precisely where to find it, in the smallest drawer of my bureau. It was written on June 1st 1801 from Caernavon in Wales, during a period of reconciliation with Adele. It is addressed to 'Mrs Beggum, corner of Waldour Street, Oxford Street London.'

'My dear Beggum, Not having been able at my departure from London to take leave of you knowing that it would distress you, being near a month that I left Town I will not delay any longer in giving you of my news, well persuaded that you will be glad to hear that I am in good health and good spirits. Yet if I flatter myself your enjoying the same blessings, I shall still be more happy in having my wishes for your Wellfare confirmed by your own hand as also that our children Charles and Ann are very well, few things in the world would afford me more enjoyment believe me than to see them to

employ their earlier days in improving their mind and their heart that they may be, when grown up, a consolation and happiness to you, will be to me the greatest satisfaction I may be permitted to enjoy in this world; may my vows and my wishes on that score be realised! -

I will not recommend you, my dear Beggum, to give your earnest cares and attentions to their principles, yours having always been those of a good and well behave woman, they could never be under a better guardian and monitress than you, so I am perfectly easy in regard of it when at home as also in regard to their health as you have been always to them a good mother, they will, when in age be sensible of it and prove in return to be dutiful children to you in being the comforts and supports of your old days. So it shall be, I have seen you a good daughter to your mother, an affectionate wife to me and tender mother to your two offsprings, God will reward you as he is always just towards the deserving and who are in fear of him and place their confidence in all his great good ness and mercy –

No doubt you'll have been agreeably surprised when informed that I was to travel in England, instead of going to the continent as I intended, as it would be to long to relate was I to enter into the causes and details of it, I will content myself in saying that I am a little more happy than I had been for these three years past, yet I am afraid it will never turn out to be a lasting happiness; may the will of God be accomplished as he commands our fates with a heart full of gratitude we must abide to his decrees and bless him even in our misfortunes –

As I don't expect to return to London before six months at least! You must in all cases of emergencies both in regard of you or children apply to Mr Angelo who has always been one of your best friends and best wisher as he was ever to me. Believe me he will always be ready to help you when necessary, I know his good heart and readiness to oblige his friends. –

My love to the children when you see them; be careful to keep them in remembrance of their father, I have a right also in their love and affections, I would be jealous and excessively mortified was you to possess them alone and my self nothing, you see that I take care of my due!

If you write to me, direct your letter

To General de Boigne
Post Office Manchester –
You'll observe however that it must be before the 15th inst. Otherwise it would not reach me as I would have left that town –
Keep your health, Be happy? And believe me with most sincere affection for ever
Your friend Bt. De Boigne

48

1853 Lower Beeding June

'My father had such faith in Mr Angelo.' Charles has been reading his father's letter over breakfast which, the fine weather holding, we are taking in the orchard. Small fruits are already clearly visible on the branches, I think it will be a good harvest this year, of plums in particular, even though, as ever, many will fall before they ripen.

'Perhaps because he knew him from India.' I take another sip of the fine China tea that Charles has brought from London. I do not wish to start another argument.

Charles frowns. 'I began to distrust him as soon as I became more closely involved in my father's affairs and started to discover that Mr Angelo told so many lies.'

'What are you saying?' My tea spills in the saucer as I hastily set down my cup and turn to him. 'Why did you never tell me?'

'At first I thought it concerned only his business dealings. There was a particular matter of bonds issued by the Prince. Mr Angelo and his partner continually asserted that it was impossible to learn anything of them, but I obtained them by making a few enquiries from the Stock Broker and going to the vaults of my father's bank. Father left such matters in my hands from then on.'

'I never liked Mr Angelo. Nor he me.' I can scarce contain my excitement at finding my long ago prejudice upheld.

Charles takes a small bundle of letters from his pocket. 'But then I found these. My letters to my father, there are few enough. See what you make of them.'

The first is dated August 7 1806 and written from Old Hall Green, near Pucthiridge, Hertfordshire, where Charles had been a student at St Edmund's College for perhaps five years, as had five or even six of Mr Angelo's own sons. There are enquiries after his father's health, assurances as to our own and that of 'our friends', and a list of the subjects he is taking (Latin, French, Greek, Dancing, Drawing, Musick and Arithmatick.) Then there is a paragraph which, even at this distance in time, wrenches at my heart. '*I cannot help entertaining a disagreeable apprehension that I have incurred your displeasure, or maybe it is because of your indisposition...*' It was evidently a long time since he had heard from his father, which, given the circumstances of that time, seems especially unkind.

The next, of 28th February 1807, acknowledges some 'favour' of the previous October for which Charles writes that he has no words to express his gratitude, avows his love and respect for '*the best of Mothers,*' which his father has clearly recommended, and asks for guidance on his future career, although his teacher has told him he is free to choose for himself. And then he writes: '*Mr Angelo continues his friendly attentions to my mother and myself. It would be ungrateful of me not to mention this circumstance.*'

I look up to question this but Charles indicates that I should read on. In September 1809 he bemoans hearing from his father '*seldom, very seldom*' and hopes he is not being *presumptuous* in sending his own news. For he was to finish at school the following year and must choose a career and '*though you have by an almost unexampled goodness left that choice to me*', he wanted advice. Soldier or statesman? This boyish point of view makes me laugh.

Charles smiles. 'Only then did my father suggest the law as another choice, and tell me that was what his own father would have had him follow.'

In the next letter Charles writes of his sadness at not having seen his father for '*8 long years*' and hopes that he may visit when he has finished his studies, '*though I know it is almost impossible for me to hear from you.*'

'I thought it because of the war,' says Charles. 'And perhaps it was, for it is true that my father called me to him very soon after the Battle of Trafalgar. But look!' He holds up another sheaf of papers.

'These are mainly letters from Mr Angelo to my father,' he says and proceeds to point to particular passages. 'In 1799 Mr Angelo requested a loan of £1000 so that he could buy a House at Eton College for his wife to run. I do not know if he received it. In 1807 he thanks Papa for the settlement of £60 per year on his son Bennett Warren Hastings, who has obtained some Company post in Bengal, and asks for help to get a 'writership' for another son. Then he goes on to say that I am doing well at school etc. but, although he will not draw more than £100 a year on my behalf, "*he is not a boy, your cloths would not be too big for him."*'

Charles laughs. 'I think he means he would, in fact, like additional funding for my support, but really, Mother, on the grounds that I was as large as my father? My father always being of such exceptionally tall and broad stature? Mr Angelo goes on further about my having a Room of my own and becoming at Christmas a Rhetorician – I do not know why that should cost more – and concludes that though one hundred is not enough he will not draw a farthing more. What do you make of it, Mother? It was not I asking for more, I can assure you. And listen to this. In the same letter: "*not having before any opportunity of sending you any letters of your dear Charles, I enclose them in this, and take away the covers for to diminish the parcel.*" And so that he could read them? Disingenous, do you not think? Scheming perhaps? No wonder my father wrote to me so little, particularly if he had formed the impression that I was a spendthrift.

'In 1812, Mr Angelo tells my father that I am unhappy not to have heard from him in response to my three letters and that my "*distress was great*" and he *ought to "gratify"* me with a letter. A few months later he is saying that he himself is "*upset that you think I might be disguising misconduct on Charles' part. He has had extra expenses, I hope to be able to give you receipts but no more than £300 per annum. I had to draw it rather than interrupt his studies.*" Then he recommends sending me a little more in recognition of my good behaviour! You see how he manipulated our relations. I am only thankful that my father's own good sense and paternal feeling prevailed.'

'Yes indeed. So you think he also cheated your father of money?'

'It looks like it, do you not think?'

I remain silent for some moments as I try to reconcile these newly appeared representations of the past with my own recollections, but find it too much of a puzzle to unravel in one sitting. I seize on the most immediate implication. 'I wonder if he similarly misrepresented me.'

Charles nods. 'It is what I was led to question also, and with great sorrow,' he says, as he shuffles the papers and extracts one.

'It was written in 1807, there is no month given,' he says before beginning to read aloud. "*Mrs Bennett: she is very well in health and has now taken a house at Enfield; since the death of her dear daughter she has not been the same woman, wandering and distracted, and expending more than what is necessary and what she ought. All my advices have been useless and in vain and at the same time she calls on me for pecuniary assistance and friendly advice. I wish you would write to her and give her a little advice. Perhaps she will be more attentive.*"'

'Oh Charles,' I can barely speak as the memories of that terrible time near overwhelm me. Wandering and distracted? Oh yes, I wandered constantly, day and night, attempting to distract my thoughts from my grief or tire myself for a few hours of blessed sleep, however tortured by dreams it might prove. And more than once my wanderings led me to some bridge, where I considered whether to consign myself to the fast-flowing, cold waters of the Thames, and only the thought of Charles left alone in England called me to my senses. Of course much of the time I was not in my right mind and going to live near Charles' school seemed my best hope, I had such need of his company. Yet all that Mr Angelo could care to relate was of my supposed extravagance...

'How cruel!' It is anger that leads me at last to clarity of expression. 'I could almost weep anew! To think he so lacked in sympathy for my plight that he saw the limit of his duty in calling your father's attention to the fact that I was apparently spending unwisely! Most particularly when, as he knew well, I had several times written to your father begging him to satisfy my creditors but, receiving no reply, thought him careless in the extreme. But was perhaps too used to being cast aside to find it remarkable and too afraid to anger him in case all payments ceased. Now I think perhaps your father did not receive these requests.'

'I know, Mother, I have formed the same opinion.' Charles looks swiftly through the letters and finds the place. 'Listen! This is your letter to my father of August 20 1806:

"29 Newland St. My dear Genral! But once more I take up my pen to enquire after your health to which I sincerely hope you enjoy perfectly well. Nearly 12 months and not receiving an answer yet I had many unpleasant thoughts but enquiring at Mr Angelo and always finding that you are well so therefore I must conclude that my writing have given you a great displease but my dear friend you could answer it my letter – and only to said that was not your wish to do it. Certain you must know that I did not demanded you but ask of you as a favour which was according to your desire to let you know of my wishes which you did so strongly mention in your last letter. But I see how easy it is to say than to perform it. But I must confess tis not your fault, but they are not my own seeking, but as will of providents."

I am not sure of your meaning there, Mother.'

'Nor I. Perhaps I was making some excuse of my sad situation as account for my apparent bad management of my finances. I seem to have accepted it as my fault.'

'And not that of some agent handling your affairs!' Charles scans the rest of my letter. 'It seems you had incurred debts through taking the lease on the house in Newland Street which you had repeatedly begged my father to discharge, for you had nothing to sell to raise money but some old furniture, apart from the lease. *"I don't doubt I would get some money for the lease if I will sell but yet I sincerely hope you will not let me be homeless again …"'*

'I don't care if I live only on bread and cheese,' I murmur, remembering even as Charles reads. *'And to have a comfortable home for my dearest child who enjoys so much thinking this our own not that going over the shops in lodging…'*

Charles smiles at me fondly before reading on. 'And then you tell him about how well I am doing at school, that I am a credit to him whom everyone knows as his supporter and how you hope he may soon see you himself.' And listen to this, I don't know if it makes me more sad or angry to read it: *"I shall write you 2 double letter in every post day till I have answer….let me beg of you to spend 5 minutes to write few lines…I remain my dear friend yours for ever H Bennett."'*

'Poor young woman.' I sigh deeply and Charles looks up in surprise. 'It is all so long ago I can hardly recognise myself in these words,' I explain. 'And my English has most certainly improved since then!'

'Thank God you had real friends, Mother, in the Walkers and others who soon secured your removal here. For I do not think my father would otherwise have understood the necessity of you being properly accommodated. I have read your other letters to him also, after Ann...'

'Let me have them? And Ann's also. Then pray excuse me for I would go inside and read them alone.'

***

When I am installed in my chamber and have called on Mary to bring my pipe, I take up Ann's letter in trembling fingers and kiss the page on which she wrote so long ago. I see that Charles has thoughtfully added a translation, for she had written in French, and begin to read.

"May 17 1802". To an address in Paris that I cannot decipher. She first enquires as to his health and that of *'my dear uncle'*- Joseph, I daresay, for I know he was in London for their baptisms. She continues:

'Maman is astonished not to have yet received your news. Every day she waits for a letter. I am still at Mrs Barker's at North End (Hammersmith) and am very well and happy there. You should know, Papa, that nothing would make me happier than to hear from you. My brother is well as is Mama and send you their best wishes. Please give my aunts and uncles my regards. Accept my dear father, all due respect and believe me to hold you in the most tender affection, Your obedient daughter Ann Bennett.'

I do not remember if she read this to me before it was sent but, on turning it over, see that I have added a hasty message on the back. *'When you write to me don't direct at Oxford St because I am going to take house in the country.'* And yet I did not, not then. I wonder also why he kept only this letter from his daughter for there must have been others. And then I begin to remember and understand that perhaps it was this letter that changed his heart and might have mended all our lives.

49

1802 London Summer

Mary Walker has called me to her house, warning that she has unexpected news. She is seated on a low couch, bids me sit beside her and regards me gravely. In anticipation, I clench my fists in my lap. Not so long ago she told me she had heard that, Benoit and his new wife being yet again estranged, he had sold Portland Place, she had gone back to her parents in Brompton Square and he was in a mood to end his life. Since then, however, I knew he had travelled with Joseph in Germany, where he had appeared to be having a lively social life, and was currently living in Paris. Perhaps he is ill.

'There is news of my husband?'

She nods, and again pauses.

'Is he well?'

She takes a breath. 'The General wishes to know if you will go with Ann and live in Savoy where he has recently bought a large chateau.' She consults the letter he has written her. 'It is called Buisson Rond, at a town called Chambery.' She puts down the letter and regards me, clearly uncertain as to my response.

It is immediate and quite without premeditation. I clasp my hands to my breast as my heartbeats quicken, a surge of joy courses through my being and I feel I should prostrate myself in praise to the Almighty who has steered my husband to his senses and delivered me from my abandonment. I can scarcely speak. 'When?'

Mary is surprised, I guess expecting more query, more discussion. 'Oh well, I daresay... John!' She calls her husband, clasps my left hand in hers and addresses him when he enters. 'Dear Helena wishes to know how soon you may arrange the passports.'

'My dear!' he comes closer and kisses my hand. 'I am very happy for you. In fact, it is Mr Angelo and Mr Richard Johnson, who are our principal agents in the matter, but I shall assist wherever I may.'

I am so eager to inform Ann that I decide to take a coach to Hammersmith that very day. Called from her class, she arrives as anxious as I felt so few hours since, kisses my cheek and is puzzled at my glad expression, then turns ecstatic as she understands why I have come.

'Oh Mama!' She throws her arms around me and kisses me many times before standing back. 'Can it be true?' And then, ever sensitive of the sentiments of others, and perhaps expecting some fear or reticence on my part, she asks: 'Shall you be glad also?'

'Oh yes,' I hasten to assure her. 'It is the fulfilment of my deepest desire, but, having long since abandoned hopes of reconciliation, I do find it hard to believe.' Indeed, during the journey I have thought how impossible I should have thought this turn of events so short a time ago. I have also had time to consider some practicalities which have a little tempered my initial bliss. 'Only it is an entirely strange country and I do not speak their language.'

'I will teach you mother.' She stands in front of me, a hand on each of my shoulders, she is already almost as tall as I, and for a moment, seems the elder as she gives me reassurance. 'Or perhaps I shall no longer go to school but have tutors at home, with whom we may both study. And, oh Mama, we shall be together, and with dear Papa also.' She clasps her hands to her breast and whirls away from me to gaze from the window, as if at this new and glorious future.

'And shall you expect me to study your romantic novels also?' I join her at the window and put an arm around her waist. I am constantly teasing her of late for all the hours she thus expends, for in truth some of these stories seem to me of dubious character and a poor guide to the complexity of life.

'But do you not see, *Maman*,' she turns to me, still in a state of high excitement. 'Sometimes goodness and patience *are* rewarded. Our story *is* to have a happy ending.'

She kisses my cheek and I reach with my other hand to stroke her hair. It is not the moment to deflate her expectations and, I reflect, very likely she will be happy for I am certain her father will delight in her company if not in my own.

'And Charles will come to stay for his holidays, unless he changes his school also and comes to live with us,' she adds. 'And we shall be happy again as before. We shall be happy ever after.'

She paints a pretty picture. Which all too soon begins to fade.

1853 Lower Beeding June

'Oh ma'am, don't weep so, I came as soon as I could.' It is Mary with my pipe. 'Shall I call Mr Charles?'

'No.' Charles does not like my smoking. 'Or yes, that would be better. And pray put the pipe to one side. Perhaps I may not need it after all.'

I hear her calling and, shortly after, Charles hastens in with Mary close behind.

I have dried my eyes.

'Mother? Are you ill?'

'I was remembering the time when it seemed I was to be reunited with your father.' Charles looks quizzical. 'Perhaps you do not remember clearly, being often away at school.'

'Remind me now. Oh Mary, you may stay,' for she is about to leave us. ''Tis better you understand what ails your mistress.'

'Then both of you must take a seat for it is quite a tale.' Charles sits on the bed beside me while Mary perches on the stool at my dressing table. 'Your father sent word that he wished Ann and I to go and live in his new chateau in Savoy. Where Charles has lived these many years,' I add for Mary's benefit. 'At first we were eagerly awaiting a date for our departure, but we started to lose heart as the months and then years passed. I even moved from my lodgings and took a lease on a house with a small garden –the one in Newland Street, Charles, which was on the outskirts of London as it was then, and enjoyed much healthier air. Still no passports were to be had, despite the apparent best efforts of my husband's agents.'

Charles snorts his disbelief but I am uncertain. 'It is possible,' I shrug. 'War broke out again, the peace lasted a year at most. But then I thought maybe your father had changed his mind for, in early 1804, I heard that he had bought another house in France, a large chateau near Paris, where he had asked Her to come and live.' I look at Mary. 'His other wife.' Mary remains confused but I do not stop to explain further. 'Which she did later that year and was joined not long after by her parents, the Marquis d'Osmond and his wife.'

Charles nods. 'She had first to arrange for their names to be erased from the list of émigrés.' He is thoughtful. 'But why did not you go, Mother, when Ann did? Why did she travel alone?'

'I think it was easier to arrange matters for Ann, she being his daughter, while I was of uncertain relation in English law. Unless he had changed his mind, about asking me to go. But I do not think that was the case, if only since he needed me to care for her.'

'I think he wanted you to go, Mother. My uncle Joseph once told me that my father told him he only wished his wife was more like you.'

'I am very glad you think so. I have always hoped that he did. Howsoever, even for Ann the only possible route was via Holland for which she set sail in September 1804. There she was looked after by a respectable family while waiting for a passport. But then, while travelling overland to France, she fell ill in Brussels, caught some fever, and, arriving at the chateau, took to her bed whence she never again rose.' I hear Mary inhale sharply but do not look at her. I must finish while I have strength to speak. 'As Charles knows, she died twelve days later in her father's arms.'

There is a long silence.

'What happened then?' asks Mary at last. 'Did you not still go to your husband? Did he not need you even more? Or wish to comfort you?'

Charles answers for me. 'My father found it hard to understand another's heart,' he says slowly. 'Despite his many other excellent qualities, for he was extremely generous to the poor and needy and he funded much construction for the benefit of the public, schools, hospitals ....' He takes my hand. 'Have you yet read the letters you wrote him? It is quite clear from them that he had no thought for how you felt when he wrote to you, seeking your sympathy in his loss when yours was so much greater.'

'Perhaps I destroyed most of his letters to me for that very reason, for surely it must have been he that informed me of Ann's death.'

'Let me read one to you and you will see.'

'I should be about my work.' Mary stands up to leave us, demonstrating, I reflect, a fine sense of decorum, given her customary curiosity. I smile at her quickly in farewell, for I see that this time Charles intends to let her go. He takes up the pages from the bedside where I have dropped them and reads.

'According to your wishes I shall write few lines but I don't know what to write as to your sorry misfortunes which you must know by your own feelings mine must be greater and as to what you complaining against me that not giving you any consolation which assure you was entirely out of my power to done it.'

'How could he be so unaware of your own grief, Mother?' Charles is shaking his head in disbelief. 'Were you not angry at his lack of care for you?'

I gaze at my son, who is ever well-intentioned and possesses a general benevolence of which I am the current focus. In his youth he certainly knew sadness and some hardship, but he has long enjoyed wealth and happiness far beyond my hopes or expectations and I rejoice for him. But I have also privately remarked that this same good fortune has somewhat blunted his understanding of others less favoured. Perhaps he was always of a simpler disposition, certainly if compared with his sister. No doubt in this particular matter he has been disturbed to discover what seems so mean an aspect of the one to whom he owes so much, and with whom he lived for so many years in apparent accord, and so at last feels sympathy for me in my past suffering. Yet I wonder if he will comprehend my true feelings at that time. Perhaps no one could.

'Not at all,' I say. 'I was glad to be of some comfort.'

Benoit's letter, unfeeling as it seems, I found of some solace. He needed me still, to counsel his troubled soul. He wished, nay, expected me to be able to help him, and how willingly would I have taken him in my arms as I had before, or sung to him to give his suffering some bearable shape. At this time I could do no more than write, but I think it was in the expectation, or at least hope that, as Mary had surmised, he would still desire our eventual reunion.

'I see you shake your head,' I say. 'Perhaps you do not believe me. Do please continue.'

Charles clears his throat. *'"I think you ought to thank to almighty God for having many relation, friends and acquaintance ... where*

288

poor I had but very few which next to none. But however you are so good to wish to know how my health is – thank God I am well as can be expected and I am very sorry to find that your health been so indifferent, but we cannot be expect our health otherwise after such a lost. Think but from Job's troubles and how he submit his heavenly will and which we all in our daily prayer say thy will must be done on earth as it is in heaven. What we all know we have nothing brought with us nor we take with us anything, which show to us itself we have nothing to belong to us. When he plans it, he giveth and when he pleaseth, he taketh. Put all your trust in him, let him do what he please long as he please."'

Charles stops reading.

'You are troubled,' I say. 'You see that what I said was true and of benefit to me also?'

'It is this next part,' he says. 'I do not understand it. Listen. "*Let me advise you to leave of those ideas that you may have been cause of the poor dear child's death no not you but someone else be -*" He pauses, frowning. 'I cannot decipher the next words... wishing? willing to? "*... deprive of poor innocents their life. I daresay you did love her as much as I did your intentions was good I don't doubt it. She is happy an angel in heaven who pray for us there.*"'

Charles looks up. 'Well I understand the latter, though marvel that you could express it with such equanimity. And I do know my father continued to feel it was his fault. He felt he had summoned her to France for his benefit and should have left her to finish her schooling. Although more than once I told him how happy she was that he wished to see her. Only – who is the 'someone' who might have deprived her of her life? Did you think a particular person or persons had neglected Ann's care, even with deliberation? Who would do such a thing?'

Charles has not seen into the darkest corner of my heart, but he might yet guess by power of deduction if I do not rapidly deflect his suspicion. So help me God, I blamed Her, thinking her in the chateau with my husband when Ann arrived, not caring what happened to her step daughter, perhaps even interfering with her proper care. I only discovered subsequently that Madame de Boigne did not arrive at Beauregard until November. Ann died in October.

'It is a little confused,' I agree. 'I expect I meant the family who were supposed to look after her in Holland, to whom she was just a stranger and not a beloved daughter, or perhaps the servants at the chateau when she arrived, I suspected they did not give her warm clothes or light a fire for her as I should have done, or call a doctor as urgently. I do not remember but surely my mind cannot have been in an entirely logical condition, to have lost her so very soon after she had travelled any distance from me for the very first time in her life. I was crazed with grief. I needed to blame someone. Let us finish.'

'"Do pray god sake for your health you to think you have another child to take care do trie to recover your health for poor Charles sake what will become to him if anything happen to you who will take care of him like a father. No noone like yourself may. Many promises you they will take care but they will take care themselves."'

Charles looks up, again quizzical and again I seek to divert his enquiry. 'More of my madness,' I laugh.

'I thought you did then suspect Mr Angelo to some degree.'

'Perhaps you are right. Most certainly he did not have my confidence.'

Charles is satisfied. 'Then you write more kind things about me and how I have written a good many letters and will write every month and that he should write a line or two to encourage me. And then you say that his last letter of 24th July had "*easied my mind a little that you have provided for Charles and also for -* " yourself? It is unclear *–"as to myself I don't much care my care is only for Charles if not well secure. How easy one wrong him out of his right by destroying the papers. How my family are not to come to want by same means. I daresay you remember some time ago you wrote to me what you have settled in England for us not sign. But however I shall trust the providence and care..."*

'It breaks off there, Mother, and then there is only this fragment, very torn as you can see, of another letter I think it was, though it is undated, addressed to Beauregard Chateau. "*and you to do what you please only I sincerely hope you will act like a father towards your son. You know he is your son. You may have many more but you are not sure they are yours... may god grant you long life and you leave to see Charles grow up more. Sincerely wish you will send me all my child's things by safe opportunity. I beg you to answer this. I remain your humble H Bennett."*

'My dear Mother,' Charles puts down the letter and takes both my hands in his. 'Such grievous hurt you suffered on account of my father's carelessness. It cannot all have been Mr Angelo's fault.'

'It is all so long ago. It must have seemed to me then a very long time that I had had no clear indication from him of his plans for us, and I was surely afraid he would forget us entirely now that he was living with Her again in such splendour....'

Charles releases my hands, stands and walks to the window whence I can see a few high clouds still catch the last rays of the setting sun. When he turns to speak, his face is in darkness so that I cannot see his expression.

'She joined him within a month of Ann's death. In fact, she left England very soon after Ann did but took a different route. She must have known that Ann was to join her father and perhaps it speeded her own decision to agree to his requests to come to Beauregard. As it happens, they did not long remain in that fine chateau for she found it cold and cheerless, it being a wet autumn, and they repaired to Paris where she soon began to lead the successful social life for which she has become famous.'

'Which he must have hated.'

'And she might still have borne him children, as you must have feared. But some say...' he breaks off, to resume a moment after. 'Some say she never allowed him his - conjugal rights. Yes!' he sees my surprise and comes back to sit on the bed beside me. 'He was certainly never truly happy and they lived together for short periods only, he sold Beauregard after a few years, and saw her rarely over the many years before he died. And I have heard from others how she ill-treated and slandered him, even after his death, perhaps especially after his death when she has committed some of her slanders to print. Whilst continuing to live on his fortune.' He takes one of my hands again and squeezes my fingers. 'I only defended her before because to me she has always behaved well. But perhaps I am overly credulous.'

'Thank you, my dear.' I lean to kiss his cheek. 'It cannot have been easy to mediate between your parents. I have always taken comfort in seeing you recognised as his rightful heir.'

291

'Thanks to you pleading my cause.'

'Perhaps. I am glad if indeed he took such note. And, you know, I have long thought that, regardless of his philanthropy, he might not have received such honours in his native town had I been installed there.'

'Oh?'

'A second wife? The Black Princess of Buisson Rond?'

He considers. 'Then I should not now be the Comte de Boigne.' He lifts my hand to his lips. 'My father did eventually send you Ann's belongings as you had asked?'

'They are in the remaining trunk.'

'I shall help you go through them before I leave. And, as soon as I reach home, make arrangements for you to visit. And for Mary to accompany you if she is able.'

50

1853 Lower Beeding July

'Mary!' I call through the wide open kitchen window from the garden where I have been admiring my roses, which are in full glorious bloom. My nostrils are still full of their scent which, if I allowed it, would take me back to the perfume sellers in Lucknow *chowk* where *attar* of roses is their most famous product. But I am far too contented in the present day to so indulge.

Mary is on her hands and knees cleaning the grate and I resolve to ask Caroline to engage extra help to leave Mary more time to give me company. She looks round, startled to see me peering in.

'I thought we should visit Caroline in her new home before she returns to work here. Perhaps you would first help me pick a bouquet of sweet peas and see if we have enough runner beans to take also.'

She jumps to her feet, rinses her hands in a basin, lifts her bonnet from its hook on the back of the kitchen door and skips out to join me. She has thought to bring a trug in which to carry our gifts.

We walk to Caroline's cottage across meadows where the long grass is filled with buttercups, cornflowers and poppies. Ann was ever tempted to pick poppies, thinking their petals like fairy skirts, and ever disappointed when they drooped within the hour. A country girl, Mary knows better and contents herself with caressing them lightly as we pass. Butterflies of many colours hover around the flower heads, intoxicated by their perfume; bees and other insects gather their nectar with greater determination.

Silver, for he has been delighted to find us out and about, runs ecstatic in wide circles round us, occasionally haring off in pursuit of some rabbit or other creature that he has seen though we have not. The smallest wisps of cloud drift across the otherwise clear blue sky where swifts and swallows dart and dive and from every direction come the sounds of birdsong. A lone thrush and a blackbird, each perched high in the tallest trees, call out their latest compositions as if competing for the lead over the chorus of tits and finches, chiffchaff and hedge sparrows and - I cup one hand to my ear - the unmistakeable call of the nightingale.

Mary smiles as she too hears it. 'There's nothing as perfect as an English summer's day, ma'am.'

'It is a perfect day,' I agree, whilst thinking how very like it is to a spring day in Lucknow, in February, perhaps, or March, in the Residency compound, playing with Chandi and the children....

We have reached the far gate and entered the field where the Budgens' tenancy begins. James keeps a small number of goats and chickens, the milk and eggs from which, I guess, satisfy their needs but, as far as I know, yield no surplus to sell. I like to see even these few creatures for they remind me of the days when I kept animals and not just chickens and goats. There were ducks and geese, pigs, several cows, a pony with a donkey for company, besides whatever injured and unwanted pets came my way. We skirt the kitchen garden where there is a good variety of vegetables but everything looks in need of clipping or tying up and training. James has never tended it as well as he does my own and I wonder how long it will be before Caroline engineers some changes.

'Caroline's hanging out her washing, ma'am.' Mary points to the side of the cottage where immaculate white sheets flap gently in the breeze and Caroline's head is just visible, a line of clothes pegs clenched between her teeth.

She is very happy to have company, proud to show off her new domain where every room is bright and clean, well swept and tidy. The much coveted pots and pans are copper and no doubt will hang in just such a gleaming row for many years, burnished by Caroline's industry. There is the sweet smell of new bread, a kettle is steaming on the stove and we are invited to take tea. We have much to discuss: the wedding, Charles' recent visit, our impending travel, in all of which Caroline engages whilst seeming constantly on the point of revealing a secret of her own.

Finally, as we leave, she announces, hands clasping her belly: 'I'm to be a mother. Early December most like.' She sees us calculate and laughs. 'Some men needs a push or they'd never take the plunge.'

***

'We forgot to tell Caroline how much we have already sorted,' says Mary next day when we meet as agreed in the library to tackle the piles of books. 'She will be pleased.'

'She will surely be surprised! But I am resolved to make all as neat and tidy as would satisfy the hardest taskmaster.'

I am amazed at my energy and determination and by the end of the morning our work is done and the books all shelved in order of their author or in useful categories. I keep aside a few volumes of poetry and a small pile of novels that we found in Ann's trunk, which I shall keep at my bedside and from time to time gaze at where she has written her name, and perhaps even attempt to read.

"Sicilian Romance", "The Romance of the Forest", "Belinda", "The Mysteries of Udolpho".... my darling girl, how sadly were you wrong in your predictions. If our story were a romance it would have ended then, when your papa called us to him. With perhaps an epilogue which finds us in Savoy, walking in a high mountain meadow filled with bright spring flowers whose names we are learning together, and snow-capped peaks dazzling in a clear blue sky. Yet now, so many years later, I am to visit there and see these wondrous sights.

But oh, what is this book and why is it amongst these works of fiction? *"The History of the Reign of Shah Alam"* by Captain W. Franklin (ed. 1798) and, I turn a few pages, my husband was among the subscribers. Perhaps he gave it to her after her arrival in France, before it became clear that she would not recover from her illness, for she had expressed the wish to be better informed so that she might talk with him about India.

I remember when she was packing her trunk looking up at me, her face a picture of determination. 'I wish to learn everything about my father's glorious career in India,' she said. 'For I was too young to

295

understand when we were there and have but isolated memories. Do you think he will be glad?'

'You have a copy of this book already, ma'am.' Mary is peering over my shoulder. 'See.' She goes to the shelves and selects a volume without hesitation. 'I knew it from the cover.'

'So I do.' I place Ann's copy with her other books and take the second from Mary's hands. 'I think my husband sent it to me. It is about a great Emperor in whose palace I once lived, with my husband and children. I will tell you about it, one day. Oh but look here!' Before she can respond I have opened the cover and am pointing to the words therein written in my own hand.

Mary leans to see where I am pointing but as soon stands back, shame-faced.

'I cannot read, ma'am.'

'Oh Mary,' I am vexed with myself for forgetting. 'But you shall. I shall teach you myself. It will give us employment when we visit Charles. And, I hope, pleasure. Listen, it is some verses that I wrote and had quite forgotten:

"This book belongs to Mrs H. Bennett – St Leonard's Forest
If thou art borrowed by a friend
Right welcome shall he be
To read, to study, not to lend
But to return to me.

Not that imparted knowledge doth
Diminish learning store
But books I find when often lent
Return to me no more.

Read slowly – Pause frequently
Think seriously
Keep cleanly – Return duly
With the corners of the leaves not turned down."

Mary is clapping. 'Very good, ma'am! I should very much like to read and write, though I may never be so learned as are you.' She reaches out her hand. 'Shall I replace it on the shelf?''

'Yes,' I hold it out to her but as quickly take it back. 'Yet no. I shall keep my daughter's copy and send this one to Charles. What do I say! I shall *take* it to him and perhaps use it to tell my grandchildren a little of their heritage. Pray put it with the other things we intend to pack and then, if you will, I should like to take my lunch outdoors, for we are done at last.'

After Mary has left me I sit awhile to ponder. With Charles' help we made such short work of sorting my darling daughter's possessions. Her few clothes were flimsy and faded, although they had been her best. It had still been warm summer when she departed and I knew that, once arrived in France, her father would soon fit her out with the latest fashions. I wonder: would her stepmother have assisted? Would she have been as charming to Ann as Charles says she has always been to him? Perhaps there would have been no place for me in the household, once Ann was established in her new home. Perhaps I should have soon become an embarrassment to her also, which would have as surely broken my heart.

Ann did have one fine possession: a set of tortoiseshell hairbrush, comb and mirror that I gave Charles to take for Ernest's new wife. I think it had been a parting gift from the Walkers, or perhaps the Blanes. And she had my long-lost telescope which I had quite forgotten I had lent her.

***

The second week in July a small packet arrives from Charles containing some daguerrotypes of Chambery town.

'*These were made only this past week,*' he writes. '*So much superior to verbal description alone, as I am sure you will agree. You may see for yourself at last the snow-capped mountains that surround us, the castle of the King of Savoy and the road with arcaded walks that runs from it which is the Rue de Boigne. And at the far end of this is my father's statue standing atop what is known as the Fountain of the Elephants. I thought you would like to have some foresight of all this before your visit, plans for which are in hand. Early August looks most likely. Your loving Chas.*'

I cannot see my once beloved's face, but overall the likeness is true enough and the quartet of elephants an imposing and appropriate foundation for the high column on which he stands. It is a great honour, justly deserved and yet it makes me sad. Mary is similarly impressed.

'Surely you must know so many stories of his great victories and accomplishments. I should like to hear.' She traces his figure with one finger. 'But how alone he looks standing there so high, so far from human comp'ny and comfort.'

When she is gone to her work I take his likeness to my seat above the orchard and within the hour have composed for him a last *ghazal*.

My love so fine and brave in war, he never knew his heart.
He grasped what chance threw in his way but never knew his heart.
Not asking if his life would stray from his intended aim,
He did not count the sacrifice, nor thought he of the pain
He caused to those he left behind. He did not know his heart.

Chasing after phantoms, he did not follow his own heart.
He saw his friend turn foe yet still he showed no change of heart.
Once pledged he kept his word, my love honourable and true.
How blessed was I to share his life when his glory days were new.
I know I could have shared his heart. Did he love me? I never knew.

***

The following Sunday I go to church and show my friends the pictures which, to my eyes, prove that my past is not the dream it often seems.

'Tis a pleasure to see you so well,' says dear Elizabeth. 'And I know you are not thinking of moving back to town, much as I should like your company. However, I happened to see Mrs Redford the other day and I promised her I would tell you that your old rooms in North Street are soon to become again vacant.'

***

While I wait for our travel instructions I take out from another drawer of my bureau some more old letters, from my mother and my sister. Once more I read how Lucknow changed, for the better in the eyes of some: so many more glorious palaces and baghs having been built, creating such a vision of golden domes and minarets and glorious trees and flowers that visiting Europeans think they have stepped into a fairy tale. But others have said how vain and inglorious the Nawabs have become, now crowned as Kings, yet in reality the puppets of the British who, in all but name, now rule this once proud realm. Some ask how long can it be before the people tire of their oppression. For even the poets are corrupted and write only of mundane matters and romantic love.

I read of my own losses: when one by one my loved ones in India died. My parents, brother-in-law, sister...I remember when I heard that Faiz had passed away, at William's fine residence in Hyderabad, for he had succeeded in his ambition and become a most successful businessman, a banker like his step brother John. How I had envied her passing her last years in the loving household of her son whilst, according to her, assisting him in his business through her cordial relations with the Nizam.

I so missed what dear Gulzar used to call her 'jovial pen', my last link with my old life, that I asked God to take me too, for Charles had already gone to live with his father and there seemed nothing left to tie me to this earth. And, when I did not die, I discovered my saviour instead in opium dreams which turned my darkest nights into day. It was at that time that young Mr Shelley passed my way and had room in his heart to share my sadness. Mary, the second Mrs Shelley, wrote of his tenderness and how she missed him after his early death. Here is my copy of his collected poetical works that she compiled, addressed to 'The Indian Princess' for she did not know my name. I daresay no more did he.

She wrote that he left behind fragments of some drama based upon his memory of me. I should like to have seen it, to see what

299

ending he wrote for me. I have no doubt of his sympathy. The world would have been a better place had he lived on, champion of the poor and oppressed, beacon of truth in these times of greed and exploitation that cause such poverty and desperation, when more is spent on a coronation robe than a working person could earn in a whole lifetime. We have had our rebels even here in sleepy Sussex, whom our newspapers ridiculed as '*clodpoles*', omitting to report their speeches or true numbers at their meetings. But even those brave souls have, it seems, gone back to sleep. I wonder for how long.

Yet I am still here! And quite at home, like one of those flowering shrubs that has crossed the globe and taken root and survived from year to year (whilst others have taken the opposite route to comfort homesick English in their gardens there). At this time of year, when the sun is high and the days are long and the air so heavy with a thousand fragrances that I hear my sister whisper '*Let's go hawa khanna*'; when the body is stilled by the heat yet not asleep, for all the senses are alive in wonder and the mind is in a state of ecstasy, then am I content with my time and place in the world. It is enough for me.

Midnight! I wept and sobbed,
Being bereft of thee.
Then came phantoms of night,
And I was shamed.
'Phantoms of night' said I,
'Sobbing and weeping thus
You find me, who until now
Slept as you glided by.

Precious things do I lack,
Deem not the worse of me,
Whom you erstwhile deemed wise,
Grievous ill hath befallen.'
And the phantoms of the night,
Pulling the longest of faces,
By me stalked,
If I were wise or a fool

Utterly unconcerned.

4th May 1814   Goethe(from Hafiz)

EPILOGUE

Charles, Comte de Boigne, died on 21st July 1853. Helena Bennett made her last Will and Testament on 5th August. According to the copy which I have seen, she left her wardrobe, bedstead, with the feather bed, bolster and pillows, to her friend Elizabeth Etherton; 25 pounds to Mary Walker and fifty pounds to Pilford Medwin of Horsham, her friend and one of her executors. He, together with her other trustees and executors, John Walker of Barnard St, Russell Square and Michael Walker of The Strand, were, upon her death, to sell off all her assets and equally divide the net monies between her grandchildren once they attained the age of twenty-one or were married. She named Ernest, Eugene, Octave, Benoit and Paul, all sons of Charles. The witnesses were Ann Howes, wife of Michael Howes, Postmaster Horsham and Alf Aldridge, also of Horsham. There is no mention of her rings.

Helena's address is given as North Street, Horsham, late of Great Ground House in the hamlet of Lower Beeding, so it seems she did move back to her previous lodgings as Charles and her friends had wanted. She died on 27th December 1853, I hope in the company of some of her friends and perhaps of Mary Piper, of whom in my rendition Helena becomes so fond. It is unlikely that Caroline could have been present for she had not long given birth to twins. Helena was buried in the Anglican churchyard of St Mary's, Horsham, where her grave may still be seen, aligned in a north to south direction which some have thought indicates her wish to return to her Islamic origins. The inscription, now almost illegible, reads:

Requiescat in pace Helena Bennett vidua,
defuncta obit 27 Decembris 1853, aet LXXXI.
"Blessed are they that mourn for they shall be comforted."

It is also not likely that Ernest or any of her other grandchildren would have been able to attend the funeral since winter would have made travel from Savoy difficult. Perhaps they came later. Someone, maybe one of them, or one of their children, visited Caroline Budgen about fifty years later, by which time she was a very old lady herself. When writing *Fountain of the Elephants,* regarded by many as the best biography of Benoit de Boigne, Desmond Young found, in the family archives, a note of the meeting, written in French on a scrap of paper. This is how Caroline remembered 'Mrs Bennett.'

'Sallow in complexion with strange dark eyes. She would sometimes stay in bed until noon and often kept her nightcap on when at last she got up. She took no trouble at all about her dress but wore magnificent rings. She smoked long pipes, lost her temper very easily and could not be bothered with anything. She had a strange character but was exceedingly good to the poor and often sent to Horsham for bread to distribute among them. She was also very fond of animals and bought numbers of all kinds. She spent money recklessly and because she was excessively generous people could easily take advantage of her.'

When I first read about Nur Begum in William Dalrymple's lovely book, *White Mughals,* I thought how inadequate an obituary were these few sentences for someone who had lived so long and had so unusual a history and was sure that there must be a much more interesting story to tell. I hope the reader has found it so.

Acknowledgments

For much of what is known about Nur and for an introduction to the unique Euro- Indian society that developed in Lucknow in the 18th century, I am indebted to *White Mughals,* one of William Dalrymple's ground-breaking books of Indian history. I am also very grateful to him and to Olivia for their hospitality to my husband Rashmi and myself when we visited Delhi. In Lucknow I greatly appreciated the welcome extended to us by the legendary bookseller, Ram Advani, and took the opportunity to acquire in his shop most of the books I needed to understand and depict Lucknow and its inhabitants when Nur lived there. The books by Rosie Llewellyn-Jones were especially valuable, particularly on the character of Claude Martin.

I am grateful also to our very knowledgeable guide in Lucknow, Atif Arshi, to Adnan Abdul Wali for inviting us into his ancient family home in the *chowk*, and to Atif's cousin in Agra, Nadeem Rehmani, who made me look more closely at the Taj Mahal and the Fort. I was kindly given access to the Aligarh Muslim University library by the Librarian Dr Shetty and encouraged by his interest in my project and that of his Deputy Dr Amjao Ali. Our driver, Bisham Singh, was very tolerant of my vague directions and sudden desire to stop and explore when I thought I had found places where Nur and Benoit might have lived or visited. In London Nick Robins, author of *The Corporation That Changed the World,* gave me an eye-opening tour of parts of the City associated with the East India Company that made it possible for me to imagine Nur and Benoit's impressions on their visit. And I am also very grateful to our dear friend Nilesh Nathwani in Vienna who shared with me some of his knowledge of ghazals.

I owe a very special debt to Nur and Benoit's descendants, the de Boigne family. The current Comte Pierre-Edward allowed me to consult the family archives in Chambery where I found material new to me and important to my developing story. He also read a late draft of the manuscript and made several helpful suggestions including further information of which I was ignorant and very happy to incorporate. (The bookplate rhyme composed by Nur and the presentation by the Emperor of gifts to Nur's little son Ali/Charles). I am also especially grateful to his cousin, Madame Marie-Helene Kourimsky, and her husband Hans, for twice welcoming us to their home and showing us other family memorabilia. I hope that they and other members of their family will be pleased with the final product.

With the exception of some of the named servants, the characters in *The Black Princess* were real people, but most of the scenes in which they appear are imagined. The dates and stages in Nur's life follow what is known as closely as possible. There is of course much more written about Benoit but he is not my focus. For constant reminder of this fact I am extremely grateful to Todd Kingsley-Jones, my inspiring writing group leader. Without his influence, I might never have developed to such an extent the story of Nur's contemporary life in England. He also convinced me that she was looking over my shoulder and happy that I was giving her the recognition she deserves. Especially in view of the tragic events outlined in the Epilogue - of which I was not aware when I started writing - I was so anxious to resume our acquaintance that she has become a major character in my next book *The Rose Goddess*. Yet, oddly enough, it was not until my cousin Rich Voysey visualised her for his beautiful cover illustration that she seemed to come fully to life.

Finally I wish to thank Rashmi for all his support and company on all my travels; our sons Ashim, Akash and Alay, and Coralie Cubitt and Gabrielle Kimm who have all read and given helpful criticism of part or all of this book.

GLOSSARY

Aigrette	a decorative pin worn on the front of a turban
Amma	Mama
Abba	Papa
Annas	Sixteen annas made a rupee
Arsi mushaf	'mirror look' part of the wedding ceremony
Aurang	cloth producing factory
Avadh	called Oudh in British history books and maps
Ayah	nanny
Babul	song of departure from a wedding
Bagh	garden
Bahail	two-wheeled bullock cart
Bahyne	sister-in-law
Bangla	thatched house, origin of 'bungalow', though often of 2 storeys
Baradhari	light, airy building for secular meetings including music performances
Beta/beti	son/daughter (affectionate form of address)
Bhulbhulaiya	network of narrow passages at the Bara Imambara in Lucknow
Bibi	mistress
Biryani	savoury rice dish
Bismillah	ceremony to mark the beginning of a child's formal education
Budgeroo	type of barge
Cabriolet	a light one horse carriage with a hood
Caravanserai	accommodation for visiting merchants and their animals
Chhathi	ceremony six days after birth
Chacha/chachi	uncle/aunt
Chai	tea, usually spiced sweet and milky
Champak	frangipani

Channa	chick peas
Chattri	dome-shaped pavilion, often on the roof of a building
Chikan	embroidery typical of Lucknow
Chillum	aromatic tobacco paste
Chowk	bazaar
Conch	a large sea shell blown as a horn in Hindu temples
Crore	a hundred *lakh* or ten million
Dia	a small light made with a wick in oil
Doab	the region between the rivers Jumuna and Ganges
Dommis	female entertainers
*Dosset	small portion
Dupatta	long scarf worn over the head or shoulders
Durbah	public appearance/audience
Firangi	foreigner
Ganj	market
Ghat	riverside jetty
Ghazal	a form of poetry, often sung
*Goistering	loud feminine laughter
Gomasta	Middle man in trade
Hawa khana	to eat the air (lit.)
Haveli	large house or mansion
Howdah	seat mounted on the back of an elephant
Imam	Muslim religious leader
Imambara	Shia shrine where Mohammed's grandson
Hussain's	*tazias* are housed
Jagindar	holder of a *jagir*
Jagir	a grant of land from which the holder can extract revenue
Jaidad	a grant of land for the support of an army
Jali	latticed stone screen
Jamas	pyjamas

Janjar	anklets often with small bells hanging from them
Jats	people from Sind later migrating to the Punjab
Jauhar	ritual group suicide
Jiggered	surprised
Jooti	slipper with pointed curved toes
*Jug	fisherman
Katar	dagger
Ko	a distance of about 6 miles.
Kothi	house
Kumbh	water jar, often of metal
Kurta	loose collarless shirt
Lakh	a hundred thousand
Lascar	sailor or seaman
Limbupani	lemonwater
Maher	dowry
Mahout	one who trains and cares for an elephant
Majlis	mourning assembly
Mali	gardener
*Mammock	to carve badly
Mashata	female matchmaker
Masnavi	long narrative poem, of Arabic origin
Mathiya	flat crisp bread
Mehfil	music party
Mehndi	red dye used to paint a bride's hands and feet
*Moil	trouble
Muezzin	the crier who calls the faithful to prayer five times a day
Muharram	Shia period of mourning for the deaths of Husain and his family
Nani	Maternal grandmother
Naqqar khana	drum house
Naubat	kettle drums
Nau shah	new king

Nawab	regional governor under the Mughal emperors
Ninsook	or *nainsook*, a fine cotton fabric
Nuzzur	gift in tribute
Pagri	turban
Palav	the long free end of a sari
Parterre	French formal garden on a terrace raised above the ground
Pinnace	type of river boat
Pulao	savoury rice dish
Punkahwallah	servant whose function is to fan his employers
Qazi	Muslim magistrate
Rakabdar	cook
Rajputs	inhabitants of the area now known as Rajasthan
Rath	well-furnished bullock drawn covered vehicle used by noble women
Rathor	Rajput clan
Rohillas	Pathans of Afghan origin then of Rohilkhand
Rupee	The principal unit of currency as now
Sahibzada	first born son and heir
Samovar	device for making and serving tea, usually of metal
Sangeet khana	music room
Sarangi	stringed instrument
Sasurai	mother-in-law
Shimla	turban
Surah iqra	part of the Koran, the first direct revelation to the Prophet
Syce	one who cares for horses
Tabla	small drum
Talinga	originally meaning troops recruited by the British from Andra Pradesh, later often simply 'outsiders' to the province where they fought.
Talwar	sword

Tare dikhana	star gazing
Tazias	replica of Mohammed's grandson Husain's mausoleum in Iraq
Tonga	horse drawn partly covered carriage
Topi	cap
Tykhana	basement apartments used in the hot weather
Ungia	tight short blouse with half sleeves
Vizier	high-ranking political advisor or minister
Vasokht	a particular form of Urdu poetry
Wazir	alternative spelling of *vizier*
Zamindar	landowner
Zenana	women's quarters

*Old Sussex words

BIBLIOGRAPHY

Abbas, Saiyed Anwer, Lost Monuments of Lucknow, Lucknow, Author, 2009

Abbas, Saiyed Anwer, Incredible Lucknow, A Visitors' Guide, Author, 2010

Abu Taleb Mirza Khan, Travels of, during the years 1799-1801, Longman et al, 1814

Ackroyd, Peter, London, The Biography, Chatto and Windus, 2000

Ahmad, Aijaz, (ed), Ghazals of Ghalib, Oxford University Press, 1994

De la Ronciere, Bertrand, La Premiere 'Femme du General de Boigne', Helene Benett, unpublished ms, 1993

Foot, Paul, Red Shelley, Bookmarks, 1988

Graff, Violet, (ed), Lucknow, Memories of a City, Oxford India Paperbacks, 2011

Candra, Vikram, Red Earth and Pouring Rain, Faber and Faber, 1995

Dalrymple, William, City of Djinns, A Year in Delhi, Harper Collins, 1993

Dalrymple, William, The Last Mughal, The Fall of Delhi, 1857, Bloomsbury, 2006

Dalrymple, William, White Mughals, Harper Collins, 2002

Gilbert, Richard, Everyman's Sussex, Robert Scott, 1927

Llewellyn-Jones, Rosie, A Fatal Friendship, The Nawabs, the British and the City of Lucknow, Oxford University Press, 1985

Llewellyn-Jones, Rosie, A Very Ingenious Man, Claude Martin in Early Colonial India, Oxford University Press, 1992

Llewellyn-Jones, Rosie, Engaging Scoundrels, True Tales of Old Lucknow, Oxford University Press, 2000

Mason, Philip, The Men Who Ruled India, Rupa, 1985

Misra, Amaresh, Lucknow, Fire and Grace, The Story of its Renaissance, Revolution and the Aftermath, Rupa, 1998

Mourad, Kenize, In the City of Gold and Silver, The Story of Begum Hazrat Mahal, Full Circle, 2013

Oldenburg, Veena Talwar, (ed), Shaam-e-Awadh, Writings on Lucknow, Penguin, 2007

Robins, Nick, The Corporation That Changed The World, How the East India Company Shaped the Modern Multinational, Pluto Press, 2012

Rude, George, Revolutionary Europe 1783-1815, Fontana/Collins, 1964

Sharar, Abdul Halim, Lucknow, The Last Phase of an Oriental Culture, Translated and edited by E.S. Harcourt and FakhirHussain, Oxford India Paperbacks, 1994

Shelley, P.B., The Works of, Wordsworth Editions, 1994

Visram, Rozina, Ayahs, Lascars and Princes, Indians in Britain 1700-1947, Pluto Press, 1986

Young, Desmond, Fountain of the Elephants, Collins, 1959

About the Author

After ten years working as a medical sociologist in universities in Scotland, England, and Canada, Maggie Voysey Paun started writing fiction while bringing up her three sons.

Her publications include five children's books, *Sunita Makes Friends, Sunita Goes to the Zoo* (Mantra 1986), *Good Terms* and *Refugee* (Cambridge University Press, 1992 and 1993 respectively.) Several of her plays including *Norah's Story, Self Willed Women* and *An Enchanted Brew*, were read or staged in various fringe venues in London and Brighton.

She later worked for many years as a parliamentary assistant.

Most of her writing has something to do with the meeting of cultures.

The Black Princess is her second novel for adults. The first, ***Sacrifices,*** was published by PublishNation in 2016.

Ninety Days Escape from Uganda

Rashmi Paun
Pages : 396
Edition : Paperback
ISBN : 978-81-9363-139-3
Subject : Biographical Fiction

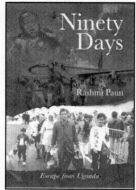

About the Book

Ninety Days is a story about what life was like for Asians in Uganda before the President ordered them all to leave, and what happened afterwards as law and order broke down and people considered themselves lucky to escape unharmed.

In August 1972 President Idi Amin announced that God had come to him in a dream and told him to order citizens of Asian origin out of the country. He declared: 'If they are not out in Ninety days, they will soon see what happens to them!'

The story centres on the Hindu Mitani family whose biggest problems before the announcement are their elder son's choice of a Muslim wife, a sister's unhappy marriage and whether or not the community should spend its money on yet another religious shrine. But as the deadline approaches and there are beatings and imprisonments they, like their friends and neighbours, become increasingly desperate to find refuge in whichever country will take them, though they must flee more or less penniless and leave all their possessions behind.

Within ninety days, 70,000 members of what had been a close community many of whom were born in Uganda, were scattered across the world, mostly in the UK, Canada, India and the US, but some others across Europe and as far afield as Australia and New Zealand.

Rashmi Paun grew up in Jinja, Uganda. In 1972, when Amin made his announcement, Rashmi was already in London, studying for a doctorate in Physics, but his parents, family and friends were forced to flee from Amin's terror.

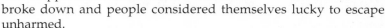

Place your order at: moonlightbooks2016@gmail.com